"Tom Matthews spins a golden story regarding the nuts and bolts of developing a leadership program at a university. Tom provides clear guidance and resources that anyone can adapt, tailor to their own needs, and make their own. Tom has left us a leadership legacy that will inspire new leadership programs across the country."
—*EDWARD O'CONNELL, Assistant Clinical Professor and Instructor for Honors and Undergraduate College of Leadership and Service, Stony Brook University*

"We have been teaching leadership at our school for years but have struggled with the notion of a formal program. Last summer at the National Leadership Symposium I was searching for ideas and had the great fortune of meeting Tom Matthews. He explained the GOLD Program outlined in this book and I immediately saw the possibilities. Four short months later we will be launching a comprehensive program involving every department within Student Affairs as well as staff and faculty members. The structure of the program is so effective because it can be tailored to the unique qualities of any institution and developed and enhanced over time. For myself and my fellow directors, we are excited to realize our hopes for a relevant, dynamic leadership program."
—*DON MORTON, Director, Center for Student Involvement, Rhode Island School of Design*

"*Building Leaders One Hour at a Time* is an excellent resource for both learning how to create short, discrete leadership development sessions as well as how to construct a comprehensive program in student leadership. All college leadership educators could benefit by having this book on their shelves!"
—*DAVID ROSCH, Ph.D., Assistant Professor in Agricultural Leadership Education, University of Illinois at Urbana-Champaign*

"*Building Leaders One Hour at a Time* is an excellent tool no matter where you are in developing your leadership program. From providing workshop ideas to establishing a theoretical and practical framework for any leadership program, this guide will help you build interdepartmental collaboration and increase student engagement on any campus. Even more exciting is how these programs are efficient in their use of resources while making a maximum impact."
—*MICHAEL PRESTON, Ed.D., Director, Office of Student Involvement, University of Central Florida*

"From the CEO to the intern and from the student to the professional, all will benefit from this insightful book. It is a cookbook for all who want to learn or improve their leadership skills. No stone is left unturned."
—*MARY ANN R. AWAD, Manager of Research, New York State United Teachers*

"In *Building Leaders One Hour at a Time*, Tom Matthews has captured a lifetime of leadership experiences and created an inventory of leadership training and development workshops that can be adapted to serve as a detailed framework for any campus leadership program in the 21st century."
—*BILL MANDICOTT, Assistant Vice President for Student and Community Involvement, Frostburg State University*

"This publication is how best practices should be done. It connects the story with the need and shows how to build a program. The worksheets connect all parts of brain-based learning [and] there is something for every thinker—analytical, structural, social, and conceptual."
—*RICH WHITNEY, Ph.D., Assistant Professor, College Student Development, Counseling & Special Education, College of Education, DePaul University*

"Tom Matthews' book *Building Leaders One Hour at a Time* is a masterful collection of lesson plans for student leadership development, together with a thoughtful story of program creation. It offers an excellent resource for teaching essential leadership competencies within the context of leader-follower relationships, service in a greater community, and the understanding of self. Those involved with NCLP, ILA, and the field of leadership will recognize the quality of scholarship that informs this amazing resource."
—*BETTY D. ROBINSON, Ph.D., Associate Professor, Leadership and Organizational Studies, University of Southern Maine*

BUILDING LEADERS ONE HOUR AT A TIME:

GUIDEBOOK FOR LEADERSHIP DEVELOPMENT

TOM MATTHEWS

For large quantity orders and promotional materials, contact publisher:
CJM Books
P.O. Box 565
East Rochester, NY 14445
www.CJMBooks.com

Photography credits: SUNY Geneseo Office of College Communications [Keith Walters and Brian Bennett].

Cover art adaptation and design by
Kristen Fuest. All rights reserved.
Text set in Adobe Garamond Pro.

ISBN-10: 0983179778
ISBN-13: 978-0-9831797-7-1

Library of Congress Control Number: 2012951453

ABSTRACT

Building Leaders One Hour at a Time tells the story of the development of the GOLD Leadership Program at SUNY Geneseo and provides lesson plans for creating user-friendly short courses in leadership and life skills. The narrative and the syllabi serve as a practical guide for organizations with limited resources to create programs through collaborative leadership.

AUTHOR'S NOTES

All proceeds from the sale of *Building Leaders One Hour at a Time* will be deposited in the Geneseo Foundation GOLD Program account and used to support the GOLD Leadership Program.

The GOLD Program includes several workshops that have been adapted from popular commercially available training programs. Each of these programs was purchased by the GOLD Program for our use in workshop classes. This book contains an explanation of how to create lesson plans to adapt the programs in a one-hour format. Because the materials are copyright protected, users will need to contact the vendor to purchase the videos and training materials. The vendor website addresses are included in the Resources Used section of the workshop pages.

COVER DESIGN

The image of the clock on the cover shows the colors of the precious metals and gemstones that identify the 10 leadership certificates that students can earn in the GOLD Program at Geneseo. The hands of the clock are set at 2:30 to represent the typical afternoon starting time for most GOLD workshops. The title of the book represents the Geneseo approach to leadership education, development, and training. Almost every workshop in the program is offered in a one-hour format.

This publication has been made possible through a generous grant from the Charles C. Jackson Foundation to the SUNY Research Foundation. Thank you to Bruce Jackson for suggesting that we share our work with other leadership educators and for assisting us in obtaining the grant for "Building Leaders One Hour at a Time: Guidebook for Leadership Development."

ABOUT THE AUTHOR

Tom Matthews is the Associate Dean of Leadership and Service at SUNY Geneseo. He earned a B.S. in Education at SUNY Plattsburgh, an M.S. in Student Personnel at SUNY Albany, and his Ed.D in Student Personnel & Higher Education from the University of South Carolina. He started his student affairs career at SUNY Brockport before moving to SUNY Geneseo as Director of Student Activities in 1967.

Tom served as Chair of the National Association for Campus Activities, has been active in regional, state, and national leadership positions, and has chaired numerous committees and presented papers and hundreds of program sessions throughout his career in organizations such as the Association of College Unions-International, the Association of Performing Arts Presenters, the International Leadership Association, the New York State United Teachers, and the American Federation of Teachers. He has also been active in United University Professions, representing over 20,000 employees in SUNY, as a local president and as statewide treasurer and vice president for professionals, and as the union's chief negotiator for two rounds of bargaining with the state of New York.

Tom is the recipient of the NYSUT Higher Education Member of the Year Award, the National Association for Campus Activities Founders Award, the Patsy Morley Outstanding Programmer Award, the Thomas E. Matthews National Association for Campus Activities East Coast Annual Student Leader Scholarship awarded annually to a student leader, the New York Leadership Educators Consortium Thomas Matthews Visionary Award, the Geneseo Alumni Association Honorary Lifetime Membership Award, the SUNY Geneseo Pride Award, the College Student Personnel Association of New York (CSPA) Outstanding Contribution to the Profession Award, and the United University Professions Nina Mitchell Award. He was also the first administrator at SUNY Geneseo to receive the SUNY Chancellor's Award for Excellence in Professional Service.

Since 2000 he has been developing the GOLD Leadership Certificate Program at Geneseo. His *Building Leaders One Hour at a Time* book is both a story about the development of the GOLD Program at SUNY Geneseo and a practitioner's guide to creating high-impact leadership development programs. Tom hopes the book will inspire others to create open and accessible leadership opportunities for anyone interested in improving his or her leadership capacity.

ACKNOWLEDGEMENTS

It would be impossible to credit everyone who has affected the GOLD Program through their books, papers, conference sessions, and hallway conversations. I cite a few in the text just to illustrate the value of reading the literature and interacting with leadership educator colleagues. I have been very fortunate to have had these experiences at a time when leadership education entered its expansion and growth period over the past 20 years. When I started working on the Leadership Certificate Program in 1999 there were a few articles on cocurricular leadership programs. By 2011, the second edition of *The Handbook for Student Leadership Development* was published, and it even contained a couple of citations and references to the SUNY Geneseo GOLD Program. There has been an explosive growth in the leadership field with new books, research, conferences, resources, and websites too numerous to even cite in this book.

However, I need to thank the administrators, faculty, and students who have helped create the GOLD Program with their support, involvement, and participation. Starting from the top, I want to thank President Christopher Dahl, Vice President of Student and Campus Life Robert Bonfiglio, and Dean of Students Leonard Sancilio for giving me the opportunity and freedom to create and nurture the program. I want to also thank all the staff members in the Center for Community for their daily assistance in managing the program, including our secretaries, Barbara Battaglia and Beth Standish, and current professional staff who teach many of our programs: Wendi Kinney, Tamara Kenney, Kay Fly, Kim Harvey, and Fatima Rodriguez-Johnson. I also want to especially thank all of our instructors in the program, including professional staff in the Division of Student and Campus Life, other campus administrators, faculty members, alumni, and students who volunteer their time to teach in the GOLD Program. There are numerous departments mentioned in the narrative that have played important roles in the GOLD Program. I also want to thank the Student Association for their continued financial support and Campus Auxiliary Services for program funding.

This program was developed to help students develop and grow their capacity for leading in the future. Several thousand students have participated and hundreds have shared their thoughts on leadership through their journals. It has been a special privilege to read their reflections and witness the practical application of leadership virtually every day.

I also want to thank the generous alumni of Geneseo, and particularly Dan Ward, who have contributed funds through the Geneseo Foundation to support the GOLD Program.

Thank you to David Rosch, Cyril Oberlander, Helen Thomas, Sherry Rhodes, and Chris Murphy at CJM Books for their valuable assistance in helping with the process of creating and framing this book. Special thanks to Kristen Fuest, Student Association Graphic Coordinator, for her amazing graphic design and layout of her first book as well as the GOLD Program website. Thank you also to the SUNY Geneseo Office of Communications, especially to Keith Walters and Brian Bennett, for providing the photographs in the book. I also want to thank my wife Betsy for her patience and understanding and support for this project. Thank you also to our sons, Jeff and Dave, and their spouses Julie and Cate, and our grandchildren, Josh, Sydney, and Rachael, for letting me take precious time on the computer to finish the book.

I also want to thank the volunteer GOLD Leader Mentors who have helped manage the program for the last 12 years. This book would not be possible without their help during the last three years. They took notes and prepared drafts of the 160 workshops that are described in this book. Although it would be impossible to mention every Mentor who worked on this project, I do need to acknowledge several Mentors who assisted in the editing and preparation of the manuscript: Bareeqah Ahmad, Bridget Denicola, Alana Eaton, Meghan Gordineer, Melissa Graham, Krista Muscarella, Chad Salitan, Brent Sanderson, and Matthew Wing.

BUILDING LEADERS
ONE HOUR AT A TIME:

GUIDEBOOK FOR LEADERSHIP DEVELOPMENT

PREFACE: HOW IT ALL BEGAN

I always ask leadership students in the Geneseo Opportunities for Leadership Development (GOLD) Program, "When did you first discover leadership happening, and when did you begin to engage in the leadership process?" For me, it started in a one-room elementary country school in Louisville, New York. I remember Mrs. Gains expecting us to help out each day. Some of us walked down the road to a farmer's well in the morning to get water to fill the water crock; others helped start the fire on cold mornings. Each year, for five years, we took on more and more tasks that required us to lead and teach the younger kids. I knew early on that I wanted to be a teacher, and I knew that leadership was happening, even if I didn't know what it was. I continued to get involved in clubs and organizations in junior and senior high and in my youth fellowship at church. I continued the leadership journey as an education major at Plattsburgh State. Looking back, I am sure I overdid it a bit with numerous leadership positions, but likely because of it, I was fortunate as a sophomore to be invited to participate in the first honors course in leadership with Dr. Redcay, a distinguished professor and administrator. I was hooked.

So, here I am, nearly 50 years later, with three degrees in education and a life-long career in student affairs, peppered along the way with some spicy leadership roles in local, state, and national organizations, enjoying life as a leadership educator. I have been blessed with the opportunity to create a new leadership development program for students at Geneseo. This book is about the last dozen years and how we created, developed, and nurtured this program.

THE GUIDEBOOK FOR LEADERSHIP

The book is divided into two parts. Part One includes seven chapters detailing the history of the SUNY Geneseo GOLD Program and the collaborative leadership used to create and develop the program. The reader will also learn how the various components of the program are organized and managed. Part Two provides lesson plan descriptions for 160 workshops that may be used by the reader as guides for organizing similar learning modules when creating or revising leadership development programs. Although this book was developed primarily to help leadership educators in higher education that have similar human resources on their campuses, these lesson plans use a one-hour format that may be adapted in secondary schools, nonprofit agencies, businesses, government agencies, or wherever a need exists to improve the leadership process within an organization. The practical use of these lesson plans will make a difference in any team or group. Just invite a local "expert" to offer a one-hour lesson on one or two critical leadership skills such as listening skills and running effective meetings and imagine the difference that might make in better relationships or more productive meetings. Participants will ask for more and people will quickly begin offering their "expertise" in your leadership program.

Scan Part Two for a treasure trove of ideas and go back to Part One to learn how to engage others in creating or expanding a practical approach to leadership development.

TABLE OF CONTENTS

CHAPTER 6 SPECIAL EVENTS AND PROGRAMS CONNECTED TO THE GOLD PROGRAM

CHAPTER 7 DATA AND ASSESSMENT AND CONCLUSIONS

PART TWO: DESCRIPTIONS OF INDIVIDUAL GOLD LEADERSHIP WORKSHOPS

DESCRIPTIONS OF INDIVIDUAL GOLD LEADERSHIP WORKSHOPS

PART 1:

The GOLD Program Design, History, and Key Elements

INTRODUCTION

This section of the book was written to give the reader insights into the development of the GOLD Program at SUNY Geneseo. The extensive campus collaboration with students, faculty, administrators, alumni, community leaders, and student affairs staff has been integral to the success of the program.

Chapter 1 includes the Mission of the GOLD Program, which is directly tied to the Mission of the College. The brief Overview of the Program highlights the design of the program in the one-hour instructional model and provides the relational model definition of leadership that is used to teach leadership as a process.

Chapter 2 reviews the history and development of the program and the critical connections with the emerging field of leadership studies and the expansion of leadership programs throughout higher education. The author traces personal leadership experiences that helped guide and shape the development of the GOLD Program and reviews the critical connections with colleagues in emerging leadership associations. The chapter concludes with an explanation of how service

was integrated into the program and introduces the collaborative approach used in expanding the program.

Chapter 3 offers a detailed explanation of the current leadership certificate packages, including descriptions of the four required workshops in each of the certificates.

Chapter 4 provides an insider guide to the operations and management of the program.

Chapter 5 explains the collaborative nature of the program within the Division of Student and Campus Life and throughout the campus and beyond that helped shape and manage the program.

Chapter 6 describes several special events and programs that are connected to the program and offers the reader possible ways to integrate campus events into a leadership program.

Chapter 7 provides the data and statistics and outcomes assessment as evidence of the success of the program.

CHAPTER 1:

The Geneseo Opportunities for Leadership Development (GOLD) Certificate Program

MISSION OF GOLD PROGRAM

The Geneseo GOLD Program seeks to prepare students for college and community leadership roles and responsibilities in service to the college and the global community. Our mission is accomplished through education, development, and training of students in an extensive series of personal development programs, institutes, leadership certificates, service learning, volunteer work, and active engagement in college and community life.

OVERVIEW OF THE PROGRAM

The national award-winning GOLD Program at Geneseo provides over 300 carefully constructed and presented, one-hour, optional workshops per year on a variety of leadership-related topics. The program uses the relational model of leadership as the guiding definition and approach to teaching and learning the leadership process. The Komives definition of leadership asserts that leadership is

> *"...a relational and ethical process of people together attempting to accomplish positive change."*

> *(Komives, Lucas, McMahon, 2007)*

The open architecture of the GOLD Program permits students to participate whether they are new students or seniors. Students may elect to take only a few workshops or earn one or more of 10 certificates by completing specific groups of workshops. They may volunteer and serve others in an extensive variety of workshop-related civic engagement opportunities.

GOLD provides students with opportunities to develop and enhance a personal philosophy of leadership that includes understanding of self, others, and community; encourages students to gain a variety of leadership experiences; uses multiple theories and models; and recognizes and rewards exemplary leadership behavior.

GOLD fulfills the need for developing leaders and fosters and encourages students to practice ethical, high-quality leadership, both as undergraduates and as future citizens of the global community.

The Geneseo Opportunities for Leadership Development Program seeks to prepare students for leadership roles and responsibilities in service to the college and the global community. Our mission is accomplished through education, development, and training of students in an extensive series of personal development programs, institutes, leadership certificates, service learning, volunteer work, and active engagement in college and community life.

– GOLD Mission Statement

"The entire college community works together to develop socially responsible citizens with skills and values important to the pursuit of an enriched life and success in the world."
– Excerpt from SUNY Geneseo's Mission Statement

"Leadership Development: Demonstrates self-confidence, understands that leadership roles are multi-faceted, and values and exemplifies ethical leadership and serves as a role model for community involvement."
– Excerpt from SUNY Geneseo's Division of Student and Campus Life Student Learning Outcomes

GOLD Program Awards

NACA Foundation
"Exemplary Practices and Model Program Award"
2002

NASPA
"Bronze Excellence Award"
2006

SUNY
"Outstanding Student Affairs Program for Leadership Development"
2007

CHAPTER 2:

History of the GOLD Program

THE EARLY YEARS

In 1967, I started my career at the State University of New York (SUNY) at Geneseo as the Director of Student Activities, and I remained happily in that position for 25 years. I worked with our student leaders to create a structure and program that delivered highly successful activities and events for the campus community. I supervised conferences and cultural programs, operated a non-credit leisure learning school for the college community, hosted Elderhostel programs, developed a campus and community summer festival, managed an Events and Scheduling office, advised student organizations and fraternities and sororities, and occasionally offered leadership training for selected student leaders. In the 1980s, I established what was then called the Geneseo Organization for Leadership Development, which consisted of an advisory committee of student leaders, faculty, and student affairs staff, who helped plan and advertise workshops for student organization leaders. I also participated in several student affairs professional organizations, including the Association of College Unions International (ACUI) and the Association of Performing Arts Administrators (APAA), and moved up the volunteer ranks in the National Association for Campus Activities (NACA) to serve two terms as Chair of the Board of Directors. Through all those years, I enjoyed going to work every day, had fun, and always felt that my work with students made a difference.

In 1992, I had an opportunity to take a leave of absence from my job to become the newly elected Vice President for Professionals at United University Professions (UUP), the statewide union representing over 20,000 faculty and professional employees of the State University of New York. For the next four years, I worked full time in that capacity, commuting 300 miles round-trip each week from Geneseo to the state capital in Albany. One of the many amazing experiences I had during those years was to serve as chief negotiator for two rounds of collective bargaining with the governor's Office of Employee Relations. Part of my preparation and training for negotiations included a week at the Harvard Negotiations Project for lawyers that was created and managed by Roger Fisher, author of *Getting to Yes*. Fisher's positive negotiations approach was especially helpful in my first round of bargaining, which was protracted and difficult, because we had to overcome ideological battles over tenure and contracting out bargaining unit work; the second round produced the most successful contract in the 30-year history of the union. What I learned through these experiences was later incorporated into the GOLD Program through a workshop I offer every year on the Fisher approach, "Developing Your Negotiation Skills."

By 1996, I came to realize that my real passion was working with students, and I knew I wanted to return to campus. From 1996 to 2000, I continued my work with the union but was able to devote half of my time to work on campus. The Director of Student Activities position could not be accomplished part time, but I was fortunate to be assigned specific tasks that could be accomplished in two and a half days per week on campus. One of those assignments was to develop the Geneseo Organization for Leadership Development program. I had a small budget from the Student Association to support a leadership retreat for student organization leaders and money to advertise workshops. I was able to work on this program and started offering a few additional leadership workshops.

We started to offer a cocurricular involvement transcript. This provided a record of each student's involvement in workshops or associated activities, and served the students in many ways both on and off campus. It was a paper copy that required a cumbersome management system, but students liked to add it to their portfolios or resumes.

In 1999, our new Vice President for Student and Campus Life, Dr. Robert Bonfiglio, met with me to discuss his thoughts on reorganizing the Student Affairs departments. I suggested that we could expand our leadership programs and that was where I wanted to focus my efforts when I returned to campus full time in 2000. This was a field exploding with new programs and initiatives, and I thought it would be fun and challenging to develop a new program for the campus. A few weeks later we talked again and he offered me a newly created job in the new Center for Community. Dr. Bonfiglio challenged me to develop a dynamic new leadership program that would be a legacy gift to the campus. He said, "Tom, I know your reputation from your leadership in NACA and what you have done at Geneseo, and I know you can create a program that will work." I was surprised and delighted. I thought, "Wow! How many people get the opportunity to create a new program late in their career?"

THE DEVELOPMENT OF THE PROGRAM

Indeed, I was challenged, and I needed to rise to the occasion and create a program that would give all of our students, not just those in leadership positions, new opportunities to engage in learning and grow as leaders.

One of my first actions was to work with the existing GOLD advisory committee to conduct a review of leadership programs using the assessment process of the Council for the Advancement of Standards in Higher Education (CAS). That review process led to a committee recommendation to create a certificate program to be used as a vehicle for offering leadership education, development, and training for students.

"I knew that standards could provide a framework for a thoughtful, educationally effective leadership development program, and certainly grounding the program in the CAS Standards has been a key component of its success."

– Dr. Robert Bonfiglio, Vice President of Student and Campus Life

I consulted widely with leadership educators at other campuses and actively reviewed the resources available through the National Clearinghouse for Leadership Programs (NCLP) at the University of Maryland. I used a grant from a college-wide committee on new initiatives to purchase all of the existing NCLP publications, and I started studying the literature on leadership education and buying as many books as I could find to expand my understanding of how to design an effective leadership program. I also read the Kellogg Foundation reports on their successful initiatives funding leadership programs and their calls for the expansion of leadership development and training of college students.

In the summer of 1999, Bill Mandicott, a Geneseo alumnus from Frostburg State University, was co-chairing a summer National Leadership Symposium at Catholic University, co-sponsored by the National Association for Campus Activities and NCLP. Mandicott invited me to attend. The faculty for that symposium included Susan Komives, Nance Lucas, and Tim McMahon, authors of a new book, *Exploring Leadership for College Students Who Want to Make a Difference,* and Joe Rost, author of *Leadership for the 21st Century.* I was deeply affected by their presentations and their work in the leadership field. Komives and her colleagues urged us to teach leadership as a process, so students would understand that leading is not just about being a leader but also about how to work effectively with others. Rost, the creator of the first doctoral program in leadership studies in the country, at the University of San Diego, shared his advice, calling on authors and educators to state very clearly their definition of leadership when writing and discussing it in their programs. His review of the leadership literature offered convincing evidence that too many authors discuss leadership without ever defining what they mean by the term. Because there were over 200 definitions at the time, it made perfect sense to me that we needed to make sure our frame of reference for teaching leadership would be clearly stated in our program. We selected the relational model of leadership, "a relational and ethical process of people together attempting to accomplish positive change," as the guiding definition and approach to leadership.

2002 National Leadership Symposium.

In the fall of 1999 I attended the second annual conference of the International Leadership Association (ILA). At the first session in the higher education leadership educator's track, I sat down next to Nancy Huber, author of *The Leader Within,* whose work calling for high standards of personal ethics in leadership resonated with me, and I decided to incorporate it into our program. We became friends, and later, the two of us co-chaired one of the National Leadership Symposiums at the Jepson School of Leadership Studies at the University of Richmond.

In the summer of 2000, at the National Leadership Symposium, I shared the draft of our new leadership certificate promotional brochure with some of the participants. The feedback was very positive, but one colleague, Craig Slack, director of the NCLP and the symposium, pointed out one important missing piece. He advised, as did several other people, that we should have a reflection component. This was one of those "aha" moments. I added a journal requirement to the program. Ten years later, I can report that the journal reflections are one of the critical components of the GOLD Program, although it did take us several tries to tweak the format and develop a good set of guidelines for writing reflections.

I kept returning to ILA every fall to participate, because the membership included leadership educators, authors, and scholars in the exploding field of leadership studies, and consultants who coach leaders in business and professional organizations. ILA became part of my ongoing education and development as a leadership educator. I was also getting acquainted with many authors and coming home from every conference with a suitcase full of new books on leadership. I met and later became personal friends with Peter Northouse, professor of communication at Western Michigan University and author of *Leadership Theories and Practice.* His book, now in its fourth edition, is one of the most widely used textbooks on leadership and is used at over 700 colleges and universities, including ours.

I should also mention that I was also fortunate to attend several program sessions by James McGregor Burns (considered the father of the leadership studies field) at ILA conferences. His passion for working on a general theory of leadership (Burns, 2007) was really his way of advocating for leadership studies to become an accepted academic field of study. I sat next to him one day during a conference session discussing a report from the ensemble of scholars he had brought together to wrestle with the impossible task of a single theory of leadership. I asked him if the motivation behind the work was primarily a question of legitimizing leadership as a discipline, and his response was a telling nod and big smile. I cherish that special connection with one of the giants in the leadership field, who coined the term "transformational leadership" in his book *Leadership* (Burns, 1982).

MERGING LEADERSHIP AND SERVICE

In 2005, Vice President Bonfiglio and Dean of Students, Leonard Sancilio, thanked me for the progress we had made with the GOLD Program and asked me to merge our leadership and service programs and expand the involvement of students in our campus volunteer efforts. I had worked closely with Kay

Fly, our Coordinator of Volunteerism and Service Learning, on developing the Sapphire Volunteerism and Service Leadership Certificate. That spring we set about the task of creating a new image that

Matthews discussing service with Vice President Bonfiglio and Dean Sancilio.

would illustrate the merger of leadership and service by adding three words to the previously wordless graphic of our logo: "volunteerism, engagement, and service." We also spent a good deal of time discussing ways we could expand our service programs and give more visibility to the existing Volunteer Center. The answer came unexpectedly, during the last week of August 2005. Just as the fall semester was getting underway, Hurricane Katrina hit the Gulf Coast. We watched the horrific images and stories on television, and students started streaming into our offices to offer assistance in the relief and recovery efforts. We realized this tragedy and our response could help us create new ways of promoting volunteer work. We invited student leaders, faculty and staff, and community leaders to a meeting to discuss ways we might collaborate to help the people on the Gulf Coast. Attendees included our county administrator, the president of the Chamber of Commerce, our local town supervisor, village mayor, members of the county coalition of churches and several local clergy, the superintendent of schools, faculty members, administrators, and numerous student organization leaders. Within an hour, we agreed to pool our efforts and create a new campus and community organization that would encompass our entire county, Livingston County, New York. Within a week, a "Livingston CARES" logo was created and a website was up and running. A month later, the Livingston County Board of Supervisors and the Harrison County, Mississippi, Board of Supervisors had passed resolutions that would lead to a 10-year agreement of Livingston CARES–led volunteer work trips to Biloxi. We also created a permanent, registered 501 (c) (3) non-profit public charity with a broad-based humanitarian mission and a campus and community board of directors.

Livingston CARES May 2010 trip. Volunteers working on house in Biloxi.

As of 2012, nearly 700 volunteers have participated in 25 week-long work trips, worked on 60 homes, and contributed thousands of dollars to help families and community organizations in Harrison County, a county chosen specifically because it was one with great need, but not one that was the focus of national attention. The operations of Livingston CARES reside in the Center for Community, and the by-laws state that the leadership and service staff members are to serve as president and secretary of the corporation and that four students serve on the Board of Directors. More information on Livingston CARES is available on the website at http://livingstoncares.geneseo.edu

Since its creation, Livingston CARES has continued to expand its operations by also focusing efforts on humanitarian needs within Livingston County through programs such as an annual volunteer service day in every town and village in the county, Geneseo Goes to Town. Livingston CARES has also created special fundraising appeals to help relief and recovery efforts after the Haiti earthquake and cholera epidemic, the Japan tsunami, the 2011 tornados, the 2011 New York floods, and most recently Hurricane Sandy. Special project funds have also been established to build and support a school in Nicaragua, assist a school in Ghana, help families break the cycle of poverty in Guatemala, and aid the HEROS mentoring program for high school students in three Livingston County school districts.

Livingston CARES projects and programs have been integrated into the GOLD Program through the increased emphasis on community service in our Sapphire and Diamond leadership certificates.

Lori Ames, Diamond Certificate Box Tops for Education Project.

Students in the program are encouraged to engage in service and pursue their passions about issues and causes that have personal meaning and possible connections to graduate work and careers (see p. 31 for a description of the Diamond Certificate and p. 36 for a description of the Sapphire Certificate). New workshops have been created to prepare students to lead service trips, explore service options such as VISTA, and develop service projects in other countries as well as locally in Livingston County. In addition to Livingston CARES, for several years, Kay Fly, Coordinator of Student Volunteerism and Service Learning, and I have been participating in Community Resource Network (CRN), a community network of service organizations and agencies that meets four times a year to share information on programs and services. I volunteered to serve as treasurer and have continued in that role for the last 10 years. In 2011, at our request, the College agreed to host the CRN website and listserv to demonstrate our commitment and thanks to the community agencies that place our volunteers and supervise their service projects and programs. We have also had our GOLD instructors conduct workshops at CRN meetings as an outreach service to the community agencies, and we invite members to attend on-campus GOLD programs. Several agency members have GOLD accounts and take advantage of popular sessions like "Who Moved My Cheese?" and "FISH!®" CRN also assisted us in the creation of our first annual Volunteer and Service Awards Dinner, held at the end of March 2012, to recognize student organizations, student volunteers, and community agencies for their volunteer efforts.

One of the outcomes of merging leadership and service was the creation of our new Diamond Civic Engagement Leadership Certificate. The certificate grew out of our participation in the American Democracy Project and conversations connected to our involvement in a campus-wide task force that recommended developing programs on transformational learning. Our service initiatives fit into the concept of transformative learning, and the new certificate provides an option for students to share their engagement stories and be recognized for their community service.

Although we have made great strides through Livingston CARES, CRN, and the Diamond Certificate initiatives to make connections and help our students with increased volunteer and service options, the possibilities for integrating the GOLD Program with our community service initiatives still seem endless.

DEVELOPING AND NAMING LEADERSHIP CERTIFICATES

In 1999, the media started focusing on the upcoming 2000 Olympics. At the time, we were engaged in developing the new GOLD Program and shifting and sorting possible approaches and terms to use in marketing the program to students. Leadership programs in the past were offered as GOLD workshops and it made sense to keep and use that name. Our planning committee included students, faculty, and student affairs staff. The president of the Student Association, Nicole Duxbury, was on the committee and she suggested that we offer certificates as an incentive for students to stay involved in the program. This was another "aha" moment and quickly led to the structure of the program as a Leadership Certificate Program with Bronze, Silver, and Gold certificates, similar to the Olympic medals. We launched the program in August 2000, just after the summer Olympic Games, with our three precious metal titles.

Two years later, we created two new certificates in collaboration with the directors of our Multicultural Programs and Services and Volunteerism and Service Learning programs. We decided to use gemstones in the names as a way of marketing the new certificates and decided to use Opal for the Diversity and Cultural Competency Certificate and Sapphire for the Volunteerism and Service Leadership Certificate. The following year, a task force working on ways to increase professionalism among student employees on the campus developed an employee training series and we added it to the GOLD Program with the Emerald label as the Student Employee Development Certificate. Because most of the workshops in this certificate were taught by our Career Development staff, the series later evolved into the Emerald Career and Professional Development Leadership Certificate.

In 2006, the library faculty approached us with a proposal to offer a series of workshops on Leadership in the Information Age. This certificate evolved from the fact that most of our librarians taught information sessions on use of library resources and research and were interested in offering similar sessions in the GOLD Program. Originally, I was not sure how we would make a meaningful connection between information management and leadership. The deal was sealed when the librarians pointed out that almost every student research paper and presentation involves the ethical use of information. Perhaps because Bernie Madoff was front-page news at the time, I immediately made the connection and agreed to work with the library faculty on the development of the new certificate to help our students understand the issues and use and manipulate information with the highest possible ethical standards. The Ruby Certificate, then, has a direct connection to our mission of preparing ethical leaders. Ruby was selected as the label for the new certificate that was offered for the first time in the fall of 2006 and was updated and retitled in the fall of 2011 as the Information Management and Digital Leadership Certificate.

For several years I participated in the college-wide American Democracy Committee and was sent with other Geneseo faculty and staff members to several national conferences on civic engagement sponsored by the American Association of Colleges and Universities. We collaborated on campus events and programs that were frequently incorporated into the GOLD Program for credit as either Sapphire or Gold workshops. In 2008, David Parfitt, Director of the Teaching and Learning Center, and I also participated together in an all-campus strategic planning committee, the Six Big Ideas Committee. We started talking about ways we could challenge students to engage in community service and social justice activism and decided to create a new leadership certificate focused on civic engagement. The certificate was conceived as a second capstone experience for students, similar in scope to the Gold level certificate with a required project and paper in addition to the eight workshops and journals. It made sense to label this certificate with the Diamond gemstone title. The first iteration of the new certificate required students to engage with a community partner on a sustainable project. A handful of students responded and created significant projects, such as the Ghana Project that has now expanded into a campus-wide program with relationships between SUNY Geneseo and Kwame Nkrumah University of Science & Technology in Ghana. The second iteration expanded the certificate from civic to community engagement and added social justice activities.

Adding social justice to the mix also led to new workshops and a social justice series. Because many of our faculty members are engaged in a wide variety of social justice issues and often give presentations on topics related to their area of research or interests, we started asking them to offer a one-hour version of their work in GOLD workshops. Every faculty member we asked to teach a workshop has done so, and several have taught the workshops multiple times during the last three years. They sometimes struggle with the limitations of the one-hour format, but quickly realize they are having an impact when they see the positive comments on the evaluation summary sheets we send to them after a workshop

Also in 2008, we decided to offer a Platinum Leadership Certificate as a bonus to students who complete all of the other available leadership certificates. As this certificate is currently only awarded to those who have attended 36 required workshops and another 36 optional workshops, very few students actually earn the Platinum Leadership Certificate.

In 2007, the College established a College Task Force on Sustainability to study environmental issues and make recommendations on instituting and promoting sustainability as a core value of the College. The task force included students, faculty, and administers who were committed to reducing the carbon footprint of the campus. In 2010–2011, the Task Force asked if we would consider offering a leadership in sustainability certificate. The task force was particularly interested in offering a program through GOLD because the College was having to cut some programs due to the economic crisis and was not in a position to add a minor in sustainability. Our model of offering inexpensive one-hour workshops with four required modules and additional optional modules made sense to the Sustainability Task Force as a way of promoting sustainability in an affordable format without committing additional scarce resources. The faculty agreed to teach the workshops without expecting additional compensation and committed to repeat the required workshops each semester. I agreed to integrate the new series into the GOLD Program and coordinate and market it to students through our promotional pieces and our website.

Although we started the GOLD Program in 2000 with a package of three core certificates (Bronze, Silver, and Gold) that teach skills, self-understanding, and knowledge of leadership theories, we expanded the program to include six critical components to help our students prepare for leadership roles in their careers and life in the global community. The next chapter describes the three core certificates in the Gold sequence and the six optional stand-alone certificates.

"I'm now a biology teacher, but over the past four years, have built up an Interact Club (service fraternity, high school version of Rotary) to over 200 high school student members and a student executive board of 15. We are extremely active, with over 100 events over the school year and over 4,200 volunteer hours. Our high activity level has resulted in a need to help supervise the club service events and I have been able to pull five like-minded teachers in as assistants. Running this massive club with 15 student leaders and five adults under my direction would not have been possible without learning the basics of leadership and volunteerism. My experiences in the GOLD Program directly relate to my successes with the Interact Club (and with teaching). I immediately wanted to give the same sort of basic skills to my Interact students, but unfortunately, there is no GOLD Program for high school students! (A great idea!!) The only program they've been able to participate in yearly is the True Colors® seminar on personality types and how to interact with those of differing personalities from yours. Every time I attend, I'm reminded of those GOLD seminars! If I could go back right now and attend more, I would!"

– Julia Kogut, Class of 2005

CHAPTER 3:

GOLD Program Design:
Ten Current Leadership Certificates

TEN CURRENT LEADERSHIP CERTIFICATES

When we first started presenting workshops, students were loud and clear about their preference for one-hour programs rather than longer ones. Our challenge, given the time constraints of students, was to create effective learning modules in one-hour formats that would work within the academic calendar and typical daily class schedule. Almost all sessions are currently offered in the afternoon from 2:30–3:30 p.m. in order to avoid competing activities when students are otherwise engaged. Most recently, student responses on the 2009 research survey Multi Institutional Study of Leadership (Center for Student Studies and the National Clearinghouse of Leadership Programs, 2009) confirmed that a one-hour time block continues to be the preferred format for leadership programs.

Diamond Community Mapping discussion with Wes Kennison.

The centerpiece of the GOLD Program is an innovative and extensive certificate program that currently offers 10 leadership certificates to students. There are three core certificates in the Gold sequence (Bronze, Silver, and Gold) and six optional stand-alone certificates plus the honorary certificate (Platinum) awarded for the completion of all nine certificates.

Core Leadership Certificates

- Bronze Life Skills and Leadership Certificate
- Silver Practicing Leadership Certificate
- Gold Personal Leadership Model Certificate

Jade Sustainability Certificate exercise with Kristi Hannam.

Specialized and Optional Leadership Certificates

- Diamond Leadership in Community Engagement and Social Justice Certificate
- Emerald Leadership in Career and Professional Development Certificate
- Jade Leadership in Sustainability Certificate
- Opal Diversity and Cultural Competency Certificate
- Ruby Certificate for Information Management and Digital Age Leadership
- Sapphire Volunteerism and Service Leadership Certificate
- Platinum Leadership Certificate

Sapphire Volunteer Involvement reflection session with Kay Fly.

Each certificate includes four required workshops and four optional workshops that students select. Personal journal reflections are also required for each of the eight workshops to complete each certificate. The tenth certificate, Platinum, is awarded to students who complete all of the other nine.

BRONZE LIFE SKILLS AND LEADERSHIP CERTIFICATE

The Bronze Certificate provides an introduction to new perspectives on leaders and leadership, suggests pathways for personal growth and development, and offers a range of individual and group leadership and life skills. The Bronze Certificate is awarded upon completion of eight workshops, including the four required workshops (Leadership Concepts, Personal Development Session, Listening Skills, and Presentation Skills) and submission of journal reflections for each of eight workshops.

BRONZE HIGHLIGHTED INSTRUCTOR:
Kim Harvey teaching a Bronze workshop.

GOLD Mentors preparing for Time Management Workshop.

BRONZE REQUIRED WORKSHOPS

LEADERSHIP CONCEPTS:

Everyone has an opinion about leaders and what constitutes effective leadership. Everyone can be a leader, and most of us will be called upon to lead at one time or another. Start or continue your leadership journey with this introductory session to the GOLD Program and to the fascinating world of leadership concepts, myths, and possibilities.

PERSONAL DEVELOPMENT SESSION:

The GOLD Leader Mentor volunteer staff has been trained to assist you in developing a personal plan for successfully completing the GOLD Certificate Program. You need to register for this session just like all other workshops. Make an appointment at the GOLD Leadership Center in MacVittie College Union 114, or call 245-5884, or email gold@geneseo.edu. The mentor staff is available between 12–8 p.m. Monday through Thursday and 12–5 p.m. on Fridays.

LISTENING SKILLS:

What makes someone a "good listener"? Think of his/her characteristics. What can prevent someone from listening carefully? This session will examine listening skills and offer ways to improve these critical skills.

PRESENTATION SKILLS:

This workshop is designed to help students learn the foundational skills of developing and organizing effective speeches and presentations. Strategies to overcome fear of speaking in public and resources to make effective presentations will be discussed.

SILVER PRACTICING LEADERSHIP CERTIFICATE

The Silver Certificate offers additional skill development, assists students in higher level group development, explores the range of personal learning and leadership styles, and helps students discover their strengths and effective leadership practices. The Silver Certificate is awarded upon completion of the Bronze Certificate and eight workshops, including the four required workshops (Leadership Styles, Running Effective Meetings, Student Leadership Practices Inventory, and Teambuilding), as well as submission of journal reflections for each workshop.

SILVER REQUIRED WORKSHOPS

LEADERSHIP STYLES:

Each individual has a leadership style that s/he prefers to use and to follow. It is valuable to recognize that different situations call for different leadership styles. In this interactive workshop you will learn about different leadership styles and you will review some of the effective uses of these leadership styles.

RUNNING EFFECTIVE MEETINGS:

Running an effective and efficient meeting is the key to getting your members to keep coming back, and we'll give you tips on how to do just that! This program will address issues like agenda setting, necessary parliamentary procedure, committee meetings, and dealing with unruly members.

STUDENT LEADERSHIP PRACTICES INVENTORY (SLPI™):

Students participating in this workshop need to be involved in one or more organizations or groups in order to effectively utilize the SLPI™ instruments. They receive a code to go online and complete the Leadership Practices Inventory and to invite specific individuals (observers) to provide feedback on leadership practices. This inventory is provided FREE to students who complete the process. The Student Association covers the cost of the SLPI™, but the $15 fee is billed to individuals who do not complete the process after the code has been assigned. A printed inventory report will be provided to each individual at the workshop.

TEAMBUILDING:

Teambuilding is critical to the success of any group that must work together. This session will cover the appropriate sequencing of activities and some basic tools for developing and enhancing teamwork. This workshop is an active learning session.

SILVER HIGHLIGHTED INSTRUCTOR:
Chip Matthews teaching FISH!® Workshop.

Student Team preparing for Silver Negotiating Skills Workshop.

GOLD PERSONAL LEADERSHIP MODEL CERTIFICATE

The Gold Certificate provides opportunities to explore a wide variety of leadership theories and models in the context of the historical development of leadership as an emerging field of study, examines individual leadership theories, assists students in developing a personal leadership model, and requires students to demonstrate an understanding of a minimum of eight of the major leadership theories. The Gold Certificate is awarded upon completion of the Silver Certificate and eight workshops, including the four required workshops (Creating and Leading Inclusive Environments, Developing a Personal Leadership Model, History of Leadership, and Leadership Identity Development) and submission of journal reflections for each workshop plus a written Personal Leadership Model. Students are required to prepare and submit a set of three documents that describe their leadership journey, an analysis of a minimum of eight leadership theories, and a statement of their current beliefs about leadership. This capstone assignment comprises the written Personal Leadership Model.

GOLD HIGHLIGHTED INSTRUCTOR:
Tamara Kenney leading workshop on Servant Leadership.

Anne Burns, George Sullivan, and Michelle Plyem receive Prize Paper Awards for GOLD Personal Leadership Model Papers.

GOLD REQUIRED WORKSHOPS

CREATING AND LEADING INCLUSIVE ENVIRONMENTS:

In any career and at any level, you will find yourself working within a diverse atmosphere. With a wide range of diversity, how do you identify differences? How do you ensure everyone feels they are a key member? How do you create a welcoming environment? These are tricky but critical skills a leader must possess to create a positive and productive team.

DEVELOPING A PERSONAL LEADERSHIP MODEL:

The Gold level of the Leadership Certificate Program requires students to articulate written and verbal statements of their personal philosophy of leadership. This informal coaching session will provide students with an opportunity to work on their model with the assistance of the instructor. Reference materials and resources will be available.

HISTORY OF LEADERSHIP:

Students will learn the history of leadership and review 16 theoretical approaches to leadership.

LEADERSHIP IDENTITY DEVELOPMENT:

When did you first discover that there was such a thing as a leader? When did you decide that you could be a leader? When did you first experience leading? Can you remember what you did? Where do you think you are in the developmental process of leading? This session, based on research on leadership identity development, will assist students in preparing the required Personal Leadership Model.

DIAMOND LEADERSHIP IN COMMUNITY ENGAGEMENT AND SOCIAL JUSTICE CERTIFICATE

The Diamond Civic Engagement Leadership Certificate is designed to prepare students for lifelong engagement and involvement in community life through individual and collective actions designed to identify and address issues of public concern. Students utilize many of the leadership skills offered in the Bronze, Silver, Emerald, and Sapphire certificates to successfully complete this certificate. Civic engagement begins with volunteering and service and requires a higher level of commitment that involves working with others in a campus or community-based project or social justice issue. Students begin this certificate by taking the first three required workshops (What Is Civic and Community Engagement?, Community Mapping, and Community Engagement & Social Justice Activity Preparation). The last required workshop, Community Engagement & Social Justice Activity, is a presentation that students make on Geneseo Recognizing Excellence and Talent (GREAT) Day, the annual college symposium in April. Each student presents his/her reflections on his/her engagement project or social justice activity. Students are encouraged to pursue projects that reflect their personal passions and interests and may be related to careers and future lives as engaged citizens. The Diamond Certificate will be awarded upon completion of eight workshops, including the four required workshops and completion of a project or involvement in a social justice reflection paper.

DIAMOND REQUIRED WORKSHOPS

WHAT IS CIVIC AND COMMUNITY ENGAGEMENT?:
Engaging in one's community includes personal action to join a group that is interesting to you, work on a cause or social justice issue that you are passionate about, help with community projects, participate in local political party activities, or simply serve on the planning or clean-up committee for a community event. Practicing civic and community leadership develops from engaging with others in the leadership process.

COMMUNITY MAPPING:
Civic engagement begins with mapping your community. Every community has a unique history, a specific demographic composition, overlapping organizations and institutions, and a particular matrix of human economic and geographic resources. This workshop will provide a conceptual and practical understanding of how individuals and/or groups may overcome obstacles and leverage resources to accomplish goals and positive change through civic engagement.

COMMUNITY ENGAGEMENT AND SOCIAL JUSTICE ACTIVITY PREPARATION:
Leaders recognize they are part of a larger social community, and any problems of that community are therefore also problems for the individual leader. Students pursuing this leadership certificate may choose to either work on a community project with a local agency or engage in multiple activities related to a social justice issue. This session is designed to help you work through the process of deciding which track to follow and what types of projects or issues will be the best fit for your interests and timeframe. We will help you define the nature of the service and activities you will be doing and help you develop an engagement plan.

COMMUNITY ENGAGEMENT AND SOCIAL JUSTICE ACTIVITIES STRUCTURED REFLECTION:
Leaders must be able to think clearly about complex issues and act in appropriate and responsible ways. In order to make connections between your community engagement activities and the larger social community, you will be required to reflect on your experience in a structured manner and to make a brief presentation in the GREAT Day Program. A written reflection and/or structured report on the service or social justice activities is required to complete the certificate.

EMERALD LEADERSHIP IN CAREER AND EMPLOYEE DEVELOPMENT CERTIFICATE

The Emerald Certificate was designed to help students develop and apply lifelong career development skills as a student employee, a full-time career professional, or both. Students learn strategies to navigate workplace issues, develop an awareness of appropriate behavior in professional settings, and prepare for the transition to a career after college. Workshops provide opportunities to enhance personal and professional skills that are workplace expectations and help prepare students for promotions and higher-level supervisory positions. The Emerald Certificate is awarded upon completion of eight workshops, including the four required workshops (Career Quest—Assessing Your Competencies, Skills, Values, and Goals; Networking/Informational Interviewing Strategies; Job Interviewing Skills; Reflecting on Your College Experiences and Marketing Your Skills), and submission of journal reflections for each of eight workshops.

EMERALD HIGHLIGHTED INSTRUCTOR:
Liz Seager helping students reflect on college experience.

Kerrie Bondi sharing career advice at Emerald workshop.

EMERALD REQUIRED WORKSHOPS

CAREER QUEST—ASSESSING YOUR COMPETENCIES, SKILLS, VALUES, AND GOALS:

Are you certain about your academic or career plans? Do you need some direction? Career Development staff will help you uncover your competencies, interests, skills, and values, and the role those traits will play in your life after Geneseo. Participants will be required to complete the FOCUS series of assessments prior to class, will be introduced to the career decision-making process as well as goal setting, and will learn how to research career opportunities. There's so much you can do to smooth the path from campus to career. Let us help you identify your options!

NETWORKING/INFORMATIONAL INTERVIEWING STRATEGIES:

Nearly every day of your life you have an opportunity to make connections and build relationships. The people you know and even people you don't know can influence the direction your life may take. If you don't know how to talk to people about your future, then this workshop is for you. Come and learn how to introduce yourself (even to those you know) and discover what questions to ask to help you in your career decision making.

JOB INTERVIEWING SKILLS:

Learn how to answer a variety of questions that you will most likely face during that moment of truth in your job search...the interview! Be prepared to learn and practice open-ended, opinion, and those all-important Behavioral-Based Interview questions, to name a few.

REFLECTING ON YOUR COLLEGE EXPERIENCE AND MARKETING YOUR SKILLS:

This session will focus on helping you build your career at Geneseo and prepare for life after college. Learn how to identify what you've accomplished as a student and employee and how to market it to future employers for other jobs on or off campus.

JADE LEADERSHIP IN SUSTAINABILITY CERTIFICATE

The Jade Certificate is designed to help students recognize the importance of sustainability issues in their personal and professional lives and to understand their responsibilities as individuals and community members to promote and encourage sustainable practices. The Jade certificate provides both a theoretical and practical foundation for students looking to take on leadership roles in the movement to build a more sustainable society.

The Jade Certificate is awarded upon completion of eight workshops, including the four required workshops (Beyond the 3 Rs: An Education for Living in Ethical and Sustainable Ways; From Preservation to Conservation to Sustainability and Intergenerational Equity; If Sustainability Is the Solution, What Is the Problem?; The Historical Origins of the Current Environmental Crisis) and submission of journal reflections for each of eight workshops.

JADE REQUIRED WORKSHOPS

BEYOND THE 3 RS: AN EDUCATION FOR LIVING IN ETHICAL AND SUSTAINABLE WAYS:

At the center of most sustainability education is a focus on the 3Rs: Reduce, Reuse, and Recycle. Unfortunately, most of us, because it's easier, put recycling at the center of our efforts rather than use it as a last resort. What would it look like if we all believed—and acted as if—it was our ethical obligation not to consume, but to conserve; to, as the catch-phrase puts it, live simply so that others may simply live? Is this even feasible in a country operating under a system Oliver James calls "selfish capitalism"?

FROM PRESERVATION TO CONSERVATION TO SUSTAINABILITY AND INTERGENERATIONAL EQUITY:

This workshop will help participants better understand the terms and concepts surrounding environmental issues in general and sustainability specifically. In order to be a successful leader in sustainability it is critical to have working definitions of the important terms that are used by academics, politicians, and the media. We will specifically discuss the differences between preservation, conservation, and sustainability. Particular attention will be given to different definitions and concepts of sustainability with a discussion of both intergenerational equity and intragenerational equity.

IF SUSTAINABILITY IS THE SOLUTION, WHAT IS THE PROBLEM?:

All people on the planet participate in activities that impact the environment through use of power sources and water, heat, transportation, food consumption, and waste production. The impacts of these activities differ depending on the technologies used and the number of people involved. This seminar will help participants better understand environmental issues related to overpopulation, consumption, pollution, climate change, etc., that result from human activities and have led to the rise of sustainability as a mindset/strategy to mitigate these problems. The workshop will follow the theme of "Think Globally, Act Locally" by examining the issues from a global perspective, considering the campus community's carbon footprint, and helping participants understand their individual contributions to the problems through the use of an ecological footprint calculator.

THE HISTORICAL ORIGINS OF THE CURRENT ENVIRONMENTAL CRISIS:

This workshop will trace the historical roots of the current environmental crisis to the ideology of the U.S. environmental movement as a reaction to the ongoing collapse of Manifest Destiny. The environmental movement will be analyzed as series of six alternative frames—conservationism, preservationism, ecocentrism, social ecology, deep ecology, and ecofeminism—each of which has challenged, in varying ways, the underlying assumptions of Manifest Destiny. The role played by frame disputes, organizational legitimization, resource mobilization and partitioning, and the emergence of second-generation environmental issues in the growth and diversification of the movement will also be discussed.

OPAL DIVERSITY AND CULTURAL COMPETENCY LEADERSHIP CERTIFICATE

The Opal Certificate is designed to help students recognize and understand that all environments are diverse, and that diverse environments are complex and challenging, present a wealth of opportunity, and are constantly changing. Students are introduced to the skill sets needed to be better able to address the challenges, as well as recognize and mine the opportunities that diversity presents. Upon completion of the program, the student will be more comfortable working as a member of a diverse team, better able to recognize cross-cultural barriers that can hinder communication, and less likely to make assumptions about others based on superficial traits and characteristics. The Opal Certificate is awarded upon completion of eight workshops, including the four required workshops (Developing Inter-Group Relationships, Cross-Cultural Problem Solving, Identity Expression, and Taking the Next Steps) and submission of journal reflections for each of the eight workshops.

OPAL HIGHLIGHTED INSTRUCTOR:
Fatima Rodriguez Johnson leading Opal work-shop discussion.

Opal session on taking adversity out of diversity with Maura Cullen.

OPAL REQUIRED WORKSHOPS

DEVELOPING INTER-GROUP RELATIONSHIPS:
Acquiring the ability to interact with people of different backgrounds is a process. It depends on our awareness and comfort level with diverse groups. This workshop will examine our relationships with individuals different from ourselves.

CROSS-CULTURAL PROBLEM SOLVING:
This session will use a model created as a process for collaboratively understanding and addressing conflicts and issues related to difference, discrimination, and inter-group tensions in a school context. Learn to apply this model in solving cross-cultural problems.

IDENTITY EXPRESSION:
Everyone has multiple identities. This session will demonstrate how people express their different identities and provide a new understanding of the wide range of diversity that exists in our daily interactions with other people.

TAKING THE NEXT STEPS:
In this workshop, participants will share their experiences, reflect on the workshops they participated in and the growth that they experienced. Participants will also create a Personal Action Plan for the future.

RUBY CERTIFICATE FOR INFORMATION MANAGEMENT AND DIGITAL LEADERSHIP

The Ruby Certificate is designed to help students become discerning members of the increasingly digital world, able to find and evaluate information quickly and present their own work professionally. Upon completion of the certificate, students will be capable of evaluating sources of information for accuracy and relevancy, confident in their ability to do solid research crucial to the decision-making process, aware of the ethical issues involving the use of information, and able to create effective multimedia presentations. Through particular useful for students in their first and second years of college, these skills will help anyone save precious time by increasing efficiency in their personal and professional lives.

RUBY REQUIRED WORKSHOPS

CREATING E-PORTFOLIOS FOR THE JOB MARKET:

An e-portfolio is a means of showcasing your accomplishments in digital format. It demonstrates your skills and competencies and is a reflection of who you are. Come and learn how to create your own free e-portfolio and add various forms of digital content, such as documents, videos, presentations, and photos.

CRITICAL INQUIRY IN RESEARCH:

Great leaders gather information and critically analyze the facts before making good decisions. Attendees at this workshop will discover helpful tips and strategies that are used in any kind of database to help improve their searches, save time, and determine the best quality resources for their research.

FAIR USE? YOUR RIGHTS AS A USER AND CREATOR OF DIGITAL CONTENT:

Can you be sued for using an image you found online? Is writing fan fiction legal? When you get inspired by something you read online and create something new from it, do you own it? After discussing scenarios, attendees will appreciate the fine line between fair use and copyright infringement, and will recognize the difference between student and professional behavior.

SOCIAL NETWORKING FOR PROFESSIONALS:

Become familiar with some of the social media technologies the savvy professional will need, including social networks, social bookmarking, and other relevant Web 2.0 applications. The focus of this workshop is to encourage students to establish good habits that lead to a professional online representation of themselves. Participants are encouraged to take advantage of presenting themselves in a positive manner in order to reap the benefits later in life.

RUBY HIGHLIGHTED INSTRUCTOR:
Steve Dresbach teaching technical skills at Ruby workshop.

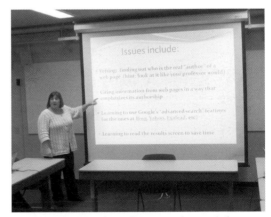

Sue Ann Brainard teaching a Ruby workshop on fair use of digital content.

SAPPHIRE VOLUNTEERISM AND SERVICE LEADERSHIP CERTIFICATE

The Sapphire Certificate is designed to help students interested in volunteering to recognize and understand the opportunities, responsibilities, service, and leadership performed by volunteers for the greater good of society. The Sapphire Certificate program provides a conceptual framework for volunteerism, offers basic information on the do's and don'ts of volunteering, offers skill-building training, encourages reflection on the experiences, and introduces a range of theoretical models of volunteerism and leadership. The Sapphire Certificate is awarded upon completion of eight workshops, including the four required workshops (Volunteerism, Engagement and Service; Volunteer Fair; Rights and Responsibilities of Volunteers; and Volunteer Involvement Reflection), submission of journal reflections for each of the eight workshops, and evidence of 20 hours of volunteer work or participation in service learning projects.

SAPPHIRE REQUIRED WORKSHOPS

VOLUNTEERISM, ENGAGEMENT, AND SERVICE:

Volunteerism is an active form of exercising leadership for the common good. This session is an introduction to volunteerism, community engagement, and service learning. Students will learn a conceptual framework for volunteer service and explore the myriad of opportunities to volunteer in the Geneseo and the Greater Livingston and Monroe County area, or the Livingston County CARES programs and other projects, including work trips to Harrison County, Mississippi. Learn how to get the most out of your volunteer experience by choosing a volunteer and service opportunity that will benefit you as well as the recipients.

VOLUNTEER FAIR:

Representatives from college and community organizations will be present to recruit volunteers and explain their programs and services. Students involved in the GOLD programs and the Sapphire Certificate program should attend and visit with as many organizations as possible in order to discover the range of possibilities for volunteer involvement. Sapphire Certificate candidates will need to visit at least 10, complete additional paper work, and submit a reflection.

RIGHTS AND RESPONSIBILITIES OF VOLUNTEERS:

As a volunteer you have rights and responsibilities. This session will provide you with both a set of expectations for you as a volunteer and expectations from the people that direct your volunteer work. You will learn the basic do's and don'ts of volunteer work.

VOLUNTEER INVOLVEMENT REFLECTION:

All students pursuing the Sapphire Volunteerism & Service Leadership Certificate are required to complete a minimum of 20 hours of service in a volunteer activity. The SUNY Geneseo Volunteer Center will assist students in finding volunteer opportunities, or students may use other service activities to fulfill the requirement. This session will provide an opportunity for students to share their volunteer experiences.

ANNUAL LEADERSHIP AWARDS AND RECOGNITION CEREMONY

At the end of the academic year, the Division of Student and Campus Life sponsors an awards ceremony to recognize student leaders and organizations for their outstanding contributions to the campus community. The one-hour ceremony is held in the College Union Ballroom during the 2:30–3:30 p.m. common hour in order to make the program easily accessible to students, faculty, and staff. Over 20 major awards are presented by the departments within the Division. Students who have completed GOLD Leadership Certificates during the year are also recognized in the awards program and presented with a signed leadership certificate as part of the ceremony. Students are required to submit a request for a printed certificate and to affirm that they will be present at the ceremony to receive their certificates.

ABOVE:
Vice President Bonfiglio challenging student leaders at awards ceremony.

ABOVE:
President Dahl congratulates Senior Mentor Kaitlyn Dennehy.

ABOVE:
Senior Gold Mentors recognized at awards ceremony.

ABOVE:
2012 Annual Leadership Awards Recognition Ceremony.

CHAPTER 4:

Key Operational Elements of the GOLD Program

STAFFING AND HUMAN RESOURCES

The GOLD Program staff consists of one full-time administrator responsible for developing and supervising the college-wide leadership and service program and a full-time secretary who also assists the coordinator of multicultural programs and services and the coordinator of volunteerism and service. Two or three work-study and temporary service student employees also assist in the daily and weekly paper and electronic work to support the program. The full-time staff members are housed in the Center for Community on the third floor of the College Union. Other staff members include the Dean of Students, the Assistant Dean for Student Conduct and Community Standards, the Coordinator of Greek Life and Off-Campus Living, and one additional secretary. The GOLD Program is also supported by 25 volunteer GOLD Leader Mentors who operate the GOLD Leadership Center and assist the director in managing the program.

GOLD PROGRAM BUDGET

The GOLD Leadership Certificate Program is supported by three sources of funding. State appropriations provide funding for the salaries of the Director, secretary, and student clerical staff, including some funds for operations and programs. Additional program funds are provided by Campus Auxiliary Services, by the Student Association, and from gifts to the Geneseo Foundation GOLD account. The current program operating budget is approximately $25,000, exclusive of salaries, and that provides over 300 programs to more than 6,000 participants annually.

The largest expense in our annual GOLD budget is the hard copies of the catalog. For several years we printed a catalog each semester and distributed copies to every on-campus room in each of the residence halls. The student government budget committee eventually withdrew their allocation for the printed catalog, primarily because the students felt the catalog was not necessary because the same information is available on the GOLD website. I was able to secure funding from our Campus Auxiliary

Ward Scholars from left to right: Chad Salitan, Dan Ward, Jim Rogers, George Sullivan, and Elizabeth Lawrence.

Services grants one year and from an alumni donor another year. During that same period, we decided to reduce the cost by printing one catalog for the entire year instead of printing a catalog each semester. The change required scheduling the entire year in advance. Although some of our faculty instructors are not always able to determine their class obligations for the entire year, we have been able to adjust to a full-year schedule with very few changes and deviations from the printed catalog. The catalog has also been reformatted to cut the number of pages by using three index formats: dates, certificates, and alpha titles and descriptions. Printing costs for nametags, handouts, and other paper supplies are covered in the three budget sources. The Student Association budget includes funding for a Martin Luther King, Jr., Day of Leadership and Service lunch and other supplies and expenses. The printing of handouts, promotional fliers, nametags, postage, and temporary service student office assistants are items included in our state GOLD Program account.

GOLD Program instructors do not normally receive any compensation or honorariums for teaching workshops. Most of our instructors are faculty, administrators, students, and alumni who are asked to teach a workshop related to their area of specialty, research, or interests. Given the large number of workshops each year (350) and instructors (100), we could not afford to offer even a modest honorarium to them all. We thank our instructors by providing evaluation feedback summary sheets, writing thank-you emails and notes, and giving modest GOLD specialty gifts such as clocks, coffee mugs, water bottles, notepads, or other low-budget items. We also try to make sure instructor names and titles are included in our GOLD catalogs and posted on the GOLD website. We also do our best to let department heads and supervisors know how much we appreciate the instructors' contributions to the program. Teaching faculty frequently cite their service to the GOLD Program in annual reports and portfolios for tenure and promotion. Administrators also cite their contributions in annual reports and in documents used for discretionary salary increases and promotions. Alumni cite their presentations in social media such as LinkedIn and Facebook. **Our instructors clearly demonstrate a strong commitment to community service through their contributions to the GOLD Program.**

RD Ryan Moton teaching Group Dynamics.

Presenting GOLD workshops is often perceived as an honor. Residence Life staff and young professionals seem honored to be asked to teach in the program, and they frequently offer to create new workshops in order to gain teaching experience. Senior staff members sometimes turn over a topic to a new staff member to give them an opportunity to teach in the program. GOLD Leader Mentors may offer to develop a workshop on a new topic, and I will sometimes ask mentors to develop a program that we would like to offer the following year. Alumni typically come back to campus to share their stories and consider it an honor to be asked to teach in the program. I often receive phone calls or emails from former students I have worked with who would like to return to campus and teach a workshop. Although we do not usually offer honorariums to alumni, we occasionally help with the cost of lodging and meals during their visit.

For the past several years we have had a modest allocation from the Student Association to use for speakers and consultant fees. Each year, I have used the teambuilding guru, Dr. Jim Cain, author of eight texts on team- and community-building activities. Cain has been a frequent presenter and a friend of the GOLD Program and each year he trains our GOLD Leader Mentor staff on teaching our required teambuilding workshops, always doing an excellent job. Cain has also co-authored the leadership curriculum for the C5 Youth Foundation and the Thrive Foundation/4H curriculum in California. More information on his books, activities, train-the-trainer workshops, facilitation skills, and teambuilding props are available at www.teamworkandteamplay.com. I was very fortunate to meet Cain as I was developing the program, and we have become good professional friends. He lives nearby and we have always been able to work out a training session for the mentors early each fall.

The speaker's budget typically co-sponsors one or two outside speakers in collaboration with Residence Life, the student Contemporary Forum committee, Multicultural Programs and Services, or departments, depending on a theme or topic that might be selected. Most years, Residence Life and GOLD collaborate on an outside speaker whose presentation also doubles as an in-service program for our Resident Assistants. In 2011, we brought Scott Allen to share his work on emotionally intelligent leadership. Other years, we have been fortunate to have Maura Cullen, Nancy Hunter Denny, Arun Gandhi, Jonathan Kozol, and Chad Prepraeke as speakers.

GOLD LEADER MENTOR STAFF

In 2000, it seemed clear that we would not be able to offer a quality leadership development program with one administrator and one secretary. We realized that we could not afford to pay students to assist with the program, so we reached out to key student leaders on campus and invited them to become GOLD Leader Mentors. We started with eight students who accepted the offer to become our first group of volunteers. As we built the curriculum for the program we involved the GOLD Leader Mentors as peer

GOLD Mentor Bronze Personal Development Session.

advisors, mentors, and teachers in the program. One of the required workshops at the Silver level of the program is Teambuilding. It made perfect sense to have Mentors teach their peers basic team and group development theory in a fun and interactive teambuilding workshop. The GOLD Mentors also developed and offered a time management workshop. Both of these workshops were highly rated and quickly became popular GOLD workshops.

In order to attract and maintain a quality volunteer team, I started offering the Mentor staff a directed study that took the form of a one-credit weekly class on leadership. The directed study continued for several semesters until it was reformatted into a one-credit course available only to GOLD Mentors that could be taken for a maximum of four semesters. The course consists of a weekly one-hour meeting with a variety of leadership-related activities and required class presentations by the Mentors. The course title, focus, and books are changed each semester to achieve a balance of learning between the theoretical approaches and the application of leadership.

In 2005, we expanded the requirements for earning each certificate from six to eight workshops, which afforded us the opportunity to add one required workshop and one optional workshop for each certificate. One of the reasons for the expansion was that the Mentor staff had recommended that each student working on the Bronze, Silver, and Gold sequence should have a one-on-one advisement session with a Mentor. We decided to add a "Personal Development Session" and make it a required

GOLD Mentor Krista Muscarella teaching Bronze workshop.

workshop. We developed a structured, 30–40 minute interview between a Mentor and a student that is designed to elicit information about the mentee's past leadership experiences in high school or college, personal interests to help the Mentor connect the student to an existing student organization, goals and aspirations for the future, planning and strategies for learning and earning leadership certificates, and information on our Cocurricular Involvement Transcript. In order to earn one Bronze credit, the student is required to write and submit a journal reflection on their Personal Development Session. Typically, the students indicate that the Mentor session was very helpful and akin to positive experiences with similar discussions they had at the high school level with guidance counselors. The addition of this requirement is among the best innovations we have made since the start of the program. The Mentors have become real mentors to their peers in the program and they are making a significant and positive difference for students. Mentors are also expected to follow up at least once during the first semester after the session with each mentee. The mentee journals for these sessions are overwhelmingly positive.

Each GOLD Mentor is required to be on-duty and staff the GOLD Leadership Center for two office hours each week and to attend a one-hour weekly meeting that is also the Mentor one-credit class. The GOLD Leadership Center is open and staffed with at least one Mentor from Monday through Thursday 12–8 p.m. and on Fridays from 12–5 p.m.

Mentors serve as hosts for GOLD workshops and work as a team to schedule Mentors at each workshop. This is a major task as there are over 150 workshops per semester and more than 12 workshops offered each week. Mentors are expected to continue attending workshops and working on certificates, and they frequently host workshops that they are also taking for credit in the program. Hosting consists of greeting participants as they arrive at a workshop, helping with the sign-in registration at the workshop, distributing evaluation sheets, introducing the instructor, cleaning up the room after a workshop, and bringing all the registration materials back to the Center for Community for administrative processing.

The GOLD Leader Mentors have functioned as an advisory group for the GOLD Program since the launching of the GOLD Leadership Certificate Program in 2000. We have vetted every program change and modification with the Mentors; each of the six optional leadership certificates was reviewed by the Mentors prior to implementation. I do recall some resistance from Mentors to adding the sustainability certificate, but I later realized the reluctance came from the realization that Mentors would need to complete an additional eight workshops in order to be awarded the Platinum Certificate.

GOLD LEADERSHIP CENTER

GOLD Leadership Center mural.

One of the first things I asked for after assuming the responsibilities of developing a new leadership program was to have a home for the program in the center of campus. We needed a place for the Mentor staff to work and a place where students could come and feel comfortable talking to the Mentors. The Vice President agreed and included the idea in his planning for updating and remodeling the College Union.

During 2000–2001, our GOLD Leadership Center was temporarily located in a makeshift office in an underutilized art gallery in the College Union. We shared the space with the Student Arts and Exhibits committee of the Student Association. In the second year of the program we moved the temporary leadership center to a small office in the student office area of the College Union, and in the third year we moved again to a larger office area closer to some of the College Union meeting rooms that are used for workshops. The size of the staff was expanded from a handful to 15 Mentors and expanded again to over 20 Mentors a couple of years later when we moved the Mentors into a new GOLD Leadership Center set aside exclusively for the GOLD Program to use as an office, library, and meeting room space for workshops. Setting aside a large room in the College Union was a major milestone in the development of the program and a clear indication that GOLD had become a significant part of the culture of the institution.

In addition to serving as an office and workshop room, the GOLD Leadership Center also houses a permanent collection of leadership books and resources that are available for loan to the campus community. The entire collection has been cataloged by the College library staff and is accessible through the Milne Library online database. We started the collection in the late 1990s with a $5,000 grant from a fund administered by a College committee charged with encouraging new and innovative programs. In addition to creating and teaching a leadership class using faculty colleagues in business, communication, and political science, I also started offering one-hour leadership workshops. It made sense to create a leadership library to support these new leadership activities. The grant was approved and I spent a few months acquiring the best available books and materials to use in studying and teaching leadership. Since its establishment, we have continued to update the library each year and have added to the collection, which now includes many of the classic and current leadership books as well as an extensive collection of teambuilding and experiential learning materials and games. The Mentor staff is responsible for monitoring the use of the leadership library. The collection can be reviewed at <geneseo.edu/aleph/gold.asp>. An annotated bibliography of the collection is also available on the resources pages of the GOLD website.

REGISTRATION AND RECORDS

During the initial stages of planning and development of the GOLD Program, we knew we had to create a system to manage our registration and certificate information. Fortunately, our Computer Information Technology (CIT) department was able to assign a student to work on a registration and records system for the new program. Although we had no idea how large and complicated the program would become, we did agree that the system would be used by students to register in advance for

GOLD Leadership Center Library.

workshops and by our office to confirm attendance. In addition, we wanted the students to have access 24/7 to their records. At that time, in 2000, the College had not yet converted records from using social security numbers to student-assigned identification numbers, and our system instructed students to provide social security numbers as their account number. Within a year or two, we had to convert our records to the new student ID system, but students created their own accounts and did not always enter correct identification information.

The system was designed during the summer of 2000 and was up and running for registration when we launched the new program in September. As with any new program and particularly with a custom-designed system, there were minor problems that needed to be fixed throughout the first year. One of the changes we made just prior to printing our first brochure was the requirement that students submit a written journal reflection for each of the six workshops they intended to use to complete a certificate. The registration system had not been designed with a way to submit journals, so students were instructed to write their journals and attach them to an email to be sent to the Director. For the first few months I eagerly opened my email each day to read and print out journals from students. I was keeping a file on each student with copies of their journals and had to keep checking folders to determine when a student had submitted the necessary journals to earn a certificate. Emails and journals piled up and I soon realized we needed a better way to maintain journals records. Would it be possible for students to submit journals directly into their GOLD account where I could read and accept them in one transaction? CIT agreed that we could modify the program, but the student who had designed the original program had graduated, and I needed to either wait for several months for another programmer to work on the modification or hire and pay the alumnus as an independent contractor to write the software. I decided not to wait and asked the graduate to design the system. He worked on the software, and we tested the design, but it did not work properly. He was not available that summer to fix the bugs. CIT helped find another student, Nathan Fixler, who was staying on as a programmer after graduation, and I hired him to work as a consultant. He was able to fix the software and students could now submit their journals into their accounts. The system automatically notifies me when a journal is submitted, and I am able to read and approve the journals. Fixler has continued as a software consultant for the last nine years and has made several upgrades and improvements in the program. Because the system software contains over 39,000 lines of customized code, we have been fortunate to have his expertise available on nights and weekends to service our program.

In 2009–2010, we negotiated an agreement with the University of Massachusetts at Dartmouth giving them the right to adapt the SUNY Geneseo GOLD Certificate Program model, including the replication of our registration system. The agreement included conversion of our system to their computer technology information system requirements. Fixler agreed to work on the conversion project and to concurrently upgrade our computer software to incorporate the latest technology requirements of our CIT department. The University of Massachusetts at Dartmouth system was completed in 2011 and is currently used to manage their version of the GOLD Program.

The GOLD Program registration system database includes records for every student who has ever registered and attended a GOLD workshop since the fall of 2000. Students start the program by going to the GOLD website and creating their own personal GOLD account. Faculty, staff, and community residents may also create their own personal GOLD accounts by using a separate page in the registration system.

GOLD name tags at every workshop.

Since the program launched in 2000, we have asked students to register in advance for our workshops and programs. Although we always welcome anyone to attend a workshop even if they have not registered in advance, the students generally understand that GOLD expects them to register for workshops. The message is reinforced at every workshop because we prepare a GOLD nametag with each name printed on a stick-on label. I have been asked why we spend the time and money to prepare nametags for every workshop, and my response is that participants are not just numbers in our program. The nametags that have the first name in large print also help instructors get to know students in the program and call on them by name in a discussion or during a question-and-answer period. These are prepared by Barbara Battaglia, secretary in the Center for Community office.

The GOLD registration software requires that each workshop be entered into the system with an assigned CRN number, title, certificate designation, description, date, beginning and ending times, location, and the name, title, and affiliation of each instructor. The software permits administrative editing, reassignment of certificate designation for individual students, alpha list of individuals registered for a workshop, alpha lists for students on wait lists, direct emails to all participants in a specific workshop or to all user accounts, attendance confirmation lists and no-shows for individual workshops, detailed views of current active workshops by semester, and detailed views of all workshops since inception.

The GOLD registration software includes a file for new instructors with name, title, and affiliation. The system will display a registration order number by assigned instructor number and an alpha list to edit information on instructors. Edits automatically appear in any workshop file that is in the system, either live or inactive files.

The registration software permits a student to access his/her GOLD account 24/7 and allows him/her to add/drop a workshop anytime in advance until 9 a.m. on the day of a workshop, when the registration is frozen to permit printing registration lists and name tags for each of the workshops for the day. Students are required to sign in at each workshop. The registration forms are returned to the Director's office and Barbara Battaglia uses the administrative system software to confirm attendance and print a paper copy, which is stapled to the signed registration forms as a back-up record.

The GOLD registration software student records display personal information, including the Geneseo ID number (which is also the GOLD account number), name, and preferred name. The student records also display all workshops that the student registered for and attended or did not attend; status level for Bronze, Silver, and Gold; and access to journals that may also be downloaded to Word files.

The development of the computer software started in 2000 continues to be a work-in-progress, as we have added components to the program and discovered needs we did not know existed. I had not anticipated that athletic coaches might want to know how many workshops their team captains had taken two years ago or how many journal reflections were submitted last year. Our experience working with Jamie Jacquart and the computer technology staff at the University of Massachusetts at Dartmouth to adapt the computer software program for them helped us expand our thinking about ways we could expand our use of all those ones and zeros in our database.

There are many software programs available that leadership educators use to manage their programs; many, like ours, are custom-designed by CIT staff and tailor-made to meet the needs of the program. Others are available by license agreements with commercial software companies. Although we never envisioned sharing our software, we did share it with U Mass Dartmouth knowing that others might also be interested in purchasing the system. Campuses interested in the system should direct an inquiry to the Director of the GOLD Leadership Program.

SELECTING THE BEST TIME AND PLACE FOR PROGRAMS

In the 1990s when we first started offering leadership workshops, the weekly academic schedule included two "common hours" each week on Tuesdays and Thursdays from 12:30–2 p.m. when there were very few classes scheduled. When we launched the GOLD Leadership Certificate Program in the fall of 2000, we scheduled virtually all workshops on Tuesdays and Thursdays between 12:45–1:45 p.m. to make it convenient for students in the middle of the day in the center of campus within easy walking distance of classes. We were off and running with the program, and attendance was increasing each semester.

Unexpectedly, the Provost and the College Senate changed the academic schedule to one "common hour" on Wednesdays. The change to a single day meant that students could only participate in one GOLD workshop each week and would have difficulty pursuing more than one certificate in any given semester. The new schedule would start the next academic year, so we spent several months figuring out how we could schedule the workshops to maintain the growth of the program. By that time, we were attracting over 2,000 participants each year, and we wanted to expand options for students. We decided to offer workshops during the new "common hour" on Wednesdays from 2:30–3:30 p.m., offer workshops during the same class period on Mondays, and still offer workshops on Tuesdays. It was a risk we had to take, and it worked for students because they now had three opportunities every week to participate in the program. We knew that we were competing with classes except on Wednesdays, but we also knew that class loads, except for science majors with labs, are not as heavy in late afternoons. The challenge actually turned into an opportunity to expand the program.

Afternoon workshop in MacVittie College Union Hunt Room.

Programs for students need to be conveniently scheduled, located, and in the right facilities. To be successful, the Leadership Program had to be scheduled in the College Union during the day when students were available and had free time. I also knew that students expect consistency and reliability and need to know they can count on whatever we are offering to happen. We were able to negotiate the use of the larger key rooms in the College Union during the three time blocks each week and these rooms are held for the GOLD Program throughout the academic year. We know there are also times when we might have to move for a special event, but there is always complete cooperation with the events office to find an appropriate room for a workshop. Each March we put a hold on the rooms we need, including the MacVittie College Union Ballroom for programs such as the Volunteer Fair, Etiquette Dinner, Women's Leadership Conference, Live Green Day, and the Annual Leadership Awards and Recognition Ceremony.

STUDENT REFLECTIVE JOURNALS

Students are required in almost all workshops to complete a journal reflection on the workshop. In the last few years, I have come to realize more and more how powerful these reflections are for students. I read literally dozens of journals almost every day. I am able to get a good sense of what students are learning, because the first of the three parts of a journal asks the students to summarize what they learned (learning outcomes). The second part asks the students to share a real-life story from their personal experience that is connected to the workshop. This part is sometimes the most difficult for students and the one that I most frequently send back to rewrite because of the tendency of students to make generalizations instead of sharing a specific story. Sometimes a student may not have a real-life

"I have used reflection in every aspect of my career and I know that it all started at Geneseo with your program."

– Jared Chester

(J.D. Candidate, May 2013 Indiana University Maurer School of Law, Bloomington)

experience to share and I have to then make a judgment call to either send it back for rewriting or just accept the generalization. The third part asks students to share how they plan to use the information learned, and students are able to articulate either how they have already used the information or how it will help them in a leadership situation, in class, or with roommates, a friend, or parent.

The journal stories that students share are frequently so powerful that I get goose bumps and have even shed a tear or two reading about how they are connecting the content or what they take away from a workshop. Except for my reading, journal reflections are confidential unless students identify them to be shared with a supervisor, such as a Resident Assistant journal that includes the Residence Director's email address, which is noted as a permission to share. I also occasionally copy a few journals (minus any identifiers) and send them to an instructor to let them know the impact s/he has had on a student participating in their workshop. Journals often include personal stories of changed attitudes, behaviors, and actions by students. Reading student journal entries from the workshops is one of the best parts of my job. I learn every day about the positive impact of the program. How often do most of us get to read an affirmation of the difference our work is making in the lives of students? I do almost every day.

A journal is either deemed acceptable or the student is asked to rewrite and resubmit. Do I wish I had time to respond or make comments? Yes, but I do not, so I accept the typos and run-on sentences or refer students to a writing lab if the errors are sloppy habits that need attention.

Although journaling and reflective writing are not new forms of pedagogy, there is a significant body of literature supporting journaling as an effective teaching tool. Hiemstra (2001) and Baker (2004) cite research studies and make the strong case for reflective journaling.

Sample student journal.

Listening Skills, 2/16/11

I learned…

This workshop focused on the elements of being a good listener, and how listening skills affect your comprehension of topics and your relationships. One fact that I found stunning was that people really only hear 25–50% of everything we physically "hear." This is why we should all practice active listening, which is the conscious effort to hear and understand what someone is saying. This helps eliminate some of the bad habits people have when conversing like assuming they know an answer ahead of time, always trying to be helpful, treating a conversation as a competition, trying to impress others, and even paying too much attention to details rather than the point of the conversation. Things we can do to be more active and mindful listeners include paying attention, giving visual cues that we are listening, providing structured feedback, avoid interrupting the speaker, and responding appropriately.

My story connected to this workshop is…

I pride myself on being a good listener, and I do believe that I exhibit many of these traits when conversing with someone. However, watching my mother interact with my father, my friends, or her colleagues makes it obvious that she is a far superior listener. She does exactly what this seminar says an active listener must do. She nods occasionally to show she's listening, keeps her comments to a minimum, but when she does interrupt it is helpful but not overbearing, and she never assumes to know the conclusion of the conversation. While we went through all the aspects of active listening I could attribute them very easily to my mother, which was really very interesting for me.

I plan to…

I certainly plan to be more mindful of the impression I give to people who are expecting me to listen to them, especially as far as physical cues go. Everyone knows the feeling of speaking to someone who clearly is not interested, and I hope to never accidentally give that impression. This seminar points out obvious things that many people simply forget about, or have never thought deeply about, and by exposing students to the fact that these small things do matter I believe it will make myself and the other participants far more conscious of being an active listener.

CHAPTER 5:

Collaborative Nature
of the GOLD Program

COLLABORATION IN STUDENT AND CAMPUS LIFE

In 2000, we enlisted the support of other departments in the Division of Student and Campus Life to help us develop the program, teach workshops, and market the new program to students. Residence Life was one of our biggest allies in the creation of the program. To enhance and develop their staff's personal skills and leadership capacity, we partnered with them in creating workshops that would appeal to the Resident Assistants (RAs) and at the same time offer in-service training opportunities.

Dr. Celia Easton, Dean of Residential Living & Professor of English, teaching the Write for Success workshop.

During the fall and spring semesters of our first year, RAs were required to participate in five GOLD workshops each semester. Because we have over 100 RAs on campus, we were able to kickstart the program with a critical mass of students attending our workshops. Although many of the RAs became strong supporters of the new program, we soon realized that requiring attendance at five workshops each semester was too high an expectation, and RAs were expressing concern about the additional work. During the second year of the program, we mutually agreed that we should cut the required number of workshops back to two per semester. The change made sense and has remained in effect for the last 11 years. In 2009, Residence Life and GOLD developed a GOLD workshop guide for the RA staff with suggested workshops for new, mid-level, and senior RAs. The guide is used by the Residence Directors to suggest appropriate and developmental workshops for each RA.

In 2005, by mutual agreement with Residence Life, we added a requirement that Resident Assistants must also submit a journal reflection for their two required workshops, which are copied and sent to their Residence Directors.

Also in 2005, the Division of Student and Campus Life set an expectation that all student employees in the division take two GOLD workshops each semester as an in-service educational component of their employment to help enhance and develop their personal skills and leadership capacity. Supervisors are encouraged to meet with individual students and suggest workshops appropriate for the individual that also meet the needs of the department. Although not every department or supervisor takes the time to ensure compliance with this policy for all student employees, students frequently disclose in journals that they took a workshop because they had to and then add a comment about enjoying the session or having an "aha" learning moment.

The MacVittie College Union and Activities (CU&A) Department requires all student employees and their College Union Student Managers to help enhance and develop their personal skills and leadership capacity by attending two workshops and submitting journal reflections. The MacVittie College Union and Activities Department supervises the recognition process for student organizations. Officers of new student groups seeking recognition must attend two Gold workshops, including completion of a journal entry for each, as a partial requirement of obtaining recognition. The journal entries are submitted with the New Organization Recognition Application. All of the professional staff in the department teach multiple workshops in the GOLD Program. In addition, the CU&A Director teaches the Accelerated Leaders Institute (ALI) with the Director of the GOLD Program. The College Union staff welcomes the additional traffic in the building generated by students attending GOLD workshops. The College Union professional and student manager staff also provide continual assistance with room usage and technical support and assistance with equipment problems for workshop instructors.

Emerti Athletic Director Marilyn Moore teaching a Silver workshop.

At Geneseo, the Department of Athletics and Recreation reports to the Vice President of Student and Campus Life. In 2008, the department started encouraging student athletes who aspire to team leadership roles to participate in the GOLD Program. Although the requirement is not a hard and fast rule for all teams, several coaches expect/require athletes who serve as team captains or co-captains to take the introductory Leadership Concepts workshop and, where possible, to also earn the Bronze Leadership Certificate. We also share the GOLD activity of current athletes each semester with the Athletic Department; one of the full-time professional staff in the athletic department serves as a liaison with GOLD to monitor the level of involvement of athletes in the program. Both the immediate past director and current Director of Intercollegiate Athletics have been strong advocates for leadership development and support the GOLD Program as an integral part of in-service training of athletes. The retired Director continues to teach an Emerald Certificate workshop on "Is It Your Job or Your Passion? Visioning Your Future" and the lacrosse coach teaches a Gold Certificate workshop on "Teaching/Coaching Leadership." We anticipate the collaboration will continue to expand as we develop and offer more leadership workshops that appeal to student athletes.

Learning to remember bread vs. drinks at Emerald Eating Etiquette Dinner.

We reached out to involve the Office of Career Development in the creation and development of the GOLD Program. The Director and counselors in the department have been teaching workshops every semester since the fall of 2000. We identified interviewing skills and resume writing as key skills needed by every student and these workshops were offered initially as Bronze Life Skills and incorporated as required workshops when we added the Emerald Career and Professional Development Certificate as an option in the program. Career Development and GOLD collaborated to create two very popular events that have been offered for several years: the Career Connections Brunch, held on Homecoming Weekend, and the Etiquette Dinner in March. Both events attract over 100 students to learn networking and etiquette skills.

In 2007–2008, the Office of Career Development experienced a drop in student attendance at office-sponsored workshops while the career workshops offered in the GOLD Program attracted larger numbers of students. The staff in both offices worked together to create the Emerald Career and Professional Development Certificate. Currently, the Career Development staff members teach an average of 12 workshops multiple times per year, including four required workshops. The majority of Career Development workshops are now offered as part of the Emerald Leadership Certificate and the average attendance ranges from 15 to 35 students per workshop. Sixty-eight students have completed the Emerald Certificate since 2008. Several new workshops have been developed by the Career Development staff and the GOLD Program supports these new workshops by providing an opportunity to market the new topics to students and registering students for the sessions.

Inter-Greek Council Executive Board members are strongly encouraged to participate in GOLD workshops. Leaders of Greek letter social organizations who face disciplinary sanctions are frequently required to work on their personal development by attending life skills and leadership skills in the GOLD Program and one recent sanction required all current members of a fraternity to earn the Bronze Leadership Certificate as a condition of working on re-recognition. Although the Director will sometimes observe a student forced to take GOLD workshops displaying resentment, most students share their experience and write about the helpfulness of the workshops to their future as Greek leaders. The Office of Community Standards and Conduct and College Conduct Review Boards also require individuals to take specific GOLD workshops as a vehicle to learning skills appropriate to the infractions. Students will often disclose that information in their journal reflections. Student Orientation Coordinators are also expected to participate in GOLD workshops to learn skills appropriate to their specific assignments. The Office of Multicultural Programs and Services requires Multicultural Fellows to participate in a leadership program, and GOLD workshops may be used to fulfill this requirement. All Livingston CARES volunteer work trip coordinators and team leaders are required to attend a GOLD workshop designed specifically for service trips. Big Brothers/Big Sisters volunteers are encouraged to participate in a GOLD workshop on Child Abuse and student mentors in the HEROS high school mentoring program are required to attend a GOLD workshop on mentoring. All new student employees in their first semester of employment in the division also attend a new student employees workshop session designed as a welcome, orientation, and training session. Students may earn credit toward the Emerald Career and Professional Development Certificate because the workshop emphasizes appropriate office etiquette and behavior in a professional work environment.

COLLABORATION BEYOND STUDENT AND CAMPUS LIFE

Bringing cocurricular learning into focus is a key element in the success of the GOLD Program, which has developed into an effective vehicle for delivering quality educational programs to the campus community. Several specific campus needs fulfilled by GOLD include: the School of Business relies on the GOLD Program to deliver the bulk of the Professional Development Events required by all majors for graduation; the Division of Student & Campus Life requires all student employees, including Resident Assistants, in the division to participate in GOLD workshops each semester as partial fulfillment of in-service education requirements; and Milne Library offers its digital and information management workshops through the GOLD Program. In addition, a new leadership certificate on sustainability, developed by the campus task force on sustainability, was offered for the first time during the 2011–2012 year as a low-cost alternative to adding a minor during a very difficult funding period for public higher education in New York State.

The GOLD workshops provide leadership development, education, and training opportunities to student leaders, and there is regular collaboration with all departments, staff, and students engaged in services and programs related to student life. New student organization officers are required by the Department of College Union and Activities to participate in GOLD workshops. The Student Association is committed to the program and provides a significant portion of the GOLD Program budget from the student activity fee.

GOLD regularly collaborates with Academic Affairs and numerous academic departments. In 2011-2012, 39 faculty, 57 administrators, and 36 alumni and guest presenters taught GOLD workshops. The School of Business designated 82 GOLD workshops as Professional Development Events that fulfill a graduation requirement for business majors. The School of Business faculty approached me in 2002 about working with their department on a new graduation requirement being proposed to the College Senate that would mandate attendance at a minimum of two Professional Development Events (PD Events) each semester for all business majors. (I had taught courses in the School of Business for several years and was teaching their Labor Relations class at the time the discussions occurred.) This opportunity to collaborate was another indication that the GOLD Program was succeeding in its efforts to develop and educate future leaders. The faculty asked if they could select workshops that would fulfill their expectations of professional development experiences for their majors. The GOLD Program obligation would be to process Scantron forms for business majors attending workshops and return them to the School of Business for their permanent academic records. Although the collaboration required more paper work for GOLD, it meant that most of the business majors would likely participate in the GOLD Program at least a few times each year. The College Senate approved the graduation requirement and we have been working with the School of Business and offering at least thirty PD Event workshops every semester as an option for business majors. We identify and label each workshop that is selected by the business faculty as a PD Event. Typically, the PD Event workshops are career and professional development sessions such as resume writing, job interviewing, diversity training, and topics such as teambuilding that are not typically included in the academic courses, but are critical skills needed by business graduates.

Even though we stress the fact that all of our workshops are open to all students at any time that they are free and would like to register, non-business students will sometimes see (PD Event) posted after the title of a workshop and conclude that it is just for business majors. We have to continually remind students that they are welcome at any workshop. As a general practice, we do not offer workshops for special groups and we frequently suggest that one of the benefits of the GOLD Program is that practically every workshop will have a mix of all types of majors and classes and student profiles.

GOLD cosponsors the annual Women's Leadership Conference with the Women's Leadership Institute. The Ruby Certificate for Information Management and Digital Leadership is a collaborative effort with Milne Library, and the Emerald Career and Professional Development Certificate is cosponsored with the Office of Career Development. The Milne library staff also catalogs the resources in the GOLD leadership library and includes the holdings in its electronic database.

Other examples of collaboration include joint sponsorships with Alumni and Advancement to bring alumni to campus for workshops and programs, joint sponsorship of etiquette dinners and luncheons with The Office of Career Development, providing speakers to the Chamber of Commerce breakfast series, participating in the Community Resource Network, and working with community groups to host meet-the-candidates for local and regional political elections.

> *"The GOLD Program plays an important role in the overall educational experience of our School of Business students. The collaboration between the GOLD Program and the School of Business has been successful in providing our students access to high-quality professional development experiences."*
>
> *– Dr. Michael Schinski, Dean of the School of Business*

COLLEGES, UNIVERSITIES AND SECONDARY SCHOOLS HOSTED BY GOLD PROGRAM DIRECTOR FOR SITE VISITS, CONSULTATIONS, AND EXTENDED CONFERENCE CALLS

Alfred University 2006

Angelo State University 2006

Buffalo State 2004

Cicero-North Syracuse High School 2006

Clark University 2005

College of St. Benedict and St. John's (MN) 2006

Cornell University 2011

Ehime University Leaders School, Japan 2008

Hiram College 2005

Ithaca College 2004

Mansfield University 2004

Marquette University 2005

Mt. Allison University, NB, Canada (Consultant 2010)

Northwestern University 2005

University of Iowa in Iowa City 2006

University of Massachusetts at Dartmouth (Consultant 2009-2010)

University of Montana 2005

University of North Carolina at Ashville 2007

Pierce College 2005

Radford University 2005

Seattle University 2005

SUNY College of Old Westbury 2007

SUNY Potsdam 2005

SUNY Purchase 2009

SUNY Stony Brook 2012

Syracuse University 2012

Wilfred Laurier University 2003

York University, Toronto 2007

CHAPTER 6:

Special Events and Programs Connected to the GOLD Program

The GOLD Program expanded over time by incorporating new programs and collaborating with other departments to offer new opportunities for students to build their portfolios of leadership and life skills. Students are encouraged to learn from successful leaders, study personal finance, and participate in several major events that are connected and integrated into the GOLD Program.

PEARLS OF WISDOM SERIES

As the GOLD Program developed over the last several years, we expanded our efforts to invite guest speakers (primarily alumni) to come to campus and share their career and personal stories with students in the GOLD Program. Having worked at the College for over 40 years, I have been able to reach out and invite many alumni friends whom I worked with when they were undergraduates. Most are delighted to be asked and are thrilled to have the chance to return to their alma mater for a visit.

Bruce Jordan, Class of 1966, actor and producer, sharing his life story at a Pearls of Wisdom workshop.

We started the initiative as "Dialogues With Successful Leaders." We learned that the label "dialogues" intimidated some students and they shied away from attending, perhaps thinking they would be required to talk. The feedback led us to rename the series "Pearls of Wisdom From Successful Leaders." Each workshop in the series is specific with a title and description tailored to the key words identifying the career or significant accomplishments of the individual. A few examples from our 2011–2012 series include:

Greg O'Connell, Class of 1964, sharing his story on revitalizing America's Main Street.

- **Pearls of Wisdom From Successful Leaders: From SA President to Federal Prosecutor to Corporate Manager** *(Jeffrey Cramer, Esq., Managing Director, Kroll) (Silver Practicing Leadership)*

- **Pearls of Wisdom From Successful Leaders: From the Classroom to the NYS Assembly Chambers** *(Barbara Lifton, New York State Assemblywoman) (Silver Practicing Leadership) or (Emerald Volunteerism and Service)*

- **Pearls of Wisdom From Successful Leaders: A Career in Special Ed to CEO of ARC of Monroe** *(Barbara Wale, CEO, ARC of Monroe County) (Emerald Career and Employee Development)*

SUNY Chancellor Zimpher sharing perspectives on transformational leadership at the Pearls of Wisdom series.

- **Pearls of Wisdom From Successful Leaders: From the Wadsworth Stage to the World Stage** *(Bruce Jordan, adaptor, actor, producer, Broadway director) (Emerald Career and Employee Development) or (Diamond Leadership in Community Engagement and Social Justice)*

Our Alumni Association and the College Advancement Division has been very helpful with the series by providing additional contact information and connection points for the alumni whom we invite back to speak in the series. The Communications Department frequently sends a photographer to capture images for use in alumni publications, and the President and the Executive Staff are often available to meet and greet the alumni participating in the program.

We also promote the series as an opportunity for students to make connections with "movers and shakers" in the professional world. We suggest that seniors should use these sessions as part of their networking efforts as they begin looking for their first job after college.

Almost without exception, students report the hour spent in these sessions to be a wise use of their time. Most often, students also describe the sessions as inspiring and helpful to preparing for their expected career. We also target market the sessions to majors that have either a direct connection to the speaker's profession or to majors and departments from which the speaker obtained his/her degree. Faculty will often recommend a specific session to students and sometimes even give extra credit in a class for attendance at sessions.

PERSONAL FINANCE SERIES

Dean Schinski teaching personal finance workshop.

In 2009, Key Bank indicated to the College that they were interested in contributing to a program that would educate students about personal finance. The local branch of Key Bank is adjacent to the campus, and students use the bank for checking accounts and ATM services. Bank tellers and staff frequently interact with students who have little knowledge or skills in managing their personal finances. Students write checks with insufficient funds and accrue bank fees and often have no clue of ways to avoid charges on their bank accounts. Personal Finance is not included in academic courses, although it had been offered on occasion as an elective for business majors. The College Advancement staff asked if we might incorporate personal finance into the GOLD Program as a response to the Key Bank request. I responded affirmatively and asked one of our GOLD Leader Mentors, Nate Stevens, a senior business finance major at the time, to develop a series of workshops that we could add to the program in the fall of 2009. I also asked Stevens to consult widely with students through surveys to help determine what workshops they might attend if offered. As Stevens worked on this project, we also needed to figure out how to market the series. Should we offer another certificate on personal finance? Should we offer workshops with no credit or should we incorporate them into one of the existing certificates? I posed these questions to the GOLD Leader Mentor staff and asked for their advice. They responded that personal finance workshops should be for credit and should be incorporated into an existing certificate. Based on these suggestions, we decided to expand our description of the entry level Bronze Leadership Skills Certificate and rename it the Bronze Life Skills and Leadership Certificate. This would permit students an option of taking one or more skills workshops on personal finance in addition to the four required workshops that focus on leadership. Although we knew that this might mean a student would take fewer core leadership workshops, we also knew that managing one's personal life is also critical to being an effective leader.

At the end of the spring semester, Stevens submitted his report and recommendations on adding a personal finance series to the program. The report included survey data from students, proposed workshop titles, and descriptions of each workshop that we should offer. I shared his report with the Dean of the

School of Business, Dr. Michael Schinski, and asked for his advice and help in implementing the Personal Finance Series. Schinski agreed to teach the introductory workshop each semester and to help us recruit other instructors. One of the suggestions from Stevens was to recruit finance majors who manage the business school's student stock fund to teach a workshop on investing in the stock market. Student peers would share their experience managing real money in a stock fund. Schinski supported this suggestion and arranged for the majors to do the first session in the spring of 2010.

We invited the local Key Bank branch manager, Bonnie Swanson, to teach a workshop on managing money and understanding how FICO scores affect personal finance. We also invited Chad Reflin, director of Rochester's Credit Education Bureau, to offer the bureau's packaged program entitled "Navigating the Credit Road." We had worked with Reflin on occasion in the past and knew that his materials were very helpful to students. Another recommendation was to offer a workshop on managing student loans and financing graduate school. We asked Archie Cureton, our Director of Financial Aid, to teach this workshop, which would be particularly helpful to seniors transitioning to graduate school or into their first job out of college. The last recommendation was to offer a session on building personal wealth, including information on benefits such as retirement options and 401(k) plans. We asked Kevin Gavagan, a financial planner/investment manager and graduate of Geneseo whom I knew, to come back to campus to share his advice on how to get started with investments.

We developed a marketing piece on the Personal Finance Series and offered all of these workshops in the fall of 2009 and repeated them again in the spring of 2010. The series was very successful, and every workshop attracted between 20–50 students. The student evaluations were very positive and the journal reflections clearly indicated the value of the sessions to students. Students reported having almost no knowledge of personal finance or the compounding value of investments or how finance credit works. After several months of experience offering these workshops and reading evaluation and journal comments, there was no doubt that this series was becoming an important component of our leadership and life skills education. We repeated the series in 2010–2011 and again in the 2011–2012 academic year.

The Personal Finance Series continues to be very popular with students. Key Bank has expressed their appreciation for the inclusion of the Personal Finance Series in the GOLD Program and has continued to make a generous gift to the College each year to support the program. GOLD has joined the Cash Course program offered through the National Endowment for Financial Education (NEFE), a non-profit foundation dedicated to educating college students about personal finance. A committee of student mentors investigated ways we might help students use online resources in individual personal finance sessions. We are offering the Cash Course for Bronze credit workshop sessions in 2012–2013.

SUMMER LEADERSHIP SYMPOSIUM

In 2010, the Division of Student and Campus Life staff collaborated to create a new leadership opportunity for key student leaders associated with all of the departments in the division. The Leadership Symposium was held just before classes started for the fall semester. Invited participants included resident assistants, captains of intercollegiate athletic teams, orientation advisors, GOLD Leader Mentors, student government officers, Inter Greek Council officers, student healthguards, and students involved in mandatory training sessions for new incoming students. The first symposium included small- and large-group discussions on leadership and what it means to be an ethical leader. The student participants also received Bystander Intervention Training and led small-group discussions on bystander intervention with all new students during their first night on campus. The symposium was very successful, involving over 200 student leaders, and the Vice President of Student and Campus Life and the department heads agreed that it should become an annual event to welcome our key student leaders back to campus and offer them another leadership experience.

Students enjoying Leadership Symposium

The second Leadership Symposium, equally successful, occurred the following year, just before fall classes started. The key student leaders connected to each of the departments in the Division of Student and Campus Life were invited and expected to participate. The program was developed by a committee representing all of the Student and Campus Life departments. The program was pared back from day-long to an afternoon program ending with dinner. A keynote speaker kicked off the symposium with a speech including engaging activities related to learning outcomes for the year on developing effective communication skills, the division theme. Students then had an opportunity to attend one of 13 GOLD one-hour workshops on communication skills. After the workshops, all participants attended a Bystander Intervention Training session to prepare them in leading discussions with new students the next evening.

The symposium has now been established as an annual program for key student leaders and the format for future years will include GOLD workshops related to the learning outcomes and theme for the year. Students are able to earn one GOLD workshop credit and apply it to an appropriate leadership certificate. Resident Assistants are able to use the symposium workshop as one of their two required GOLD workshops for the fall semester. The challenge will be to recruit instructors to teach workshops on a day just before the new students arrive when most faculty and student affairs staff are busy preparing for the new academic year. However, it is a terrific opportunity to engage student leaders in the GOLD Program. The Vice President is now expecting GOLD and the Center for Community staff to play a lead role in planning and executing the symposium.

MARTIN LUTHER KING, JR., DAY OF LEADERSHIP AND SERVICE

Martin Luther King, Jr., Day service project for homebound senior citizens.

In the fall of 2010, New York Campus Compact encouraged campuses to create service opportunities on Martin Luther King Day by offering small grants to assist with expenses. We reached out to the Livingston County Office for the Aging and several campus departments and asked them to join with us in creating a leadership and service day that we could offer on campus. Committee members from Volunteerism and Service, Multicultural Programs and Services, College Union and Activities, Student Association, GOLD Mentors, Alliance for Community Enrichment (ACE), and the Office for the Aging were excited and enthusiastic about developing a program.

On January 17, 2011, we offered our first Martin Luther King, Jr., Day of Leadership and Service. Twenty-five senior citizens from the Livingston County Office for the Aging Foster Grandparent Program came to campus and joined 60 student leaders for the program. We invited a very popular Distinguished Teaching Professor of History, Dr. William Cook, to open the program with his perspective on the King Legacy. Participants then had a choice of attending one of five GOLD workshops on volunteerism and service. After intergenerational lunch discussions, volunteers worked on service projects designed to help 400 homebound, low-income senior citizens in the Meals-on-Wheels program. Volunteers made dry soup mixes, wrote greeting card notes, and assembled personal care kits for the homebound. Evaluations and feedback on the program were very positive, with 97% (N= 68) of the evaluation survey participants rating the program either a 4 or 5 on the excellent side of a 5-point scale. Every department and student group involved as well as the Office for the Aging agreed that we should continue the program and make it an annual event.

The second annual Martin Luther King, Jr., Day of Leadership and Service occurred on January 16, 2012, with the same format, the same departments and agencies, and similar service components. We expanded the GOLD involvement by offering credit for attendance in our Opal Diversity and Cultural Competency and our Sapphire Volunteerism and Service Certificates. We also continued offering one GOLD credit for participating in one of the five one-hour workshops built into the program for the day. We now have an annual event that ties leadership and service together to engage students and community residents in an inter-generational program. Workshops and service occur on the same day. In 2011, students earned credit for participating in workshops; in 2012, they were able to also earn credit for their service on that day. In 2012, 100% (N=58) of the evaluation survey participants rated the program either a 4 or 5 on the excellent side of a 5-point scale.

WOMEN'S LEADERSHIP CONFERENCE

In 2008, the Provost and the Vice President of Student and Campus Life agreed that a new program, the Women's Leadership Institute (WLI), under development by the Access Opportunity Programs (AOP) staff, should receive financial support and a connection to the GOLD Program. The staff and students were planning a program at the end of the academic year that included a dinner and a guest speaker. The Vice President agreed to help with the finances by moving some of his small grants funding to GOLD so we could help with the planning and funding of the dinner and speaker. The speaker was Tre Jordan, Research Associate for the American Planning Association, and an alumnus of Geneseo. The event was very successful, and we developed a good working relationship between GOLD and the Women's Leadership Institute.

"The Women's Leadership Institute (WLI) carries out its mission to support the development of young women in leadership roles through the Five Pearls of WLI: Leadership, Networking, Service, Advocacy, and Support. It was only fitting that WLI would seek a collaboration with the GOLD Program, and the Women in Leadership Conference was the best vehicle for that collaboration."
– Patricia Gonzalez

Later that year, Patricia Gonzalez from the AOP staff and I agreed to start the planning process much earlier so we could include the program in our GOLD schedule for the year and offer students credit for attending. We added another sponsor, the Klainer Center for Women in Business that is housed in our School of Business, and we moved the event to early March to avoid the hectic competition of events in the last few weeks of the semester. In 2009, Summit Federal Credit Union provided funding for the dinner, and Laurie Baker, Senior Vice President and COO and a Geneseo alumna, gave the keynote address. We also started a new tradition of honoring the speaker with the awarding of an honorary GOLD Leadership Certificate. Our guest speakers for the programs have all been distinguished alumna from a variety of professions, including Erika Rottenberg, Senior Counsel for LinkedIn (2010); Jackie Norris, Senior Advisor at Corporation for National and Community Service (CNCS) and former Chief of Staff for Michelle Obama (2011); and Tiffany Courtney, Director of Financial Reporting, Philadelphia Industrial Development Corporation (2012). In addition to the keynote alumna speakers, most of the panelists at the individual GOLD workshop sessions at the Women's Leadership Conference are also graduates of the College. Several have been so well received that the students on the planning committee wanted to invite them back each year to share their stories and their positive advice to our undergraduate women. Topics have also been repeated multiple times, including Breaking the Glass Ceiling, Power Couples, Financing Your Life, Women's Health Issues, Community Engagement, and Personal Branding.

The 2012 program included a fourth sponsor, the Geneseo Alumni Association Board of Directors. The treasurer of the board, Mark Kane, who had been teaching ethics workshops for the GOLD Program for several years, made an appointment to see me in June of 2011 to tell me that the board members intended to make a contribution to the GOLD Program and were interested in sponsoring a special event. It made perfect sense to me that the event should be the Women's Leadership Conference that had featured mostly alumna as speakers and guests. The board members were pleased and readily agreed to contribute their funds to the Women's Leadership Conference.

Students involved in the WLI program are encouraged to attend GOLD workshops and earn leadership certificates. I also share journal reflections from WLI students who indicate that the director of the program, Patricia Gonzalez, should receive a copy of the reflection. In addition to taking basic Bronze leadership skills workshops, many students in WLI also participate in the Emerald Career and Professional Development workshops.

VOLUNTEER FAIR

Working at a community garden.

For over 20 years, the Volunteer Center has hosted two Volunteer Fairs each year, one in the early fall and a second early in the spring semester. Community organizations that need and often depend on student volunteers staff tables at the fair in our MacVittie College Union Ballroom. The fairs run from 10 a.m.–3 p.m. and typically attract over 30 organization representatives and over 500 students. Attendance is monitored through the registration sheets at each agency table. In 2005, when we increased the requirements for earning certificates from six to eight workshops, we decided to make attendance at a Volunteer Fair one of the four required workshops for completing the Sapphire Volunteerism and Service Leadership Certificate. We knew from several years of experience that students were often not aware of the depth and breadth of opportunities for service and it made sense to encourage attendance at the Volunteer Fairs where they would have easy access to volunteer possibilities.

At each Volunteer Fair, GOLD Leader Mentors staff a GOLD information table at which students who have registered in advance in the GOLD registration system are asked to stop by and sign in just as they do at any workshop. Students who have not registered for the Sapphire credit in advance may also sign the sheet for credit. The Mentors give each student an instruction slip that tells them to visit a minimum of 10 agencies represented in the room and report on which agencies they visited in their journal reflection for the "workshop." The slip also asks them to share their plans on what volunteer work and groups they intend to pursue. Although we do not always get journal reports immediately after the fairs, we do often get a good sense of what attracts students to volunteer and we share that information with the Volunteer Center coordinator.

STUDENT ORGANIZATION EXPO

Each semester, the College Union and Activities staff invite all student organizations to an event where they can set up a table exhibit displaying their activities and have an opportunity to recruit new members. This semi-annual event has increased in popularity each year with over 150 participating organizations. Almost from the beginning of the GOLD Program, we have offered attendance at this event for credit as a "workshop." The GOLD Leader Mentors staff a registration table at the expo and students

Students registering at the Student Expo.

who have registered in advance for Bronze Certificate credit are asked to stop by and sign in. Students not pre-registered my also sign in and register for Bronze credit. Each student is given an instruction slip that asks them to visit a minimum of 10 student organization tables and then report in a journal on their experience and their plans for joining student groups.

Students in the GOLD Program are advised by the GOLD Leader Mentors in the Personal Development Sessions and at the required Leadership Concepts workshop that the GOLD Leadership Program is intended to be an applied program as opposed to a theoretical program. Students are encouraged to get involved in student organizations and take what they are learning in GOLD workshops and figure out how to apply and use their skills and knowledge in real-life experiences. The Mentors and Director reinforce that message frequently with students in the GOLD Program.

The Student Organization Expo provides a great opportunity each semester for both new and upper-class students to make new connections and seize opportunities for practicing leadership. Student journal reflections confirm that students are taking advantage of the Expo to join student organizations.

CANDIDATE FORUMS

Meeting and greeting political candidates.

During the even-year election cycles in New York State, we typically invite candidates running for public office to come to campus to meet students. We have hosted candidate meet-and-greets in the College Union Lobby during high-traffic daytime hours and have sponsored public candidate forums in the early evening hours. Attendance has varied widely depending on the candidates and the current issues in the election cycle. We have offered credit to student participants in these events toward either the Sapphire Volunteerism and Service or the Diamond Community Engagement and Social Justice Leadership certificates. We also connect these events to our campus-wide voter registration drives that state law requires public campuses to do each year. Presidential election years typically draw the largest number of students to register, meet candidates, and vote in an election.

THE COCURRICULAR INVOLVEMENT TRANSCRIPT

The Geneseo Cocurricular Involvement Transcript, originally on paper but then transitioned to an electronic version through an off-campus server, was ultimately integrated into our on-campus electronic information technologies. It is now online and accessible 24/7 to students through the GOLD website. Students create a personal account and are able to enter information to create and edit their transcripts at any time. They may print an unofficial version at any time. They may also choose to request an official version of their e-portfolio that contains a background seal of the college, the word "official," and a signature with a raised seal.

Copies of the transcript are free to the students, but students are required to provide the name and email address of an individual for each activity listed who could verify the information they have entered into the record. As the administrator of the system, I approve and sign the official transcripts.

On campus, Residence Life as well as other departments in the Division of Student and Campus Life request copies of the unofficial Cocurricular Involvement Transcript when students apply to be a Resident Assistant, or for other student employee positions. Other departments, such as the Geneseo Foundation, which provides scholarships to students, also recommend that copies of the transcript be attached to scholarship applications, and an increasing number of academic departments ask for copies of transcripts to assist in deliberations regarding honors and awards. The Career Development staff members have also suggested that transcripts be added to placement files or used at interviews or with follow-up letters to employers.

Details on the transcript and a sample are available on the GOLD website at http://gold.geneseo.edu/description.html

Geneseo

STATE UNIVERSITY *of* NEW YORK AT GENESEO

⊰ OFFICIAL COCURRICULAR INVOLVEMENT TRANSCRIPT ⊱

STUDENT: Student Name
STUDENT ID: 000223333
EXPECTED GRADUATION: 5/1/2010

ACTIVITY	DATES	POSITION/ROLE	DESCRIPTION OF INVOLVEMENT	AREA OF DEVELOPMENT
CAMPUS ORGANIZATION ACTIVITIES				
Activities Commission	04/08-04/09	Mac's Place Coordinator	Hosted monthly programs that featured local musicians. Creted marketing campaign and worked with a budget.	Initiative Problem Solving
Class Council - Class of 2010	09/07-05/08	Secretary	Helped organize and plan activities for the sophomore class. Took minutes at all Executive Board meetings. Created flyers and brochures for Class activities.	Delegation Skills Leadership Skills Short & Long Range Planning
Inter-Residence Council	09/06-05/06	Hall Representative	Attended IRC and Hall Council meetings. Voted on fuding for Residence Life programs.	Effective Group Member Financial Management
CAMPUS ORGANIZATION ACTIVITIES				
Activities Commission	04/08-04/09	Mac's Place Coordinator	Hosted monthly programs that featured local musicians. Creted marketing campaign and worked with a budget.	Initiative Problem Solving
Class Council - Class of 2010	09/07-05/08	Secretary	Helped organize and plan activities for the sophomore class. Took minutes at all Executive Board meetings. Created flyers and brochures for Class activities.	Delegation Skills Leadership Skills Short & Long Range Planning
CAMPUS ORGANIZATION ACTIVITIES				
Activities Commission	04/08-04/09	Mac's Place Coordinator	Hosted monthly programs that featured local musicians. Creted marketing campaign and worked with a budget.	Initiative Problem Solving
Class Council - Class of 2010	09/07-05/08	Secretary	Helped organize and plan activities for the sophomore class. Took minutes at all Executive Board meetings. Created flyers and brochures for Class activities.	Delegation Skills Leadership Skills Short & Long Range Planning
Inter-Residence Council	09/06-05/06	Hall Representative	Attended IRC and Hall Council meetings. Voted on fuding for Residence Life programs.	Effective Group Member Financial Management

End of Transcript Record

The information presented on this transcript regarding organization involvement is student reported.

Thomas Matthews | 585-245-5857 | matthews@geneseo.edu

Associate Dean of Leadership and Service

Sample Cocurricular Involvement Transcript.

CHAPTER 7:

Data and Assessment and Conclusions

DATA AND STATISTICS

The GOLD workshops that are offered each year are available to all students, faculty, staff, and residents of the community. They are free opportunities to learn and to develop both life and leadership skills. They are free opportunities to learn and to develop leadership abilities and/or other skills. Students may register and participate in any workshop any time it is offered. Students participate and take workshops for many different reasons and are welcome to attend as few or as many of the workshops as they have the time or interest in attending. Students may earn certificates at any time during their college career. Some students earn one or two certificates in their first year, and then return to the program to complete other certificates in their junior or senior year. Other students elect to complete certificates in their first two years. The program allows students to participate as their schedules permit and at various times and semesters throughout their time at the College. Each year students are awarded approximately 150–175 leadership certificates.

In 2012, the GOLD Leadership Program completed its eleventh year of operation, and the number of students attending one or more workshops continues to increase.

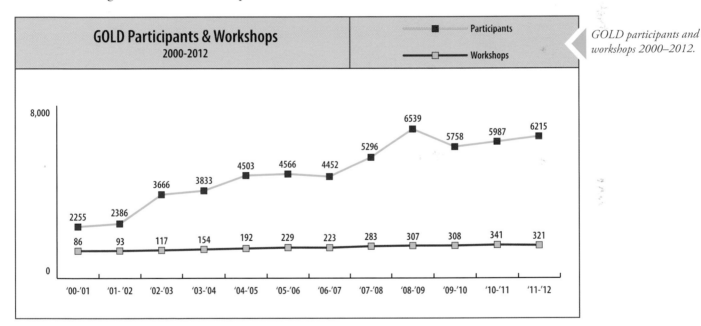

GOLD participants and workshops 2000–2012.

Both the number of participants and the number of workshops have more than doubled since the inception of the program in the fall of 2000. Currently, there are 6,046 active GOLD accounts (including recent alumni from 2010, 2011, 2012, and local residents), and 508 students are actively submitting journals and pursuing one or more of the nine leadership certificates. During 2011–2012, 1,288 students, or 24% of Geneseo undergraduates, participated in one or more GOLD workshops and earned 150 certificates.

The GOLD Program and the Leadership Certificate Program have earned a reputation for providing reliable and high quality workshops and programs to the campus community. GOLD catalogs with descriptions of the workshops and the schedule are distributed to students through Residence Life, and copies are also available in the MacVittie College Union. In addition, faculty, professionals, and administrative support staff at the college receive copies of the GOLD catalog. Student employees in the Division of Student & Campus Life, including the Resident Assistants, are required to take two GOLD workshops each semester as part of their in-service professional development. Athletes who aspire to be team leaders and team captains are also required to participate in the GOLD Program. Virtually every business major participates in GOLD workshops to fulfill their Professional Development Event requirement for graduation. All programs are open to the community, and the GOLD program is frequently cited as one of the programs of distinction at the College. The Director has made numerous presentations on the GOLD Program at local community organizations, regional and national conferences, and at several International Leadership Association conferences. The Director has hosted and/or consulted with over 30 colleges and universities on developing leadership programs, including three from Canada (Mount Allison University, York University, and Wilfred Laurier University), and one from Matsuyma, Japan (Ehime University Leaders School). He has also consulted with the University of Massachusetts at Dartmouth on their adaptation of the GOLD Program as a certificate program for undergraduates. GOLD received the National Association for Campus Activities Exemplary Practices and Model Programs Award in 2002, the Bronze NASPA Excellence Award in 2006, and the State University of New York Outstanding Student Affairs Program for Leadership Development Award in 2007. Our SUNY Geneseo community service programs that are connected to our leadership and service initiatives have also been recognized for the past six years on The President's Higher Education Community Service Honor Roll and for three years "with distinction" by the Corporation for National and Community Service (CNCS).

OUTCOMES ASSESSMENT

The GOLD Program has demonstrated success in addressing student needs through the depth and breadth of the dozens of educational workshops available to the campus community. For example, many of the skill sessions are filled to capacity of 50 on a regular basis, and the average attendance at all workshops is 19. The program clearly has a positive impact on student learning. Each workshop includes individual evaluations from students. The Director and staff compile the evaluations and provide summary sheets with all comments to each instructor. In evaluation data from Fall 2009 through Spring 2012 (three years) that included **responses from 7,324 participants, 93% indicated "I learned more**

GOLD Program evaluations.

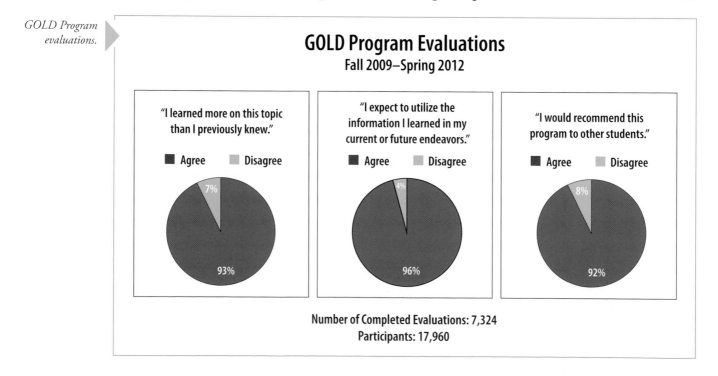

GOLD Program Evaluations
Fall 2009–Spring 2012

"I learned more on this topic than I previously knew."

■ Agree   ■ Disagree

7%

93%

"I expect to utilize the information I learned in my current or future endeavors."

■ Agree   ■ Disagree

4%

96%

"I would recommend this program to other students."

■ Agree   ■ Disagree

8%

92%

Number of Completed Evaluations: 7,324
Participants: 17,960

on this topic than I previously knew," 96% reported that "I expect to utilize the information in my current or future endeavors," and 92% indicated that "I would recommend this program to other students."

In 2011–2012, I also instituted a new assessment procedure for each of the certificates. Each student completing a certificate receives an email requiring the student to complete a Google Survey Document before a certificate is awarded. Each survey is specific to the individual certificate and questions include both Likert scale responses and narrative responses. After reviewing the data and narrative comments, we have made some adjustments in three of the leadership certificates. In the summer of 2012, we also surveyed alumni who earned one or more certificates in the program. **Of 120 respondents, 94% indicated "The GOLD Program helped me to become a more effective leader," 96% reported "Looking back, participating in the GOLD Program was a good use of my time at Geneseo," and 93% indicated they would recommend the program to current Geneseo students.**

The journal reflections regularly include the "aha" moments and statements that GOLD programs make a difference and fulfill student needs. During the last couple of years, we have been sharing a few journals (without names) with instructors to give them a sense of the impact they are having on students. Most instructors respond with an email thanking us for letting them know that students are learning and frequently reporting on actions they have taken to make positive changes in their own behaviors or how they are helping others. There is also very strong evidence of the effectiveness of the GOLD Program in the Personal Leadership Model papers required as the final capstone experience prior to earning the Gold Certificate. Exit interviews are conducted with all students who have earned the Gold Certificate, and every student has reported significant and positive changes in their beliefs about leaders and in their practice of leadership.

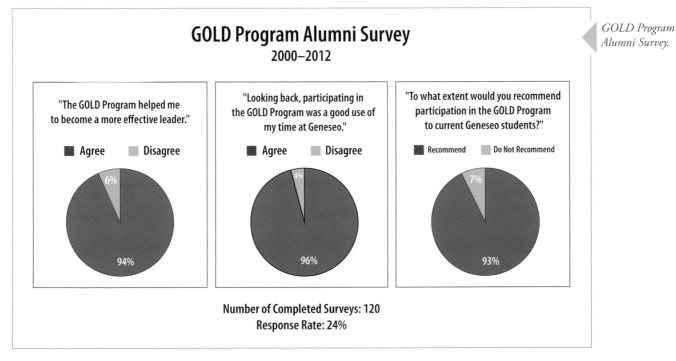

GOLD Program Alumni Survey.

The GOLD Program is clearly relevant to the mission of the college, which "combines a rigorous curriculum and a rich cocurricular life to create a learning-centered environment" and "develop[s] socially responsible citizens with skills and values important to the pursuit of an enriched life and success in the world." It delivers on that promise through an open and accessible program that has campus-wide support and significant student participation.

The students are expected to learn and to practice leadership and to be able to articulate a personal leadership philosophy, and they are awarded certificates, as well as other leadership recognition, for their participation and achievements at the annual awards ceremony held at the end of each academic year. The GOLD Leadership Program plays an important role in the cocurricular life of the campus, and student leaders regularly emerge from the participants in the GOLD Program. A significant number of awards and honors for leadership and service at the annual awards ceremony and at commencement are earned by students who have earned multiple leadership certificates in the GOLD Program.

CONCLUSIONS

Geneseo responded to the call from the W. K. Kellogg Foundation (2000) to expand leadership programs in higher education. We read the literature; talked with colleagues in leadership education; used the CAS standards to review our existing leadership program; consulted widely with other Geneseo faculty, staff, and students; and networked with educators and scholars to determine a framework and direction in launching a new approach to leadership education, training, and development. Our research and instincts paid off as we built the program from a modest beginning of three leadership certificates in 2000 with 86 workshops and 2,255 participants into a highly successful program frequently cited as one of the hallmarks of transformational learning at Geneseo (2012). In 2011–2012 the program provided educational opportunities that served 24% of the student body in 321 workshops and attracted 6,046 participants.

The growth of the GOLD Program parallels the explosive growth of leadership programs throughout the country and around the globe. There are now invaluable resources for anyone charged with developing a new college leadership program such as NCLP and ILA. The NCLP Leadership Educators Institute (LEI) is designed for people entering the field. There is an annual summer National Leadership Symposium and ILA conference. These memberships and conferences have informed my thinking and contributed to the GOLD Program in countless ways, such as workshop content, books and resources in our library, strategies used in marketing, and even the theoretical foundations and practical applications of leadership that we use in the program.

Leadership education is an expanding field because higher education needs to prepare future generations to lead. Higher education is duty bound to make a difference and set the bar high for preparing honest and ethical leaders who will practice good leadership (Kellerman, 2004).

Part One of this book traced the history and development of the SUNY Geneseo GOLD Program, explained the context and framework of the 10 leadership certificates, detailed key operational elements of the programs, suggested ways to foster collaborative leadership in a program, connected campus events to leadership, and cited the data and evidence of the learning taking place through the GOLD Program. Over the past dozen years numerous colleges and universities have inquired about the program. We wanted to share the story and the details about how we have made it work for our campus. Even though every campus has a different culture, our story will hopefully inspire others to create open, accessible, and collaborative leadership programs.

Part Two offers over 160 lesson plans for the one-hour modules that are used to deliver the education and learning that is taking place in the GOLD Program. Writing and editing the work of over 70 instructors has been a monumental task that has been three years in development. Instructors, mentors, student participants/journal authors, work-study and other temporary service student employees, and the clerical and professional staff in the Center for Community and the Division of Student and Campus Life have all contributed to the lesson plans in Part Two.

We are sharing these workshop descriptions and lesson plans to help other leadership educators develop their programs. Most campuses have human resources and people who will gladly volunteer to teach a one-hour lesson on their area of expertise or organize a lesson based a module needed in a leadership program. These lesson plans and the PowerPoints and handouts (available on buildingleadersonehouratatime.com by user code) may be used to enlist volunteer instructors to adapt a learning module for any leadership program.

"I participated in the GOLD Program throughout my four years at Geneseo. During that time, I developed invaluable leadership skills, while enjoying myself and making new friends. When I interviewed to get into medical school, I was asked about my role in the GOLD Program. Four years later, during my residency interviews, program directors were particularly interested in my time spent in the GOLD Program. It was clear that both programs valued leadership skills highly among their applicants. Now that I'm in residency, the leadership skills that I learned through GOLD help me every day in the hospital. I have no doubt in my mind that I would not be the confident leader I am today without the help of the teachers, mentors, and lecturers of Geneseo's GOLD program. Thank you!"

– Dr. Jessica Capasso

"I would encourage anyone in the GOLD program to take it very seriously, and to realize in a much broader sense that how we all relate to one another is extremely vital. The tools, techniques, mindsets, and attitudes that can be developed through this program—if you choose to pursue them and investigate them, and sincerely write in your journals—will certainly be a worthwhile investment for you down the road."

– Jesse Parent

"The GOLD program has aided me in growing into the person and leader I am today. I started utilizing these great workshops as a student-athlete and a future educator. Participating in the Bronze and Silver certificates has molded my personal morals and beliefs of leadership and the kind of leader I wanted to be. This really helped me during my time as an athlete and now, as a coach. I am able to demonstrate good leadership and offer advice to the athletes on topics I learned about in the GOLD program, including time management, teamwork, and listening skills."

– Alyssa Polosky, All-American women's basketball player (2009–2011), assistant coach (2011–present)

"The diversity of topics covered by each of the available certificates broadened my understanding of leadership beyond a surface level and more fully prepared me for graduate study and employment. "

– Rebecca Coons, Class of 2010

"The lessons I learned from the GOLD Program constantly prove worthwhile to me in my professional life. I believe that I am one of the best in my professional organization at running meetings due to the training I received with GOLD."

– Jessica Bowen (Powell), Class of 2007

PART 2:

Descriptions of Individual GOLD Leadership Workshops

INTRODUCTION

This section of the book consists of 160 GOLD workshop descriptions that have been offered in the program. The descriptions are in alphabetical order by title with a notation of the certificate(s) that apply. The reader should also know that 36 required workshops (four in each of the nine different certificates) are offered at least twice each year (once per semester) and several at the bronze and silver level are offered more times to meet the demand for seats. Each description was initially drafted by a GOLD Leader Mentor who participated in the workshop. The drafts were edited, shared with the instructors, and edited again for content and style. The final version of each workshop has been approved by the individual instructor whose name appears in the workshop description.

Each workshop includes the title, the applicable certificates, the description that appears on the website and in the GOLD annual catalog, the learning outcomes, activities/content of the workshop, and a listing of the resources used by the instructor. Individuals who purchase this book may access (some but not all of) the current handouts and PowerPoint materials cited as Resources Used for workshops on the book's website at the following URL: *http://www.buildingleadersonehouratatime.com/resources.html*. New and updated resources will be added to the files available on this website.

WORKSHOPS BY CERTIFICATE

BRONZE LIFE SKILLS AND LEADERSHIP CERTIFICATE

SILVER PRACTICING LEADERSHIP CERTIFICATE

GOLD PERSONAL LEADERSHIP MODEL CERTIFICATE

DIAMOND LEADERSHIP IN COMMUNITY ENGAGEMENT AND SOCIAL JUSTICE CERTIFICATE

EMERALD LEADERSHIP IN CAREER AND EMPLOYEE DEVELOPMENT CERTIFICATE

JADE LEADERSHIP IN SUSTAINABILITY CERTIFICATE

OPAL DIVERSITY AND CULTURAL COMPETENCY LEADERSHIP CERTIFICATE

RUBY CERTIFICATE FOR INFORMATION MANAGEMENT AND DIGITAL LEADERSHIP

SAPPHIRE VOLUNTEERISM AND SERVICE LEADERSHIP CERTIFICATE

BUILDING LEADERS ONE HOUR AT A TIME:

DESCRIPTIONS OF INDIVIDUAL GOLD LEADERSHIP WORKSHOPS

WHAT TO LOOK FOR IN THE WORKSHOP SECTION

Below is a chart used to explain what you will find in the coming section of workshops. Use this diagram to navigate through the many workshops outlined in the coming pages.

All workshops are assigned to one or more certificate levels.

Alphabetical listing of the titles of 150 workshops offered.

Contains name and title of current instructor(s).

Description of the workshop as it appears in the GOLD catalog and website; used to address and attract students.

A NEW LOOK AT DIVERSITY

CERTIFICATE: Gold | **INSTRUCTOR:** Dr. Robert Owens, Distinguished Teaching Professor, Communicative Disorders

"I plan to use my understanding of diversity by acknowledging that there will be significant differences between members of a group—as every person is from differing sub-cultures, but also appreciating this diversity. With a greater diversity of people representing sub-cultures within a group, diverse ideas may come about."

Ilyssa, sophomore, 2009

Each workshop includes a quote from a student journal, with the student's first name, grade level when they attended the workshop, and year of attendance.

WORKSHOP DESCRIPTION

So much of the history of this country is steeped in black and white that we often forget that diversity is all around us. In this workshop, participants step out of the race/ethnicity paradigm to examine cultural diversity from a new point of view. Two highly interactive activities will help bring each participant to a new understanding—and we'll have LOTS of fun, too.

What the student should take from the workshop.

LEARNING OUTCOMES

Upon completion of this workshop, participants will:
- Be able to explain the differences between race, ethnicity, and culture.
- Have examined cultural diversity from a new point of view as they step out of the race/ethnicity paradigm.
- Be able to describe how the majority of Americans differ from other cultures.

Contains a combination of content and activities that the instructor uses to teach the workshop.

WORKSHOP ACTIVITIES

- Participants pick up a Handout on Cultural Competence and a few Post-it® Notes. After a brief introduction, the participants are asked what they consider "race" to be. The instructor states that race is not important unless people actually make it so. The instructor continues by asking the group what "ethnicity" is. Ethnicity is explained as sometimes a nationality, a nation's language, or a shared history. The group is asked what "culture" is, and a story is told to illustrate the definition.
- An outline of an iceberg in water is drawn on a white erase or easel board. Icebergs have a small part that is above water and a much larger part that is under water. This is an analogy to characteristics of a person. There are many ways to label a person purely on how they look—their race, gender, etc. These are the things that are generally "above the water." There are even more ways to categorize someone based on what cannot be seen on the surface—their religion or ambitions, for example—and these are the things under the water's surface.
- An exercise is conducted in order to have participants come up with as many ways they can to characterize someone and label these characteristics as either above or below the water. Each difference is written on a Post-it® Note and placed on the iceberg either above or below the water.
- As part of the iceberg exercise, the participants decide as a group whether or not they agree with the placement of the Post-it® Notes. This is a great opportunity for a meaningful discussion about how we judge and interact with people. If the group decides that a Post-it® Note should be moved they can put it completely above, completely below, or in the middle of the iceberg.
- The instructor then explains the Handout on Cultural Competence, which provides examples of how the majority of Americans differ from other cultures.
- At the end of the workshop, participants reflect on how they personally interact with other people, and consider how other people might view these interactions.

RESOURCES USED

Owens, R. (2008). *Handout on Cultural Competence.* Adapted from Almanza, H., & Moseley, W. (1980). Curriculum adaptations and modification for culturally diverse handicapped children. *Exceptional Children, 46*(8), 608-614.

Includes citations of the handouts, PowerPoints, and other references used by the instructor. Purchasing this book will give the owner access to a password-protected website where these materials will be posted. Copyrighted materials have citations, which can be used to access these resources.

A NEW LOOK AT DIVERSITY

CERTIFICATE: Gold | **INSTRUCTOR:** Dr. Robert Owens, Distinguished Teaching Professor, Communicative Disorders

"I plan to use my understanding of diversity by acknowledging that there will be significant differences between members of a group—as every person is from differing sub-cultures, but also appreciating this diversity. With a greater diversity of people representing sub-cultures within a group, diverse ideas may come about."

Ilyssa, sophomore, 2009

WORKSHOP DESCRIPTION

So much of the history of this country is steeped in black and white that we often forget that diversity is all around us. In this workshop, participants step out of the race/ethnicity paradigm to examine cultural diversity from a new point of view. Two highly interactive activities will help bring each participant to a new understanding—and we'll have lots of fun, too.

LEARNING OUTCOMES

Upon completion of this workshop, participants will:

- Be able to explain the differences between race, ethnicity, and culture.
- Have examined cultural diversity from a new point of view as they step out of the race/ethnicity paradigm.
- Be able to describe how the majority of Americans differ from other cultures.

WORKSHOP ACTIVITIES

- Participants pick up a *Handout on Cultural Competence* and a few Post-it® Notes. After a brief introduction, the participants are asked what they consider "race" to be. The instructor states that race is not important unless people actually make it so. The instructor continues by asking the group what "ethnicity" is. Ethnicity is explained as sometimes a nationality, a nation's language, or a shared history. The group is asked what "culture" is, and a story is told to illustrate the definition.
- An outline of an iceberg in water is drawn on a white erase or easel board. Icebergs have a small part that is above water and a much larger part that is under water. This is an analogy to characteristics of a person. There are many ways to label a person purely on how they look—their race, gender, etc. These are the things that are generally "above the water." There are even more ways to categorize someone based on what cannot be seen on the surface—their religion or ambitions, for example—and these are the things under the water's surface.
- An exercise is conducted in order to have participants come up with as many ways they can to characterize someone and label these characteristics as either above or below the water. Each difference is written on a Post-it® Note and placed on the iceberg either above or below the water.
- As part of the iceberg exercise, the participants decide as a group whether or not they agree with the placement of the Post-it® Notes. This is a great opportunity for a meaningful discussion about how we judge and interact with people. If the group decides that a Post-it® Note should be moved they can put it completely above, completely below, or in the middle of the iceberg.
- The instructor explains the *Handout on Cultural Competence*, which provides examples of how the majority of Americans differ from other cultures.
- Participants reflect on how they personally interact with other people and consider how other people might view these interactions.

RESOURCES USED

Owens, R. (2008). *Handout on Cultural Competence*. Adapted from Almanza, H., & Moseley, W. (1980). Curriculum adaptations and modification for culturally diverse handicapped children. *Exceptional Children*, 46(8), 608-614.

ACCELERATED LEADERSHIP INSTITUTE

CERTIFICATE: Bronze | **INSTRUCTOR:** Dr. Tom Matthews, Associate Dean of Leadership and Service, & Chip Matthews, Director, College Union and Activities

"The amount of information condensed into these four weeks could be compared to a semester's worth of an upper-level business class. The materials, examples, and interactions between attendees resulted in an incredible experience."
Harrison, sophomore, 2010

WORKSHOP DESCRIPTION

The Accelerated Leadership Institute (ALI) is a program designed for students who are sophomores, juniors, or transfers currently involved in student organizations and campus activities. ALI helps students gain valuable knowledge and skills that will aid them in future leadership positions on campus. ALI is a group process, and participants are expected to attend all four sessions. Topics to be covered include goal setting and getting results; communication and problem solving; motivation and teambuilding; running effective meetings; leadership styles; ethical leadership; managing your stress and time; and diversity and leadership. Students completing this program and the required journal reflections will earn Bronze certificates. This series of four 90-minute workshops provides an alternative to taking the standard eight workshops in order to complete the Bronze Life Skills and Leadership Certificate; i.e., it is an accelerated way to achieve the Bronze Certificate.

LEARNING OUTCOMES

Upon completion of this workshop, participants will:
- Understand that leadership is a process.
- Understand how to create and meet personal and organizational goals.
- Understand the critical role communication plays in organizations.
- Be able to solve problems in organizations.
- Understand motivation and the principles of team development.
- Understand the important principles of running effective meetings.
- Be able to articulate and describe their personal leadership style.
- Articulate their commitment to become a role model for ethical leadership.
- Understand the need for managing time and stress.
- Understand the concepts of diversity and cultural competency.

WORKSHOP ACTIVITIES

- The institute is limited to 20 students. The instructors take turns teaching the 10 topics covered in the institute, with assistance from other staff members in student and campus life as needed and appropriate.
- Our coordinator of multicultural programs and services, Fatima Rodriguez Johnson, facilitates the module on diversity and cultural competency.
- All participants are required to attend and complete all four 90-minute sessions and write a journal reflection on each of the four sessions. Each session is worth one Bronze credit.
- Each week the instructors use a combination of lectures, discussions, and exercises to cover each of the 10 topics. Each participant receives a handbook with articles, exercises, and homework assignments given for the second, third, and fourth sessions.

RESOURCES USED

Matthews, T. (2008.) Notebook of papers and *Handouts From Bronze Life Skills and Leadership Certificate Workshops.*

APPLYING FOR SERVICE JOBS: AMERICORPS VISTA AND ROCHESTER YOUTH YEAR

CERTIFICATE: Diamond and Sapphire | **INSTRUCTOR:** Kay Fly, Coordinator, Volunteerism & Service, and Rochester Youth Year VISTA Representatives

"This workshop provided an in-depth overview of opportunities in service jobs, especially for working in the Rochester area. This is an excellent opportunity to take a year and give back to the community. Not only does this make an outstanding impact on someone's resume, it allows someone to make a difference in the area in which they live."

Douglas, sophomore, 2008

WORKSHOP DESCRIPTION

This workshop addresses the application process and the opportunities for service through AmeriCorps VISTA and the local Rochester Youth Year program. In addition, participants are given further information about other programs to explore and provided with the resources needed to apply for a program. Also, the participants hear the personal journeys of two AmeriCorps members in their specific programs.

LEARNING OUTCOMES

Upon completion of this workshop, participants will:

- Know about the AmeriCorps organization, specifically the New York Campus Compact program and the local Rochester Youth Year Fellowship Program.
- Understand how to become involved with these programs.
- Have resources that provide further information about the programs and the application process.

WORKSHOP ACTIVITIES

- The instructor shows a 60-second video clip from the AmeriCorps website that explains the organization.
- A PowerPoint presentation is used to deliver an informative lecture about AmeriCorps. The PowerPoint contains the following topics:
    - Brief history of the AmeriCorps organization
    - Ways to get involved with the organization
    - Fast facts about the organization
    - What AmeriCorps does
    - Different branches of AmeriCorps, and what each branch does
    - AmeriCorps State and National
    - AmeriCorps VISTA
    - AmeriCorps National Civilian Community Corps (NCCC)
    - People/organizations that benefit from the AmeriCorps programs
    - Benefits of being an AmeriCorps alumnus
    - Reasons why people might want to participate in the AmeriCorps program
    - Ways to find more information about the AmeriCorps programs
- Using a separate PowerPoint presentation, an instructor with AmeriCorps experience talks about his/her own personal journey with AmeriCorps. Topics include:
    - New York Campus Compact (NYCC), which is the particular AmeriCorps program
    - What NYCC does, and what s/he personally does as an AmeriCorps VISTA volunteer at SUNY Geneseo
    - Where NYCC is located, and some fast facts about the program
    - The website where more information about the NYCC VISTA program can be found
- A final PowerPoint presentation is delivered by another instructor with AmeriCorps experience, who talks about his/

her own personal journey with AmeriCorps. Topics include:
  - Rochester Youth Year Fellowship program, which is a part of the AmeriCorps program
  - Goals of Rochester Youth Year (RYY), and why this particular program is needed
  - RYY host agencies and current fellows
  - RYY requirements, and the benefits of becoming involved
  - The website where more information can be found about RYY, and where the application could be downloaded
- The instructor shows a short video clip displaying photographs of AmeriCorps members responding to emergencies and providing disaster relief.
- The workshop ends with a question-and-answer period regarding the various AmeriCorps programs.

RESOURCES USED

AmeriCorps (2009). *Fact Sheet.* www.americorps.gov/pdf/factsheet_americorps.pdf

New York Campus Compact (2009). *PowerPoint.* www.nycampuscompact.org/uploads/1/0/6/3/10630880/campus_partner_orientation.pdf

Rochester Youth Year (2008). *Rochester Youth Year PowerPoint.*

For more information on AmeriCorps, go to www.americorps.gov

For more information on NYCC AmeriCorps VISTA, go to www.nyccvista.org

For more information on Rochester Youth Year, go to www.youthyear.org

"The best way to find yourself is to lose yourself in the service of others." –Mahatma Gandhi

ASSERTIVENESS TRAINING

CERTIFICATE: Emerald | **INSTRUCTOR:** Wendi Kinney, Coordinator of Greek Affairs and Off-Campus Living

"I learned how to stand up for my best interests while simultaneously being respectful of others. There is an 'I win, you win' outcome when someone uses assertive techniques effectively."

Elizabeth, freshman, 2009

WORKSHOP DESCRIPTION

Do you often say "yes" when you really want to say "no"? Is it difficult for you to speak up for yourself? If so, come to the Assertiveness Training workshop, where you'll learn about the differences between assertiveness and aggression, have a chance to assess your own assertiveness level, and learn new skills. This interactive workshop features activities that help participants evaluate their own behavior.

LEARNING OUTCOMES

Upon completion of this workshop, participants will:

- Understand what defines assertive behavior and how it differs from passive and aggressive behaviors.
- Have awareness of their own behavioral patterns.
- Begin identifying strategies to become appropriately assertive.

WORKSHOP ACTIVITIES

- Each participant is given a *Handout on Assertiveness Definitions*. The instructor asks for student volunteers to read each definition aloud. The goal is to familiarize the workshop participants with the terminology that is the basis of assertiveness and the different types of behavior associated with it. After the definitions are read, the participants are asked to write down personal examples for each definition.
- Participants put the terms to use in an activity using the four corners of the room. Each corner has one term taped onto the wall (assertive, passive, aggressive, and passive-aggressive). The instructor explains different situations/statements. Participants then move to the respective corner that would describe how they would personally behave in that situation. When all participants are standing in their respective corners, the instructor asks one or two people from each why they chose that particular behavior and possible ways to resolve the situation.
- Upon completion of the four corners activity, the participants are asked to return to their original seats in order to take a quiz (*Handout on Self Assessment*) to assess how assertive they are. After participants complete the quiz, the instructor asks for a show of hands how many students fall into which category.
- Participants are given *Handout on Assertiveness Strategies for Dealing With Conflict* and the instructor asks for participant input for scenarios in which they were taken advantage of or instances in which they were not assertive. The workshop concludes with a role-playing activity. Based on the scenario, two participants role play using the different strategies listed on the handout.

RESOURCES USED

Bloom, L., Coburn, K., & Pearlman, J. (2000). *The new assertive woman*. Gretna, LA: Wellness Institute Press.

Kinney, W. (2010). *Handout on Assertiveness Definitions*.

Kinney, W. (2010). *Handout on Assertiveness Strategies for Dealing With Conflict*.

Kinney, W. (2010). *Handout on Self Assessment*. Adapted from Bloom, L., Coburn, K., & Pearlman, J. (2000). *The new assertive woman*. Gretna, LA: Wellness Institute Press.

ASSESSING ATTITUDES ABOUT SUSTAINABILITY— CHALLENGES & OPPORTUNITIES FOR SUSTAINABILITY LEADERS

CERTIFICATE: Jade | **INSTRUCTOR:** Dr. Kristina Hannam, Professor of Biology

"This workshop definitely made me more aware that sustainability leaders need to make more of a presence on campus and lead by example."

Krista, senior, 2012

WORKSHOP DESCRIPTION

As individuals whose goal is to lead their community or organization through changes to bring about a more sustainable world, it is important for leaders to know the current attitudes and activities of the people they are working with. In this workshop, we will examine survey data from populations both on and off campus to assess attitudes about sustainability, and compare them to our own survey results. We will use these surveys as a starting point to discuss what the data may tell us about the challenges and opportunities for making changes at Geneseo and beyond.

LEARNING OUTCOMES

Upon completion of this workshop, participants will:
- Be able to analyze simple survey results to determine the current state of environmental attitudes and activities within their own or other communities and organizations.
- Be able to identify potential challenges to creating change through sustainability initiatives in their own community or organization, and brainstorm ways to address these challenges.
- Be able to identify areas/attitudes that may provide opportunities for productive change and brainstorm ways to leverage these for further sustainability successes.

WORKSHOP ACTIVITIES

- Participants examine data from sustainability surveys from the Geneseo campus and off-campus sources.
- After completing a survey about their own environmental attitudes and activities, participants are asked to compare survey responses from different groups on and off campus.
- Participants discuss how the attitudes reflected in the survey results may present opportunities and challenges for motivating additional change on campus and beyond.

RESOURCES USED

Hannam, K. (2011). *Assessing Attitudes About Sustainability PowerPoint.*

"All things are connected like the blood which unites us all. Man did not weave the web of life; he is merely a strand in it. Whatever he does to the web, he does to himself." –Chief Seattle

BABY MALL GAME: WILL MONEY MAKE A DIFFERENCE?

CERTIFICATE: Silver or Opal | **INSTRUCTOR:** Dr. Terry Bazzett, Professor of Psychology

"My previous ideas on this subject were very clear, but after the workshop I realized that there were several complications and no clear solutions. Bearing this in mind, I plan to think about challenges that face me in my future from several different angles and not settle on an opinion too quickly."

Nathan, freshman, 2011

WORKSHOP DESCRIPTION

Imagine if people could buy specific attributes for their future baby: What would they be? How much value do people place on height, athletic ability, and prevention of autism? This game was created just as "The Human Genome Project" was making headline news. Participants are led through a simulated "Baby Mall" where they are confronted with various issues and controversies, including the future of medical insurance, ethics, classism, and prejudice towards non-traditional parents. The game is a fun, interactive program that challenges participants to think critically about the many differences that make us who we are.

LEARNING OUTCOMES

Upon completion of this workshop, participants will:
- Have gained knowledge about the Human Genome Project.
- Have awareness of the rapid changes in our world.
- Have thought about the impact that genetic engineering may have on our future and considered related ethical questions.

WORKSHOP ACTIVITIES

- The instructor gives a brief overview of where the human race is in terms of the Human Genome Project. This leads to consideration of the possibility for parents to be able to choose what attributes their child will have by intervening with the fetus' genes.
- The workshop participants are divided into couples, with each couple given an envelope. Inside the envelope are two things. The first is fake money. Each envelope has different amounts of money. The second item in the envelope is the same for everyone, a birth announcement indicating that the couple is expecting a baby. The notice goes on to explain how they can choose attributes for their future baby. There are three categories of attributes: Physical, Behavioral, and Common Disease Prevention. The instructor has three student volunteers to act as vendors, one vendor for each of the three attributes. The vendors are stationed around the room as if the room were the Baby Mall.
- The couples discuss what attributes to buy and visit each vendor to purchase the desired attributes in the Baby Mall.
- When the instructor divides the group into couples, care should be taken to make some couples same-sex and to have some single parents. Vendors tell some couples that items are not available for them to purchase. This brings up issues of prejudice and questions of who should be in charge of this medical technology in the future. Because some of the couples will have significantly less money, there will also be issues of socioeconomic classism to be discussed.
- Controversial options, such as choosing sexuality, will provide interesting discussions. Controversial questions will also come up, such as, "Should we really be creating a perfect race?" and "What role will medical insurance play when this simulation becomes a reality?"
- At the end of the workshop, all of the participants come back together to discuss which attributes they purchased and what impressions they had based on treatment from the different vendors.

RESOURCES USED

Bazzett, T. (2005). *The Baby Mall Game*. GOLD Program Resource, SUNY Geneseo, Geneseo, NY.

BAD LEADERSHIP VS. GOOD LEADERSHIP

CERTIFICATE: Gold | **INSTRUCTOR**: Dr. Tom Matthews, Associate Dean of Leadership and Service

"This workshop is crucial for leaders like myself. It allowed me to see the distinctions between what can make someone a respected leader, or a dreadful leader."

Brooke, sophomore, 2012

WORKSHOP DESCRIPTION

Much of the discussion in the literature on leadership centers on the concept of how to be a good and effective leader. Barbara Kellerman, Research Director of the Center for Public Leadership in the Kennedy School of Government at Harvard University, concluded in her recent book, *Bad Leadership*, that one has to study the entire continuum of leadership from bad to good in order to understand the practice of leadership. Kellerman's book is the starting place for a lively discussion on the practice of leadership.

LEARNING OUTCOMES

Upon completion of this workshop, participants will:
* Be aware of the range of leadership from bad to good.
* Know the characteristics of each of the seven types of bad leadership: incompetent, rigid, intemperate, callous, corrupt, insular, and evil.
* Be able to use Kellerman's suggestions on how to move from bad leadership to good leadership.

WORKSHOP ACTIVITIES

* The instructor offers a brief explanation as to why it is important to consider the concept of bad leadership and Kellerman's book on *Bad Leadership: What It Is, How It Happens, Why It Matters*.
* The *Handout on Bad Leadership Definitions* is distributed and each participant is asked to define leadership and give a definition of good vs. bad leadership. Participants are also asked to share three examples of good leaders and three examples of bad leaders. Workshop participants discuss their definitions and examples in pairs. The entire group then shares some of their answers. Examples typically include celebrity leaders or leaders they have worked with in their lives. Commonalities among the examples are considered. This activity concludes with the instructor sharing Barbara Kellerman's answers.
* The *Handout on Selected Thoughts from Kellerman on Bad vs. Good Leadership* is reviewed. Kellerman's work is discussed and select thoughts from her book are shared. The seven types of bad leadership are evaluated.
* Using the reverse side of the second handout (*Handout on Selected Thoughts from Kellerman on Bad vs. Good Leadership*), a discussion is led on Kellerman's suggestions for moving from bad to good leadership. If time permits, the instructor uses the *Handout on Characteristics of Admired Leaders* by Kouzes and Posner. Participants are asked to rank a list of characteristics of a leader they would follow, not because they have to but because they want to. Participants share their top choices. The instructor shares the results from research which indicates the number one characteristic is honesty.

RESOURCES USED

Kellerman, B. (2004). *Bad leadership: What it is, how it happens, why it matters*. Boston, MA: Harvard Business Press.

Matthews, T. (2011). *Handout on Bad Leadership Definition*.

Matthews, T. (2011). *Handout on Characteristics of Admired Leaders*. Adapted from Kouzes, J., & Posner, B. (2010). *The leadership challenge*. San Francisco, CA: Jossey-Bass.

Matthews, T. (2011). *Handout on Kellerman's Work*.

Matthews, T. (2011). *Handout on Selected Thoughts from Kellerman on Bad vs. Good Leadership*. Adapted from Kellerman, B. (2004). *Bad leadership: What it is, how it happens, why it matters*. Boston, MA: Harvard Business Press.

BAFÀ BAFÀ®

CERTIFICATE: Opal | **INSTRUCTOR:** Dr. Celia Easton, Dean for Residential Living, Professor of English

"Bafà Bafà® is a great cultural experience. As an international student, this is what I experienced when coming to the United States, and now my peers can understand what I have been through."

Karen, senior, 2011

WORKSHOP DESCRIPTION

Bafà Bafà® is a game designed to help people understand the challenges of social interaction across cultural groups. This highly interactive game has been used by thousands of groups all over the world to teach an appreciation of group differences and cross-cultural conflicts. This workshop builds on the lessons imparted by playing the game Bafà Bafà®, by Simulation Training Systems. Participants are split between an Alpha and a Beta culture, each with its own distinctive traits. At its core, Bafà Bafà® is a cultural studies game that allows participants to experience otherness, act out questions of diversity, and be conscious of their actions around other cultures. Participants are encouraged to explore differing perspectives and points of view while reflecting on their own perspectives of different cultures. This workshop is particularly well suited for the introduction of diversity education and consciousness and serves as a valuable preparation for those wishing to travel abroad.

LEARNING OUTCOMES

Upon completion of the workshop, participants will:
- Be able to discuss the experience of otherness and how that impacts interactions with diverse cultures.
- Have the ability to explain different approaches to working with other cultures.
- Be able to compare and critically analyze individual perspectives and points of view on diversity with peers.

WORKSHOP ACTIVITIES

- Workshop participants are split into two groups, the Alphas and the Betas. These groups represent two different "cultures" and each have different traditions. The Betas are taken to another room.
- Each group listens to a recording about their culture's traditions and practices the rules of their culture. Once both groups have had ample time to practice their respected cultures, the next part of the workshop is introduced.
- Members from each culture go one at a time to the other culture to try to determine the other's traditions in order to report back to their own culture. The observer is unable to talk or interact with the other culture while visiting. The observers discuss with their group what they saw and overheard.
- Once each group has sent a portion of observers to watch the other group, the instructor informs the groups that they are able to interact and try to integrate into the other society. Each group visits the other society and obtains more information on their traditions. The instructor interrupts the visit when the conversations and interactions begin to slow.
- Each group has the opportunity to discuss their findings within their own group. The instructor brings the groups back together and leads a discussion about what each culture thought about the other. Many adjectives are typically negative; why is this? Was the reason more than just a language barrier?
- The instructor asks for participants to volunteer to share personal experiences about being immersed in a foreign culture and about being discriminated against. A discussion as to whose responsibility it is to be involved in a group (outsiders to get involved? or insiders to encourage involvement?) and the possibility of a hybrid (where the outsiders and insiders of both cultures are responsible for initiating interactions and being welcoming) concludes the workshop.

RESOURCES USED

This workshop requires the purchase of materials from Simulation Training Systems. To purchase these materials, please visit www.stsintl.com/business/bafa.html.

(n.d.). Bafà Bafà®: A Diversity, Cross-Cultural Simulation. *Simulation Training Systems: Simulations for Businesses, Schools, and Charities*. Retrieved June 16, 2011, from http://www.simulationtrainingsystems.com.

BECOMING A CHANGE AGENT THROUGH TRANSFORMATIONAL LEADERSHIP

CERTIFICATE: Gold | **INSTRUCTOR:** Kimberly Harvey, Director of New Student Programs

"To be a transformational leader one must be able to successfully function as the leader of a group, but also prepare that group for a new leader and to be successful once you are no longer in the leadership position."

Jenni, sophomore, 2011

WORKSHOP DESCRIPTION

Transformational leaders make a difference. How do individuals move from mere transactions to transformation? Learn about the theory and practice of transformational leadership and become an agent for positive change. This workshop uses small- and large-group discussions to educate students on the theory of transformational leadership. Students are taught the steps of transformational leadership that lead to a highly empowered group and also assess their ability to create a vision as a leader.

LEARNING OUTCOMES

Upon completion of this workshop, participants will:

- Be able to define transformational leadership and identify the various steps to becoming a transformational leader.
- Understand the skills associated with transformational leadership.
- Be able to identify examples of transformational leadership.

WORKSHOP ACTIVITIES

- The instructor asks the participants to complete the *Leadership Vision Questionnaire* to assess their ability to create a vision as a leader.
- The instructor presents the *Becoming a Change Agent Through Transformational Leadership* PowerPoint and leads a discussion about the steps and skills associated with transformational leadership.
- Participants are divided into small groups and are asked to describe their individual values and how their leadership styles reflects those values. The group comes back together and discuss their values as a whole.
- Participants break up into small groups again and are asked to give an example about a time when they, or someone they know, acted as a transformational leader and what the experience was like. The instructor then asks for participant volunteers to share some of these examples.
- The instructor gives a brief overview as to why people resist change. Participants are given the opportunity to share examples of instances when change was resisted.
- The workshop ends with a question-and-answer period.

RESOURCES USED

Harvey, K. (2010). *Becoming a Change Agent Through Transformational Leadership PowerPoint.*

Harvey, K. (2010). *Handout on Leadership Vision Quest.* Adapted from Northouse, P. (2009). *Introduction to leadership: Concepts and practice.* Los Angeles, CA: Sage Publications.

Looly, E. (1996). *Transformative leadership.* Ohio Literacy Resource Center. Retrieved from http://literacy.kent.edu/Oasis Leadership/over2.htm.

Northouse, P. (2009). *Introduction to leadership: Concepts and practice.* Los Angeles, CA: Sage Publications.

Pielstick, D. (n.d.). *The transforming leader—Why leaders can lead.* Retrieved from http://www.cba.nau.edu/pielstick-d Leadership/Chrspapr.html.

BECOMING AN ÜBER-EFFICIENT RESEARCHER

CERTIFICATE: Ruby | **INSTRUCTOR:** Justina Elmore, Business & Data Librarian

"Having the ability to use this program makes research papers much easier and creates more time for writing the paper rather than worrying about the proper citation format."

Melissa, junior, 2012

WORKSHOP DESCRIPTION

Find out how to use the Firefox web browser to gather, store, and create citations for research papers. Students will learn to capture and save research sources and export them into a Word document in the citation style of their choice. Through direct instruction and whole group discussion, participants learn how to use the helpful Zotero Firefox Extension, which was originally released in 2006 by the Center for History and New Media.

LEARNING OUTCOMES

Upon completion of this workshop, participants will:
- Understand the capabilities and functionality of the Zotero Firefox Extension as well as how to use all of the main buttons and folders.
- Have an understanding of how to use Zotero for multiple purposes, such as how to cite emails, web pages, and PDFs, and how to use the extension in Microsoft Word.
- Be aware of the importance of avoiding plagiarism.

WORKSHOP ACTIVITIES

Students are guided through exercises to practice creating their own Zotero library by:
- Comparing the various citation tools available to select the one that most meets their needs.
- Learning how/where to download Zotero and the word processor plugins.
- Adding items to their Zotero library using library databases and catalogs.
- Adding items to their Zotero library from sites on the free web.
- Creating folders and organizing resources into new folders.
- Importing citations into a Word document using the Zotero word processor plugin.
- Exporting bibliographies into the clipboard and Google Docs.

RESOURCES USED

No additional resources.

"Research is formalized curiosity. It is poking and prying with a purpose." –Zora Neale Hurston

BEYOND THE 3RS: AN EDUCATION FOR LIVING IN ETHICAL AND SUSTAINABLE WAYS

CERTIFICATE: Jade | **INSTRUCTOR:** Dr. Leigh O'Brien, Professor, Shear School of Education

"For me, I prioritize the future; I want to ensure that both me and my future family have a world with the same resources and opportunities that I do, and I resolve to live the principles of the 6Rs, and fight for environmentalism."

Jessica, sophomore, 2012

WORKSHOP DESCRIPTION

At the center of most sustainability education is a focus on the 3Rs: Reduce, Reuse, and Recycle. Unfortunately, most people, because it's easier, put recycling at the center of their efforts rather than use it as a last resort. What would it look like if everyone believed—and acted as if—it was the ethical obligation not to consume, but to conserve; to, as the catch-phrase puts it, live simply so that others may simply live? Is this even feasible in a country operating under a system Oliver James calls "selfish capitalism"?

LEARNING OUTCOMES

Upon completion of this workshop, participants will:

- Be able to identify and describe the 6Rs (G. Rendell, *Getting to Green*).
- Have identified at least one thing they can do to expand their own efforts to live sustainably.
- Understand at least one way they can encourage others to be more aware of the consequences of their lifestyles.

WORKSHOP ACTIVITIES

- After a brief introduction, the instructor begins the *Beyond the 3Rs* PowerPoint presentation.
- A short activity is included in the *Beyond the 3Rs* PowerPoint in which participants think about a special place for them or a time when something they cared deeply about was stolen or taken from them.
- After coming up with their answer(s), participants are encouraged to share their responses with the group as a whole.
- Then, through the PowerPoint presentation, participants are able to review the 3Rs and then learn about the 6Rs. The 3Rs refer to reduce, reuse, and recycle, whereas the 6Rs refer to rethink, resolve, reduce, re-source, re-use, and recycle.
- Participants then apply the 6Rs to their own lives, keeping in mind their special place or loss, by articulating changes that may follow.
- The workshop concludes with a question-and-answer period.

RESOURCES USED

O'Brien, L. (2011). *Beyond the 3Rs PowerPoint.*

Rendell, G. (2011). Green is not sustainable. *Ecology Campus Network.* Retrieved from http://campus.ecology.com/2011/03/17/green-is-not-sustainable/

"We do not inherit the earth from our ancestors, we borrow it from our children." –Native American Proverb

BREAKING THE GLASS CEILING

CERTIFICATE: Emerald or Opal | **INSTRUCTORS:** Guest Speakers: Sue Beaurfield-Thomas, Class of '90, Global Sales Training, United Parcel Services, and Twanda Christiansen, Class of '98, Marketing Manager for Summit Federal Credit Union

> *"The same morning of this workshop I stumbled across several internships at UPS that seemed to fit what I was looking for. However, I'm always wary about applying to companies if I don't know anyone who is working for them; I want to make sure they treat their employees well before I get involved with them."*
>
> *Annemarie, freshman, 2011*

WORKSHOP DESCRIPTION

What are some of the gender disparities in the workplace? How do women navigate a career in a male-dominated work environment? This workshop examines the hardships that women experience in achieving success in predominantly male-oriented careers. This is a lecture-style workshop in which the speakers talk about their experiences as women in business. They share the stories of their own careers, offer suggestions and encouragement, and answer any questions raised. This workshop could feature new guest speakers every time it is offered, or the same speakers could present multiple times.

LEARNING OUTCOMES

Upon completion of the workshop, participants will:
- Understand the challenges faced by women in male-dominated careers.
- Know how to face and try to overcome those challenges.

WORKSHOP ACTIVITIES

- The instructor offers advice and stories from her personal experience; this includes the importance of networking and how it helped her in the business world.
- The instructor then describes her career as a continuous learning process and informs the participants to "Never be afraid to ask questions," as well as to always expect the unexpected and be flexible in the workplace.
- The instructor asks participants to consider what they personally want. She brings up the example of asking to be considered for new positions or promotions. The instructor talks about knowing your own "market value." She asks the participants for examples of skills and traits that make people efficient.
- The second instructor contributes her own advice and experience, explaining how to pay it forward. The instructor reminds the participants that when someone reaches out to you, make sure you reach out to others. Help the new person in the office and find a mentor when you are starting out at a new job. The instructor tells the participants to not be competitive people but to work well as team members. The participants are told to learn how to help others and become the "go-to" person. The participants are advised to make the whole company successful, not just themselves. The instructor then asks the students for certain ideas about on how to become an asset to their organizations.
- The instructor then talks about jobs that may not seem like the right fit and brings up tips on how to learn from them and detach oneself from the situation. An example of this is having a bad boss or bad coworkers.
- The instructor touches on how to keep your emotions away from the workplace. An example of how to deal with difficult situations in the workplace is to think "someday that guy's going to work for me" or "that's not how I want to be treated/will treat people." The instructor reminds participants that things constantly change and that how you manage/accept/deal with change is very important. The participants are asked how they want to be defined in a work group. This helps to determine how to carry yourself and the amount of work you do.

- The participants are asked to find what they love or a specific talent or gift they have and find ways to use it at any job. Incorporating these things will make you and those around you more at ease. The instructor urges participants to push themselves to go to areas they are uncomfortable in, to make themselves better and better. The instructor asks the participants to name some mentors they have had. It is important to find a mentor, someone who has a style you respect in regard to how they treat others and how they lead. Finally, both instructors talk about how to maintain a life-work balance and the work that goes into that.
- The instructor tells the participants to always keep in mind what is important to you and what you want to achieve.
- The instructor reminds the participants to know when they are happy! While often we are always chasing after the next thing (promotion, position, etc.), at some point we may have to stop and be content.
- Another tip the instructor gives is when interviewing, ask about a company's flexibility to understand if the position will fit into your lifestyle.

RESOURCES USED

No additional resources.

"Often we women are risk averse. I needed the push. Now, more than ever, young women need more seasoned women to provide that encouragement, to take a risk, to go for it. Once a glass ceiling is broken, it stays broken." –Jennifer M. Granholm

BUILDING LEADERSHIP SKILLS THROUGH DIVERSITY, ENGAGEMENT, AND SERVICE

CERTIFICATE: Emerald | **INSTRUCTOR:** David Jordan, Teach for America Recruitment Manager, 2007 New York City Corps member

"This workshop taught participants to start with the vision of their future and work backwards. Envision what you want and work from there. The pillars presented in this workshop reminded me to keep developing all aspects of leadership, particularly in the RA position."

Samantha, junior, 2011

WORKSHOP DESCRIPTION

Learn about what graduate schools and employers seek in their candidates and how students can expand their skills and experiences throughout college to set themselves up for post-graduate success. This seminar focuses on the skills of ideal candidates, such as effective communication and leadership skills built through working in service-oriented and culturally diverse environments. There will be a specific emphasis on how participants can increase their own effectiveness as leaders.

LEARNING OUTCOMES

Upon completion of this workshop, participants will:
- Be able to identify the six pillars of what makes a great leader.
- Know how to implement the six pillars of leadership in their lives.

WORKSHOP ACTIVITIES

- The instructor discusses the context of the study in leadership and asks participants to define the term "achievement gap."
- The instructor examines each of the six pillars of leadership. After defining and explaining each pillar, the instructor has participants talk in small groups for a short time about ways in which they can implement the pillars on their college campus. Student volunteers are called on to share their practices.
- After discussing some resume tips, the instructor answers questions from the audience about leadership skills.

RESOURCES USED

   http://charactercounts.org/overview/council.php

CAREER QUEST—ASSESSING YOUR COMPETENCIES, SKILLS, VALUES, AND GOALS

CERTIFICATE: Emerald (Required) | **INSTRUCTORS:** Kerrie Bondi, Career Counselor in Career Development, and Elizabeth Seager, Associate Director of Career Development

> *"This workshop made me more confident about my major, as well as made me more aware of how careers should be picked based on your personality rather than salary."*
>
> *Katrina, sophomore, 2010*

WORKSHOP DESCRIPTION

Are students certain about their academic or career plans? Do they need some direction? Career Development staff will help uncover student interests, skills, and values, and the role those traits will play in their life after college. Participants will be required to complete the FOCUS series of assessments prior to class; will be introduced to imagery, the career development process, and workplace trends; and will learn how to research career opportunities in the Career Library. There's so much students can do to smooth the path from campus to career. Let the Career Development staff help identify the options!

LEARNING OUTCOMES

Upon completion of the workshops, participants will:

- Demonstrate an understanding of the importance and use of self-assessments to define and advance a career plan.
- Select appropriate campus resources for career exploration and development.
- Enact an individually determined next step along a career development path.

WORKSHOP ACTIVITIES

- Prior to the day of the workshop, each participant receives an email with a link to *FOCUS Self-Assessment* (Copyright 2010 Career Dimensions®, Inc.). They are asked to complete all five sections of the self-assessment and to combine their results.
- At the workshop, the participants are given the *Career Quest Syllabus* and the instructors begin an icebreaker activity by writing three careers on the board. The participants work together to fill in what is involved in each career, and the source of each piece of knowledge about the careers. They then go back and rate the reliability of each source. The purpose of this activity is to stimulate participants to think about whether their perceptions of certain careers are accurate.
- The instructors deliver a PowerPoint presentation about FOCUS, which is a mini-lecture about the importance of finding a career that matches your interests, skills, personality, and values.
- "The Job Giveaway" activity follows. Everyone stands up and listens to a list of characteristics about an unidentified career. They sit down when they hear something undesirable about that career. At the end, the job is revealed and there is a discussion about the things that people did not like about the job. This helps participants recognize what they value in a career.
- The instructors give a mini-lecture about considering interests and skills when choosing a career. The participants are led through a discussion on decision making and goal setting and asked to set goals for the next day, week, and semester.
- The instructors takes the participants to the Career Development Library and leads a tour of the facilities. The workshop ends with small-group discussions about next steps in researching or choosing a career.

RESOURCES USED

Career Dimensions®, Inc. (2008). *FOCUS PowerPoint©.*
SUNY Geneseo Office of Career Development. (2011). *Making a Career Decision.*
SUNY Geneseo Office of Career Development. (2011). *Barriers to Making a Career Decision.*
SUNY Geneseo Office of Career Development. (2011). *Career Quest Syllabus.*

CITING SOURCES IN THE SOCIAL SCIENCES

CERTIFICATE: Ruby | **INSTRUCTOR:** Tom Ottaviano, Reference Instruction Librarian, and Michelle Costello, Education & Instructional Design Librarian

> *"As I move up the educational ladder here at Geneseo, I'm sure that I will need to know how to use different citations for my different classes. I'm grateful that I now have a basic grasp on many different forms of citation."*
>
> *Matthew, junior, 2009*

WORKSHOP DESCRIPTION

Citations and other format-related issues are a critical yet time consuming part of any research paper. Learn how to efficiently use the APSA, ASA, and American Antiquity styles, and learn where to find information on other styles important to citations in the social sciences. This workshop provides participants with a guided lesson on the citation rules and procedures to follow in citing sources in the social sciences. Each participant must have a computer to work on during this hands-on workshop.

LEARNING OUTCOMES

Upon completion of this workshop, participants will:

- Know specific social science citation formats (i.e., ASA, American Antiquity, etc.).
- Understand how to find sources from a citation.
- Utilize the research tools available at the Geneseo library.

WORKSHOP ACTIVITIES

- Participants are invited to the GOLD citation example page (must be done by library faculty through Google Docs).
- The instructor asks the participants to practice deciphering citations, including what the source is, when the article/book was published, who the author(s) are, etc.
- The participants practice using library resources to find the original web pages of previously cited sources.
- Participants practice writing citations from many different sources.
- The Google Docs page consisting of citations created by the class is made available to serve as a template for the students for future citation needs.

RESOURCES USED

Ottaviano, T. (2009). *Handout on Deciphering Citations.*

> *"The way to do research is to attack the facts at the point of greatest astonishment."* –Celia Green

COMMUNITY ENGAGEMENT AND SOCIAL JUSTICE STRUCTURED REFLECTION

CERTIFICATE: Diamond (Required) | **INSTRUCTOR:** Dr. Tom Matthews, Associate Dean of Leadership and Service, and Dr. David Parfitt, Director of Teaching and Learning Center

"The reflection provided me with the opportunity to think about the project from start to finish and how the planning committee will further implement ideas after I have graduated from Geneseo."

Elizabeth, senior, 2012

WORKSHOP DESCRIPTION

Leaders must be able to think clearly about complex issues and act in an appropriate and responsible way. In order to make connections between your community engagement activities and the larger social community, you will be required to reflect on your experience in a structured manner and to make a brief presentation in the GREAT Day Program, a day when all classes are canceled for student research and project presentations. After the reflection and presentation, you will produce a written reflection and structured report on your service or social justice activities.

LEARNING OUTCOMES

Upon completion of this workshop, participants will:

- Have presented and will reflect on experience with either a community engagement project or activities related to a social justice issue.
- Be able to prepare and articulate a clear description of a project or activities related to a social justice issue.
- Have received feedback and constructive comments on a project or activities.

WORKSHOP ACTIVITIES

- Participants are allotted specific time up to a maximum of 10–15 minutes (varies depending on number of completed projects or activities) to describe their project and/or activities. (Examples include human rights advocacy, neuropsychology, Project Kenya trip to Kenya and engagement with school, bone-marrow drive, disparity, cultural differences, health insurance, box tops for schools, Ghana Project to build a school, creating a Venture Crew program, environmental issues, Martin Luther King Jr. Day of Leadership and Service, From Passive to Progressive: Transforming an Honor Society, Iaido.)
- Participants are asked to explain their project's mission statement, describe the steps involved in choosing and managing the project, acknowledge community partners in projects, share the obstacles and issues faced, and share recommendations on how to make the project and/or issues sustainable in the future.
- After each presentation the instructor and participants ask questions and discuss the project.
- Students are required to submit a project report and/or write a reflection paper on their involvement in a social justice issue. The reports are submitted in place of a journal reflection prior to earning one credit toward the certificate.

RESOURCES USED

Matthews, T. (2010). *Handout on Diamond Certificate Report Instructions.*

COMMUNITY ENGAGEMENT AND SOCIAL JUSTICE ACTIVITY PREPARATION

CERTIFICATE: Diamond (Required) | **INSTRUCTORS:** Dr. Tom Matthews, Associate Dean of Leadership and Service, and Dr. David Parfitt, Director of Teaching and Learning Center

> *"I have learned the true importance of what it means to give back to the community that has nurtured you. The whole purpose of community involvement is to build bridges to bring people together who may have never worked with each other before."*
>
> *Ryan, junior, 2011*

WORKSHOP DESCRIPTION

Leaders recognize they are part of a larger social community and any problems of that community are therefore also problems for the individual leader. Students pursuing this leadership certificate may choose to either work on a community project with a local agency or engage in multiple activities related to a social justice issue. This workshop is designed to help participants work through the process of deciding which track to follow and what types of projects or issues will be the best fit for their interests and timeframe. Instructors help participants define the nature of the service and activities they will be doing and help them develop an engagement plan to complete the Diamond Leadership Certificate.

LEARNING OUTCOMES

Upon completion of this workshop and required reflection, participants will:

- Understand the requirements of the two options available to earn the Diamond Leadership in Community Engagement and Social Justice.
- Identify a topic or area of interest for a project or social justice issue.
- Review the college resources that may be utilized in creating a community project or working on a social justice issue.
- Develop and submit a written action plan to the instructors for completing the project or engagement in a social justice issue. The action plan will be the journal submission for this workshop.
- Receive written approval of the action plan from the instructors. Credit for journal submission will indicate approval of the action plan.

WORKSHOP ACTIVITIES

- The instructors explain the development of the capstone Diamond Leadership in Community Engagement and Social Justice Certificate.
- Students are asked to introduce themselves and briefly describe possible community engagement and/or social justice issues they might be interested in pursuing.
- Instructors describe previous community engagement projects:
  - Ghana Project: A collaborative among education department, residence life, study aboard, and relationships with a university in Ghana. The project was started by a student from Ghana who wanted to build a school and expanded into a year-round initiative and recognition as a student organization.
  - Book Drive: Started by an RA involved in the Geneseo Chapter of the National Residence Hall Honorary who wanted to collect books for a competition at a regional conference. Geneseo won an award for collecting more books than all other colleges combined.
  - Senior Class Gift: A sophomore student initiated a plan to create a memorial for veterans on the campus. The project became part of the senior class gift three years later.
  - Box Tops for Schools: An education major worked with the Geneseo Central School PTA to collect box tops for school equipment.

- Boy Scouts of America Adventure Crew: Students created a college-level equivalent of Scouting for college students.
- The Kenya Project included a summer trip to Kenya and involvement with a school.
- The instructors ask students work to work in pairs or small groups to share ideas and focus on possible projects or social justice issues. Instructors ask students to report on their conversations.
- The instructors distribute a packet of materials and review the handouts that include guidelines for creating independent projects, project registration forms, service grant forms, holding account policies, SMART Goals, and project/social justice reports.
- The instructors explain the paperwork, logistics, and the final paper for completing the certificate requirements, including the final workshop on Community Engagement and Social Justice Activities Structured Reflection on GREAT Day.
- The instructors review the expectations for the journal reflection of this workshop, which will be the student action plan for completing a project or involvement in a social justice issue. Students are encouraged to use SMART Goals to establish a plan. Students pursuing a project are encouraged to collaborate with other organizations and to narrow the focus to realistic and achievable goals. Students pursuing a social justice issue are encouraged to pursue their passion for a cause or issue but also be realistic about what they can accomplish.

RESOURCES USED

Center for Community. (2011). *Handout on Community Engagement Project Registration Form.*

Center for Community. (2011). *Handout on Community Engagement Project Guidelines.*

GOLD Program. (2011). *Handout on SMART Goals.*

GOLD Program. (2011). *Handout on Community Engagement and Social Justice Activity Preparation.*

GOLD Program. (2011). *Handout on Community Service Grants for Recognized Student Organizations and Approved Community Engagement Projects.*

Livingston CARES. (2009). *Guidelines for Project Holding Accounts.*

"Never doubt that a small group of thoughtful, committed citizens can change the world; indeed, it's the only thing that ever does." –Margaret Mead

COMMUNITY MAPPING

CERTIFICATE: Diamond (Required) | **INSTRUCTOR:** Wes Kennison, Class of '79, and Faculty Fellow for International Studies

"Analyzing the small communities that I am surrounded by each day will help me map out the larger community and think about how each is interrelated."

Elizabeth, sophomore, 2010

WORKSHOP DESCRIPTION

Civic engagement begins with mapping your community. Every community has a unique history, a specific demographic composition, overlapping organizations and institutions, and a particular matrix of human, economic, and geographic resources. This workshop provides a conceptual and practical understanding of how individuals and/or groups may overcome obstacles and leverage resources to accomplish goals and positive change through civic engagement. Additionally, every community consists of organizations and people that are connected by minimal degrees of separation. This workshop serves to make participants aware of these connections and how to best utilize them within the community. This is a highly discussion-based workshop where participants are presented with a theoretical or actual problem in their local community. They then think about all of the organizations and people in the community that could contribute to solving the problem. The workshop focuses on using creativity to link these resources together.

LEARNING OUTCOMES

Upon completion of the workshop, participants will:

* Have an awareness of the extensive organizations and resources that exist within a community and the relationships between them.
* Approach community problem solving using a creative and "big-picture" perspective.
* Know how to link together the resources within a community in order to find the most effective solution to a problem.
* View a community as a web of interwoven organizations, resources, and people.
* Understand and know how to overcome the "Founders Syndrome" and egoism.

WORKSHOP ACTIVITIES

* The instructor poses a problem that needs to be solved within the community. Participants think of all of the organizations that could become involved as part of a solution to the problem. The instructor prompts the participants to think of creative solutions and to link resources together in new ways.

RESOURCES USED

Kennison, W. (2011). *Handout on Community Mapping Chart.*

"One of the marvelous things about community is that it enables us to welcome and help people in a way we couldn't as individuals. When we pool our strength and share the work and responsibility, we can welcome many people, even those in deep distress, and perhaps help them find self-confidence and inner healing." –Jean Vanier, Community and Growth

CONFLICT RESOLUTION

CERTIFICATE: Sapphire | **INSTRUCTOR:** Dr. Leonard Sancilio, Dean of Students

"In order to deal with conflict in a positive and healthy way, it is important to be open-minded and respectful."

Felicia, junior, 2011

WORKSHOP DESCRIPTION

Conflict is a part of every group and organization. Success and growth depend on the positive resolution of conflicts that occur. This workshop will provide methods and activities that can help participants effectively manage conflict and deal with difficult people in your group. The purpose of this workshop is to teach participants about peaceful and effective ways to resolve both positive and negative conflict within their organizations. They will learn about elements, causes, and ways of dealing with conflict. A group discussion atmosphere will be created where participants can share their thoughts on the definition of conflict, ways they deal with conflict, and ways in which to escalate or de-escalate a conflict. This workshop will stress the idea that conflict can be positive and how members of a group can change and learn from it.

LEARNING OUTCOMES

Upon completion of this workshop, participants will:
- Have analyzed and discussed different ways of dealing with conflict.
- Have developed an understanding about the positive effects of confronting a conflict.

WORKSHOP ACTIVITIES

- The instructor asks an introductory question about the definition of conflict. Participants are asked to form groups of three and come up with their own definition of conflict. The groups are asked to share their definitions as the instructor writes their ideas on the board. Following this discussion the instructor leads the group in a discussion of why people do not like being in conflict and why conflict is inevitable throughout your lifetime.
- The instructor goes over specific causes of conflict, asking for student input. The lecture then leads to the question of how we deal with conflict, focusing on the primary two options: fighting versus ignoring.
- The instructor explains the three necessary elements that exist for a problem to occur, which include (1) a relationship between two or more people, (2) issues surrounding the conflict, and (3) individual feelings.
- The *Different Levels of Intensity* handout is passed out, which leads to a discussion on actions that may escalate or de-escalate a conflict. Participants brainstorm different behaviors as the instructor writes their ideas on the board.
- The instructor asks the participants to visualize themselves mediating a conflict between two people. They are asked to come up with "rules for fighting fairly" that the people in conflict must abide by during the resolution. It leads to four specific rules, which are: (1) Stick to the issues, (2) Respect the other person, (3) Define the problem, and (4) Use certain language. The instructor then hands out the remaining two worksheets, "Dealing With Conflict" and "Conflict Resolution."

RESOURCES USED

Sancilio, L. (2000). *Handout on Dealing With Conflict*. Adapted from unknown source.

Sancilio, L. (2011). *Handout on Conflict—Different Levels of Intensity*. Adapted from *Conflict intensity chart: A resource for committee on ministry*. (2002). Louisville, KY: Presbyterian Church (U.S.A.).

Sancilio, L. (2011). *Handout on Conflict Resolution*. Adapted from Raider, E. S., & Gearson, J. (2000). Teaching conflict resolution skills in a workshop. In M. Deutsch & P. T. Coleman (Eds.). *Handbook of conflict resolution: Theory and practice* (pp. 499–521). San Francisco: Jossey-Bass.

CONSIDERING A GOVERNMENT JOB? LEARN STRATEGIES FOR FEDERAL AND STATE JOB SEARCHES

CERTIFICATE: Emerald | **INSTRUCTOR:** Kerrie Bondi, Career Counselor, Office of Career Development

"I look forward to the process of looking for a job, but it also scares me because I know jobs are limited. I feel this information will help me get a head start in the searching process for jobs."

Lindsay, sophomore, 2010

WORKSHOP DESCRIPTION

Our federal government is hiring tens of thousands of new employees at a steady pace, with job openings available for every interest area and at virtually every agency. This hiring surge comes at a time of high national unemployment and a renewed enthusiasm for public service, which means there will be fierce competition for federal jobs. When you're in the market for a job, shouldn't you at least consider the largest employer in New York State with the broadest array of jobs and job sites? That's the New York State government. To get a job in New York State government, you must begin by competing in a civil service examination designed to test for the knowledge, skills, and abilities needed to perform the duties of the position to be filled. If you would like help navigating the hiring process of these two large employers, you'll want to attend this workshop.

LEARNING OUTCOMES

Upon completion of the workshop, participants will:

- Be familiar with navigating the federal and state job posting web sites, including tips to make the process less overwhelming.
- Understand the variety of jobs available with both federal and state employers.
- Have an awareness of Career Development resources to assist with the process.

WORKSHOP ACTIVITIES

- This is a lecture format workshop that uses the Partnership for Public Service PowerPoint slides as well as slides provided by the New York State Department of Civil Service. Students are encouraged to ask questions throughout the presentation and to contact the presenter afterwards if they need more information or help with the application process.

RESOURCES USED

New York State Department of Civil Service. (2010). *Career Opportunities With the State of New York PowerPoint.*

Partnership for Public Service. (2009). *Making the Difference: Finding and Applying for Opportunities in Federal Service PowerPoint.*

"Choose a job you love, and you will never have to work a day in your life." –Confucius

CREATE BETTER-LOOKING REPORTS USING MICROSOFT EXCEL'S ANALYSIS TOOLS

CERTIFICATE: Ruby | **INSTRUCTOR:** Steve Dresbach, Technology Instructor

"I use Excel all the time for different classes, and I do not know all of the different techniques and formulas that it can accomplish. It is amazing what Excel can do, and now I can apply what I have learned for my own uses."

Kimberly, freshman, 2012

WORKSHOP DESCRIPTION

Learn about some of MS Excel's analysis tools to convert your lists of data into organized, attractive, easy-to-read reports. You will learn about Excel tables, pivot tables, consolidating, and scenarios.

LEARNING OUTCOMES

Upon completion of this workshop, participants will:

- Possess a basic understanding of how to use four of Microsoft Excel's analysis tools, such as tables, pivot tables, data consolidation, and scenarios.
- Be provided with introductory documents for further practice in using these analysis tools.

WORKSHOP ACTIVITIES

- The instructor outlines the basic function and use of each of the four analysis tools highlighted in the workshop.
- Students download practice spreadsheets from the library instructor's Geneseo Outbox in order to all have access to the same data.
- The instructor begins walking the participants through examples of how to use each analysis tool, beginning with simple formatting of tables; moving to pivot tables; discussing how, when, and why to consolidate data; and finally choosing the appropriate method to create scenarios using the sample data.
- The instructor details how these various tools can enhance the content and appearance of professional reports, as well as emphasizing their importance in a student's data analysis projects.

RESOURCES USED

Dresbach, S. (2011). Microsoft Excel Sample Data files.

"Learning is a treasury whose keys are queries." –Arab proverb

CREATING A CLIMATE OF CARE

CERTIFICATE: Bronze | **INSTRUCTOR:** Karen Duerr-Clark, Residence Life Area Coordinator

"Living in a residence hall requires sharing common spaces. Therefore it is necessary to clarify expectations in order to have good relationship trust with those that I live with."

Brandi, junior, 2012

WORKSHOP DESCRIPTION

Does your organization or life feel sticky? Trust is the glue that bonds great people, processes, and environments in order to ensure long-term success. Based on the book *The Speed of Trust*, by Stephen M. R. Covey and Rebecca R. Merrill, this workshop will explore the first three waves of trust—self trust, relationship trust, and organizational trust. Trust impacts us 24/7, 365 days a year, so come join this lively discussion as we look into how we can make trust the core of our personal and professional lives.

LEARNING OUTCOMES

Upon completion of this workshop, participants will:

- Demonstrate an understanding of the different waves of trust.
- Know the keys to building trust among teams and within groups.
- Be able to apply trust-building skills in current and future group and leadership roles.

WORKSHOP ACTIVITIES

- Using the core principles of *The Speed of Trust*, this interactive workshop begins with a brief explanation of three types or waves of trust: self-trust, relationship trust, and organizational trust.
- Participants engage in discussions on the nature of trust, the requirements to create and maintain trust, and the overall importance of trust. Focusing on skills and traits such as active listening, empathy, transparency, and accountability, participants use real examples and experiences to discuss how understanding these skills creates better leaders and organizations.
- Participants conclude by brainstorming together ways to strengthen groups they are already involved with or wish to become involved with.

RESOURCES USED

Covey, S. M. R., & Merrill, R. R. (2008). *The speed of trust: The one thing that changes everything.* New York: Free Press.

Harvey, K. (2009). *Creating a Climate of Care PowerPoint.* Adapted from Covey, S. M. R., & Merrill, R. R. (2008). *The speed of trust: The one thing that changes everything.* New York: Free Press.

"The best way to find out if you can trust somebody is to trust them." —Ernest Hemingway

CREATING E-PORTFOLIOS FOR THE JOB MARKET

CERTIFICATE: Ruby (Required) | **INSTRUCTOR:** Steve Dresbach, Technology Instructor

"Having an e-portfolio shows technical competence and could give me an edge on other applicants when applying to graduate schools or to a new job."

Melissa, junior, 2011

WORKSHOP DESCRIPTION

An e-portfolio is a means of showcasing your accomplishments in digital format. It demonstrates your skills and competencies and is a reflection of who you are. Come and learn how to create your own free e-portfolio and add various forms of digital content, such as documents, videos, presentations, and photos.

LEARNING OUTCOMES

Upon completion of the workshop, participants will:
- Understand how an e-portfolio can showcase your work.
- Recognize the different forms of digital content that can be placed in an e-portfolio.
- Know how to use Google Sites to create a polished e-portfolio.

WORKSHOP ACTIVITIES

- The instructor explains how an e-portfolio is a tool that can be used to supplement a resume.
- Things that can be put in a portfolio are discussed, such as examples of writings or artwork, as opposed to an e-portfolio, which can also have audio clips, such as of interviews conducted, and videos of presentations.
- Participants look at the different tools that Google offers that can be used in creating an e-portfolio.
- The steps to creating a page are discussed, such as using the first page to introduce one's self, how to add pages with files from Google Docs, and how to add PowerPoint Presentations and podcasts.
- Throughout the workshop, the instructor shares his e-portfolio with the participants and uses it as a demonstration piece.

RESOURCES USED

Laptops are required for this workshop.

"We are what we repeatedly do. Excellence, then, is not an act, but a habit..." –Aristotle

CREATING AND LEADING INCLUSIVE ENVIRONMENTS

CERTIFICATE: Gold | **INSTRUCTOR:** Fatima Rodriguez-Johnson, Coordinator, Multicultural Programs and Services

"It is important for everyone to feel wanted and to feel like they are contributing; in addition, you may find that better ideas come to the table from people you wouldn't expect them from. I believe that being able to lead an inclusive environment is a key factor in being a leader."

Jenna, sophomore, 2012

WORKSHOP DESCRIPTION

In any career and at any level, you will find yourself working in a diverse atmosphere. With a wide range of diversity, how do you identify differences? How do you ensure everyone feels they are key members? How do you create a welcoming environment? These are tricky but critical skills a leader must possess to create a positive and productive team.

LEARNING OUTCOMES

Upon completion of this workshop, participants will:

- Be able to articulate the differences between exclusive and inclusive groups.
- Understand the critical need for creating welcoming environments.

WORKSHOP ACTIVITIES

- Instructors describe previous community engagement projects and ask the following questions:
  - "How do you identify differences?"
  - "What do you do to ensure that everyone feels like they are key members of the organization?"
  - "How do you create a welcoming environment?"
- The questions stress the importance of representation, interaction, and atmosphere.
- After the participants discuss the questions in small groups, there is a large-group discussion on the same questions and about the reality of creating inclusive environments.
- The participants fill out an "organization handout" about an organization in which the atmosphere was exclusive.
- The presenter shares her story about experiences working in inclusive and exclusive environments.
- The *Creating and Leading Inclusive Environments Handout* is given to participants, followed by a discussion on how to implement these environments.

RESOURCES USED

Creating and Leading Inclusive Environments Handout. Adapted from Pious, S. (2002–2011.) Social Psychology Network. Rodriguez-Johnson, F. (2012). *Handout on Organization Experience.*

"If we cannot now end our differences, at least we can help make the world safe for diversity." –John F. Kennedy

CREATING PODCASTS AND ENHANCED PODCASTS WITH APPLE'S GARAGEBAND

CERTIFICATE: Ruby | **INSTRUCTOR:** Steve Dresbach, Technology Instructor

"I was required to give a 10–15 minute presentation on a topic of my choice for class, and the professor was looking for unique projects that consisted of more than just a PowerPoint presentation. I thought a podcast might be a different way to present my topic. I spent some time planning out a podcast and playing around with Apple's GarageBand."

Abigail, junior, 2010

WORKSHOP DESCRIPTION

Podcasting is all the rage, but what exactly are they? Podcasts are syndicated content in a multimedia file that users can download to a computer or handheld device, then listen to or watch. Do you have a subject or topic you want to talk about and distribute to the whole wide world? You need to create a podcast for others to listen to! Come to this workshop and learn the basics of recording quick audio content for the web, iPods, or other MP3 players. Then learn how to create the syndicated feed so users can subscribe to your podcasts. For this workshop, participants need access to a Mac computer with Garageband in order to learn how to use the software to make effective podcasts.

LEARNING OUTCOMES

Upon completion of this workshop, participants will:
- Understand the requirements for creating a podcast.
- Know how to use recording/editing software to record a podcast and MP3 file.
- Be able to create an RSS feed for their podcasts by using a blog and FeedBurner.

WORKSHOP ACTIVITIES

- The instructor asks participants, "What is a podcast?" and reviews some responses.
- A PowerPoint is shown that has definitions/descriptions of programs and technology. The instructor then presents his podcast and enhanced podcast (which includes artwork) as an example.
- The instructor shows a podcast on Garageband and explains how all of the tracks are related to each other.
- Participants open Garageband and create a new podcast and episode (that explains each track and how to record).
- They drag the Podcast folder to the photo section and into the audio section, then Drag VO (from the Podcast folder) to empty space (as its own track) and do the same with the other audio pieces in the folder.
- The instructor explains how the Zoom indicator can arrange them (right to left), then shows how to drag track bars to logically arrange them (top to bottom).
- Participants are allowed to play around with the program and get comfortable with the features.
- The instructor shows participants how to edit tracks and how to use the Loop Browser button.
- Participants learn "ducking" (moving up and down pointed arrows on tracks, which allows you to control which track will be louder and which will be softer when playing tracks simultaneously) and "fading" (using the down arrow volume control for track, click, and set points to control level).
- The instructor briefly explains enhanced podcasts and reminds participants how to delete pieces.
- The instructor shows how to finish/create the podcast.

RESOURCES USED

Dresbach, S. (2010). *PowerPoint on Podcasting.*

CRITICAL EVALUATION OF ENERGY USE CHOICES IN THE CONTEXT OF OUR CHANGING CLIMATE

CERTIFICATE: Diamond or Jade | **INSTRUCTOR:** Dr. Scott Giorgis, Chair and Professor of Geological Sciences

"He showed me the little things I could do to start reducing my carbon footprint and gave us the tools to calculate the impact of our decisions."

Grace, junior, 2011

WORKSHOP DESCRIPTION

How much and what kind of energy we choose to use will have a direct impact on the future trajectory of global climate change. There are many possible routes to "carbon footprint" reduction, but it is often difficult to choose the most effective option. We will examine methods for evaluating the impact of different technologies and/or lifestyle changes on your personal contribution to climate change. This is a lecture-based workshop and the presenter uses a PowerPoint presentation for a visual aid. However, the instructor highly encourages questions and discussion throughout the presentation.

LEARNING OUTCOMES

Upon completion of the workshop, participants will:

- Know how changing incandescent light bulbs to CFLs, unplugging cell phone chargers, and changing eating habits affect one's carbon footprint.
- Be able to effectively convey this information to others.

WORKSHOP ACTIVITIES

- The instructor explains the importance of being realistic when trying to encourage others to change their energy use habits and reduce their carbon footprint impact. People will probably only do a few things. Carefully choosing what you will advocate for is important to the future success of what others will actually do. Simple quantitative analysis is important to illustrate points.
- The instructor uses PowerPoint slides and graphs to illustrate the following concepts.
  - The correlation between temperature and carbon dioxide emissions is discussed.
  - The instructor describes the social justice framework and looks at what industrialized countries have done in the last 150 years. Is this fair to other people in the world? Is this fair to future generations?
- Cause and effect relationships are examined.
  - For light bulbs, participants look at cost, carbon emissions, and mercury emissions.
  - The graph which shows unplugging the cell phone charger is discussed as a good practice, but one that does not yield huge results.
  - The effect of changing dietary habits is also discussed.
- An important point emphasized is realizing that when you buy something, you take ownership of it. When you buy something, you are essentially telling the companies to keep doing what they are doing.

RESOURCES USED

Giorgis, S. (2010). *Handout on Climate and Food Article 1.*

Giorgis, S. (2010). *Handout on Climate and Food Article 2.*

Giorgis, S. (2010). *Handout on Climate and Food Excel File.*

Giorgis, S. (2010). *Critical Evaluation of Energy Use PowerPoint.*

Weber, L. C., & Matthews, H. S. (2008). Food-miles and the relative climate impacts of food choices in the United States. *Environmental Science & Technology*, 42(10), 3508–3513.

CRITICAL INQUIRY IN RESEARCH

CERTIFICATE: Ruby (Required) | **INSTRUCTORS:** Thomas Ottaviano, Reference Instruction Librarian, and Michelle Costello, Education and Instructional Design Librarian

"Gathering information is usually the hardest part of becoming knowledgeable about a topic, but now that it has just been simplified for me, I will not be as intimidated by research projects."

Abby, sophomore, 2012

WORKSHOP DESCRIPTION

Great leaders gather information and critically analyze the facts before making good decisions. Attendees at this workshop will discover helpful tips and strategies that are used in any kind of database to help improve their searches, save time, and determine the best quality resources for their research.

LEARNING OUTCOMES

Upon completion of this workshop, participants will:

- Understand the peer-review process.
- Know the components of scholarly and peer-reviewed resources.
- Know how to select the most appropriate resources for researching a topic.
- Know how to enter a research topic into a database so that it yields the best possible results.

WORKSHOP ACTIVITIES

- Find resources based on citations (the resources are interchangeable, but one should be scholarly, one should be a trade publication, and one should be popular).
- Look at a list of criteria for those resources to determine if they are popular, trade, or scholarly.
- Break down a typical research question into separate concepts. For example, in the research topic "Does a teenager's level of self-esteem affect the amount of alcohol they consume?" the concepts would be *teenager*, *self-esteem*, and *alcohol consumption*. Students are encouraged to use a research topic they will be using for a class this semester.
- Brainstorm synonyms for the different concepts.
- Add appropriate searching tricks such as Boolean terminology (AND, OR, NOT) and truncation (*) to search terms and enter them into the databases.

RESOURCES USED

Ottaviano, T. (2011). *Peer Review Process PowerPoint.* Milne Library, SUNY Geneseo.

Ottaviano, T., & Costello, M. (2011). *Handout on Critical Inquiry in Research.* Milne Library, SUNY Geneseo.

"The most all-penetrating spirit before which will open the possibility of tilting not tables, but planets, is the spirit of free human inquiry." –Dmitri Mendeleev

CROSS-CULTURAL PROBLEM SOLVING

CERTIFICATE: Opal (Required) | **INSTRUCTOR:** Fatima Rodriguez-Johnson, Coordinator, Multicultural Programs & Services

> *"One important perspective was the need to recognize differences between people and view them in a positive light, as opposed to simply ignoring them."*
>
> *Russell, sophomore, 2010*

WORKSHOP DESCRIPTION

This session will use a model created as a process for collaboratively understanding and addressing conflicts and issues related to difference, discrimination, and inter-group tensions in a school context. Participants will learn to apply this model in solving cross-cultural problems. This is a required workshop that informs participants about the cross-cultural problem-solving model, which includes six different steps. Within the interactive workshop, participants engage by working in groups, addressing a real life problem in order to further their understanding of the model.

LEARNING OUTCOMES

Upon completion of the workshop, participants will:
  * Demonstrate an understanding of the cross-cultural problem solving model.
  * Have collaborated with others to discuss multicultural issues.
  * Apply the cross-cultural problem-solving model to real-life situations.

WORKSHOP ACTIVITIES

  * Participants are presented with the question: "What are multi-cultural problems in Geneseo?" Examples can include bias-related incidents, ignorance, treating others differently due to expectations and stereotypes, holiday celebrations in schools, and how schools value and acknowledge other cultures.
  * The participants are given the handout on *Collaborative Multicultural Problem-Solving*, then read through each paragraph in the six-step model aloud. After each paragraph, there is a mini-discussion about what each step actually means.
  * The instructor chooses an example/scenario and goes through the six-step process described in the handout. This can be repeated with different examples if time allows.
  * The instructor splits the participants into four groups and provides each group with a marker and a large sheet of paper. The groups are asked to discuss the pros and cons of the six-step process and brainstorm how to make the process better.
  * After the groups have had ample time to communicate with each other and write some pros and cons of the six-step process, the instructor will ask each group to present their thoughts.
  * The workshop concludes with a discussion about the differences between fairness and equity. (Fairness: Everyone gets the same thing. Equity: Consider other factors and make sure everyone gets what they need.)

RESOURCES USED

Clark, K. (2002). *Handout on Collaborative Multicultural Problem-Solving With Case Studies.*

> *"We become not a melting pot but a beautiful mosaic. Different people, different beliefs, different yearnings, different hopes, different dreams." –Jimmy Carter*

CRUCIAL CONFRONTATIONS: WHERE DO YOU STAND?

CERTIFICATE: Bronze | **INSTRUCTOR:** Victoria Gebel, Residence Life Area Coordinator

"In the future I plan to follow the steps given in this workshop and really make an effort to stay calm when approaching crucial confrontations. What I learned in this workshop will help me get through the rest of college, my personal life, and my future career in the business world."

Kerri, freshman, 2010

WORKSHOP DESCRIPTION

This workshop will address how to break through and master the art of maintaining effective communication and relationships with others in your life. At times there may be breakdown in your relationships at work or home. When working directly with others, confrontations and disagreements arise and an effective leader knows how to deal with these. In this workshop, participants will learn to identify their own conflict style and then how to deal with confrontations from individuals of all conflict styles. Different types of confrontations will be outlined and participants will be instructed to recognize and turn confrontations into "care-frontations" while maintaining a cool head and leadership authority. Participants learn practical and effective tools to not only improve their individual performance, but their organization's overall success as well.

LEARNING OUTCOMES

Upon completion of this workshop, participants will:
- Be able to explain the characteristics of different confrontational styles.
- Demonstrate techniques to deal with confrontation effectively.
- Use effective communication to deal with confrontation.

WORKSHOP ACTIVITIES

- The instructor asks students to think about the confrontations that they typically avoid and common mistakes that are made when participants decide to confront someone.
- Using the book *Crucial Confrontations*, students are walked through various techniques and strategies as presented in this text.
- A video clip from The Office is used in a humorous way to demonstrate intervening during a conflict between two co-workers, along with a clip from Dorm Life: Episode 109—The Talent Show.

RESOURCES USED

Bramson, R. (1981). *Coping with difficult people.* New York: Dell Publishing.

Harvey, K. (2011). *Handout on Conflict Questionnaire.*

Harvey, K. (2011). *Handout on Crucial Conversations.*

Harvey, K. (2011). *Handout on Some Do's and Don'ts for Managing Difficult Interactions.* Adapted from Bramson, R. (1981). *Coping with difficult people.* New York: Dell Publishing.

Harvey, K. (2011). *Crucial Confrontations: Where Do you Stand? PowerPoint.*

Patterson, K., Grenny, J., McMillan, R., & Switzler, A. (2005). *Crucial confrontations.* New York: McGraw-Hill.

"To effectively communicate, we must realize that we are all different in the way we perceive the world and use this understanding as a guide to our communication with others." –Tony Robbins

DEVELOPING A PERSONAL LEADERSHIP MODEL

CERTIFICATE: Gold (Required) | **INSTRUCTOR:** Dr. Tom Matthews, Associate Dean of Leadership and Service

"My leadership traits have explored different situations and developed into what they are today. Engaging in numerous activities throughout my years of grade school as well as college, I realize how mature my leadership qualities have become, and understand that it is an ongoing process throughout life that must be learned, practiced, and experienced."

Aelim, sophomore, 2011

WORKSHOP DESCRIPTION

The Gold level of the Leadership Certificate Program requires students to articulate written and verbal statements of their personal philosophy of leadership. This informal coaching session will provide students with an opportunity to work on their model with the assistance of the instructor. Reference materials and resources will be available. This session is limited to students planning to complete the Gold Certificate this semester. Participants complete self-evaluation activities and individual goal-setting exercises designed to help them formulate their personal philosophies of leadership.

LEARNING OUTCOMES

Upon completion of this workshop, participants will:
- Identify their major thoughts and beliefs about leadership.
- Evaluate the consistency between their thoughts and beliefs with their actual practice of leadership.
- Understand the requirements and instructor expectations for writing the Personal Leadership Model paper, which has the three sections: leadership journey, analysis of eight leadership theories, and current conclusions and beliefs incorporated into a personal statement on the meaning of leadership.

WORKSHOP ACTIVITIES

- The instructor divides the participants into groups of four and asks them to move their chairs into small groups spread throughout the room. Each participant is asked to draw a picture of leadership. They share and explain their drawing in the small groups. This picture and explanation is a repeat of an activity used in the introductory Leadership Concepts workshop for the Bronze Certificate. The participants are asked if the depiction of leadership is the same or different from their drawing in the Leadership Concepts workshop. Typically there will be a range of responses from "identical" to "radically different," and the instructor solicits a few responses at random from the room and suggests that students are learning to view leadership in many new ways as a result of their participation in GOLD workshops and earning the Bronze, Silver, and Gold certificates.
- The participants receive the *Sixteen Questions for Leaders* handout that contains a list of deep and probing questions on leadership. The instructor ask the participants to reflect on the first six questions: What does leadership mean to me? What kind of leader do I want to be? What kind of leader do I not want to be? What best exemplifies great leadership to me? Why? How does my story and background have a bearing on what I want to do with my life? How can I draw on my story and background as a resource in my leadership? The purpose of this activity is to allow participants to reflect on their attitudes and beliefs on leadership.
- Using a second handout (a reprint of Chapter 5 of *Leading From Within,* by Nancy Huber), the participants are asked to read pages 55–58 on "A Philosophical Foundation: Assumptions, Attitudes, Values and Beliefs." The instructor asks the participants to reflect and then share with their small group four questions: What are my beliefs and values about human nature? What are my beliefs about what the purpose of leadership is? What are my beliefs about what constitutes leadership? What are my beliefs about the leadership process? This exercise is timed by the instructor with just a few minutes on each question allowed before proceeding to the next.
- Participants are then asked to read page 60 on the handout that discusses developing a personal credo. Participants then write a few "I will" credo personal statements.

- The final handout, *Developing a Personal Model of Leadership*, is handed out and reviewed by the instructor. The essay requirements are reviewed, including the three sections: a personal leadership story from the earliest recollection of leadership to the current experience, review and analysis of a minimum of eight leadership theories, and the conclusions and current beliefs about the meaning of leadership as stated in a Personal Model of Leadership. Participants are instructed to use several books listed on the handouts that are on reserve in both the college library and the leadership library in the GOLD Leadership Center. The books include two encyclopedias on leadership. Participants are also informed that three Outstanding Prize Papers will be selected and announced at the Annual Leadership Awards and Recognition Ceremony in April.
- Participants are also asked to sign up for one of the two final GOLD Leadership Presentations at which each student completing the Gold Leadership Certificate will have an opportunity to make an informal presentation on their Personal Leadership Model.

RESOURCES USED

Burns, J. (2000). A river runs through it: A metaphor for teaching Leadership Theory. Reprinted from *The Journal of Leadership Studies*, 7(3), 41–55.

Huber, N. (2001). Leading From Within: Developing Personal Direction. Reprint of Chapter 5 (pp. 53–63) from Huber, N. (1998). *A Personal Philosophy of Leadership*. Malabar, FL: Krieger Publishing Company.

Matthews, T. (2011) *Handout on Sixteen Questions for Leaders*. Adapted from an unknown source.

Matthews, T. (2011). *Handout on Developing a Personal Leadership Model.*

"I am personally convinced that one person can be a change catalyst, a 'transformer' in any situation, any organization. Such an individual is yeast that can leaven an entire loaf. It requires vision, initiative, patience, respect, persistence, courage, and faith to be a transforming leader." –Stephen R. Covey

DEVELOPING INTER-GROUP RELATIONSHIPS

CERTIFICATE: Opal (Required) | **INSTRUCTOR:** Fatima Rodriguez-Johnson, Coordinator, Multicultural Programs & Services

"It was definitely a wake-up call that I think a lot of people around me are similar to me, when in reality I have no idea what the person next to me believes or how they were raised. I must learn to address it and learn from my interactions. Assumptions are not beneficial ways to base beliefs."

Melissa, sophomore, 2010

WORKSHOP DESCRIPTION

Having the ability to interact with people of different backgrounds is a process. It depends on our awareness and comfort level with diverse groups. This workshop will examine our relationships with individuals different from ourselves. The workshop is designed to help individuals explore their own perceptions, experiences, and comfort level with diverse groups through an eye-opening activity. Ultimately, individuals will gain some insight into their own ways of thinking and can begin to apply what they've uncovered to future interactions with other groups and individuals.

LEARNING OUTCOMES

Upon completion of this workshop, participants will:

- Have explored their own perceptions, ideas, and feelings about diverse groups.
- Have increased self-awareness about the way they conceptualize diverse groups.
- Know the concept of privilege and how that relates to inter-group relationships.
- Be able to apply these ideas to new situations and experiences with diverse groups in the future.

WORKSHOP ACTIVITIES

- Everyone is asked what "inter-group relations" means. Students brainstorm answers but there is no acknowledgement of whether the students' ideas are accurate or not. Everyone is advised to think about the definitions provided.
- Participants are split into small groups. Everyone is given a paper bag with six different kinds of dried beans in it and an activity key, which lists four kinds of diversity (religion, socioeconomic status [SES], sexual orientation, and ethnicity). The activity key also lists what each of the beans represents (participants may discover their prescribed group is not listed and the list should be changed accordingly). The instructor reads a prompt and directs everyone to choose the bean (based on the key) that is most appropriate. This process is repeated for each of the four highlighted kinds of diversity. The instructor reminds the participants to be aware of how they are feeling during this process.
- Throughout the process, the instructor makes sure to clarify some of the relevant terminology. For example, the different subsets of SES (poor, low income, working, middle, high) are loosely defined. By explaining the terminology, the workshop participants' choices are based on the same general understanding of the concepts.
- Once the participants chose a bean, the instructor leads a discussion about how people felt as they were choosing their beans, if they felt forced to choose, what they noticed about their responses, what was uncomfortable, what they had not thought about before, and how this activity is relevant to leadership. The instructor comments on how people often base who they have relationships with on who looks like them because those are whom they feel most comfortable with.
- The workshop concludes with a discussion on how privilege is a defining factor in society. It is important to be honest with ourselves about who we start relationships with, our comfort level with different groups of people, our knowledge about different groups, and who we avoid and why. By gaining insight into these, we learn about ourselves, and can then be open to developing new and more accepting attitudes, perceptions, and experiences.

RESOURCES USED

Rodriguez-Johnson, F. (2010). *Handout on Activity Key.*
Rodriguez-Johnson, F. (2010). *Handout on Sample Questions.*

DEVELOPING SUPERVISION SKILLS

CERTIFICATE: Emerald | **INSTRUCTOR:** Mark Scott, Executive Director of Campus Auxiliary Services

"I understand that it takes time and practice to be a better supervisor, but with the goal in mind of being the best possible supervisor, change is the only way to improve oneself."

Michael, junior, 2010

WORKSHOP DESCRIPTION

Leading includes responsibilities for supervising others. Whether supervising employees, peers, or volunteers, there are various skills and techniques that a leader can use to improve his/her effectiveness as a supervisor. Learn tips and tools that you can use immediately in any leadership and/or employee role you may aspire to, either on campus or in the future. This workshop is conducted in a lecture and discussion format for the first half. The workshop then provides an exciting opportunity for participants to try to solve a conflict between the instructor and an upset employee.

LEARNING OUTCOMES

Upon completion of this workshop, participants will:

- Know the importance of balancing behavioral and technical skills when supervising.
- Understand the responsibilities involved with a supervising position.
- Be able to apply supervision skills to any organization or work setting.

WORKSHOP ACTIVITIES

- The instructor asks participants to introduce themselves. They are rewarded with a small prize for responding.
- Participants go through an icebreaker involving trivia where correct answers are rewarded with another small prize.
- The instructor introduces the PowerPoint and works through the bullet points in the presentation, creating discussion questions from various slides.
- Role playing is incorporated into the presentation by setting up a scene where a participant is the manager of a company and has to fire an employee. The goal of the role-playing activity is to help demonstrate the bullet points and to examine the issue of credibility.
- The instructor constantly asks for feedback from the participants on the various topics covered.
- The instructor ends the workshop by asking more trivia questions and rewarding correct answers with small prizes.

RESOURCES USED

Scott, M. (2009). *Developing Your Supervision Skills PowerPoint.*

"Surround yourself with the best people you can find, delegate authority, and don't interfere as long as the policy you've decided upon is being carried out." –Ronald Reagan

DEVELOPING YOUR NEGOTIATION SKILLS

CERTIFICATE: Sapphire or Silver | **INSTRUCTOR:** Dr. Tom Matthews, Associate Dean of Leadership and Service

"One thing that I can definitely work on is trying to view the situation in a non-subjective matter in order to effectively analyze both of the sides negotiating, and view in a clearer way the costs and benefits of each side's proposal."
Colleen, senior, 2009

WORKSHOP DESCRIPTION

We all negotiate every day with our friends, parents, spouses, classmates, professors, bosses, and members of our organizations. This session will help you develop positive strategies for win-win negotiations based on the concepts of Roger Fisher's best-selling book *Getting to Yes*. The instructor's experience includes a dissertation study on negotiations and service as a chief negotiator for two labor contracts for academic and professional faculty in SUNY.

LEARNING OUTCOMES

Upon completion of this workshop, participants will:

- Understand the constitutional protection of contract agreements.
- Be able to define the basic elements of a contract and steps required to engage in win-win negotiations.
- Understand the need for preparation prior to negotiating agreements.
- Appreciate the importance of relationships in maintain negotiated agreements.

WORKSHOP ACTIVITIES

- Participants are asked to complete a short true/false questionnaire on negotiations to complete before the session starts.
- The instructor asks for student responses to what the word "negotiate" means, then refers to a slide on a PowerPoint defining contracts. Participants are asked to define "agreement" and the instructor shares a second slide with a definition.
- Six volunteers are used to participate in a negotiations exercise. The six students meet outside in the hallway. The instructor distributes the PowerPoint handout to the rest of the participants and asks them to read the handout, then goes into the hall to divide the six volunteers into two teams. One group is assigned to be the seller of a box and the other group to be the buyer of the box. They are given time to prepare but with strict instructions to not share their bottom line throughout the negotiations.
- The participants review the seven elements of negotiations from Fisher and Utrel's *Getting Ready to Negotiate: Interests, Options, Alternatives, Legitimacy, Communication, Relationships, and Commitment.*
- The negotiating teams return and are given 10 minutes to reach an agreement on the selling/purchasing of the box. Neither the negotiators nor the other participants are informed of the bottom line, which is impossible to reach, but the teams try to figure out how to "get to yes." The instructor puts the pressure on as time runs out. Most times the teams figure out a solution.
- At the conclusion of the negotiation, the instructor asks for reactions from both teams and for observations from the other workshop participants. There is a brief discussion about the importance of good preparations and spending time trying to figure out what the other side needs in order to get to a settlement.
- The instructor then divides up the entire group into teams of six with three each on opposing sides. Each group is given a case study based on past or current campus or community issues. One side is an administrative team and the other is a student team and they are meeting to negotiate a solution to the issue. Everyone receives a handout sheet to use in preparing for negotiations. The teams are given 10 minutes to prepare and 10 minutes to negotiate a settlement. Time is called and one person from each group states the problem and the agreement reached by the teams.
- The answer sheet for the questionnaire on negotiations is passed out and there is a quick review of the major steps involved in win-win negotiations.

RESOURCES USED

The resources used in this exercise include a PowerPoint and handout on the major elements of negotiating effective agreements, a self-assessment handout on knowledge about negotiations, an answer sheet for the self-assessment, instructions for Negotiating a Box, and case studies using campus issues familiar to students.

Specific resource materials quoted and handouts distributed to participants include:

Asherman, I. (1996). *Handout Questionnaire on Negotiations*; *Handout With Answers to Questionnaire on Negotiations*, *Handout Worksheet on Planning for Negotiations*. Adapted from *50 activities to teach negotiations*. Amherst, MA: HDR Press, Inc.

Fisher, R., &, Ury, W. (1981). *Getting to yes*. New York: Penguin Books.

Matthews, T. (2005). *Handouts of Selected Case Studies on Campus and Community Issues*.

Matthews, T. (2005). *Handouts With Instructions for Sellers and for Buyers of the Box*.

Matthews, T. (2012). *PowerPoint on Negotiations*.

"Let us never negotiate out of fear. But let us never fear to negotiate." –John F. Kennedy

DINNER ETIQUETTE FOR BUSINESS & SOCIAL SETTINGS

CERTIFICATE: Emerald | **INSTRUCTORS:** Jonna Anne, Executive Chef, Campus Auxiliary Services, and Mark Cronin, Class of '88, Division Director, Strategic Health Initiatives, Upstate NY American Cancer Society

"Not only was the food superb, but I found it extremely useful and practical. Being able to practice the tips and techniques we learned in real time was very helpful. I feel much more comfortable when facing a formal or semiformal dinner situation after participating in this workshop."

Sarah, senior, 2012

WORKSHOP DESCRIPTION

Salad fork? Seafood fork? Napkin in the lap or tucked in the shirt like a bib? What should be discussed or avoided in conversation? You may not know that lunch or dinner during a day of interviews is part of the interview process and the potential employer is observing and evaluating your behavior. Networking and etiquette in formal and informal professional situations is often a confusing maze for many during the job search or first years in a new career. Whether your field of interest is human services, education, or business, knowing how to conduct yourself socially is important to success in your career. The annual Geneseo Etiquette Dinner will help you learn critical etiquette skills and knowledge. The evening will include a first-class dinner and dessert. Our speakers will guide you through the experience and even provide valuable tips on appropriate conversation. Local employers and college staff will be hosts at each table. This program requires payment of $5.00. This event is co-sponsored by the Office of Career Development, GOLD, Geneseo Alumni Association, Student Association, and CAS.

LEARNING OUTCOMES

Upon completion of this workshop, participants will:

- Remember how to meet new people and carry on appropriate table conversations.
- Understand and practice critical dinner etiquette skills in a realistic environment.

WORKSHOP ACTIVITIES

- The workshop has two distinct sections. In the pre-dinner meet and greet section, students learn about shaking hands, making eye contact, and confidence. They practice these skills by walking around, holding a water glass in their left hand, and meeting other participants. This is continued at the dinner table with their table mates and host.
- The second section is the dinner. There are several courses: soup, salad, bread, main dish, and dessert. As the courses are served, participants attempt to use the correct utensil and glasses and the speakers answer a variety of questions about eating and meeting challenges.

RESOURCES USED

Anne, J. (2009). *Handout on Dining Etiquette Guide.*
SUNY Geneseo Office of Career Development. (2011). *Handout on Networking.*

"Manners maketh man."
—*William of Wykeham (1324–1404), motto of Wincester College & New College, Oxford University, England*

DOES YOUR PERSON ATTEND SUNY GENESEO? A CREATIVE & INSIGHTFUL TWIST ON GUESS WHO?

CERTIFICATE: Opal | **INSTRUCTOR:** Garry Morgan, Residence Life Area Coordinator

"Over the past two years, I've become a very tolerant person. Everyone has to be able to step out of their generalizations of others and negative feelings they propel based on these stereotypes."

Matthew, junior, 2011

WORKSHOP DESCRIPTION

Do you think your colleagues make assumptions about others based on appearance? Come play a game of Guess Who? with a stereotypical spin. We will also discuss and devise tactics to minimize the effect these stereotypes and prejudices have on the interactions we have with other students. Participants are asked to discuss various stereotypes and prejudices associated with different groups of people. The richness of the discussion depends upon the level of participation and enthusiasm of the participants.

LEARNING OUTCOMES

Upon completion of the workshop, participants will:

- Have critically analyzed the existence, basis, and nature of stereotypes and prejudices.
- Demonstrate an understanding of tactics used to minimize the effects of these stereotypes and prejudices.
- Have an awareness of how their own beliefs and actions affect other people.

WORKSHOP ACTIVITIES

- The instructor leads a group discussion on what the participants think characterizes prejudice and stereotypes.
- The instructor asks the participants to play a "Guess Who?" type of game, where they determine who the instructor is thinking of by asking questions with only yes or no answers. This activity encourages students to free their minds of prejudices in order to make accurate guesses. The instructor explains the ground rules of the game to the participants before the game begins.
- The ground rules of the game are: confidentiality, don't take things personally and do not attack others, give everyone a chance and respect each other, stay open minded and use active listening, self-responsibility (use "I"), and participate at a comfort level but try to challenge yourself.
- The session ends with an open discussion of the lessons learned from the workshop.

RESOURCES USED

Anti-Defamation League. (2001). *Close the book on hate.* New York: Anti-Defamation League. Retrieved from www.adl.org/prejudice/closethebook.pdf

Morgan, Garry. (2011). *Guess Who? PowerPoint*

For more information on the National Conference for Community and Justice, visit www.nccj.org/
For more information on Tools for Tolerance, visit www.Tolerance/org 101
For more information on Diversity Peer Education, visit www.Mydpe.com

"Prejudice is a burden that confuses the past, threatens the future, and renders the present inaccessible." –Maya Angelou

ECOHOUSE PANEL DISCUSSION: GETTING INVOLVED

CERTIFICATE: Jade | **INSTRUCTORS:** Resident Assistants From EcoHouse and Wyoming Residence Hall

"Not only was this workshop a way to learn about a special college house, it also demonstrated real examples of how students on campus are putting their ideas about sustainability into practice."

Melissa, junior, 2012

WORKSHOP DESCRIPTION

Join a panel of EcoHouse students to learn how you can cultivate your own environmental awareness and activism. This workshop will include a holistic approach to environmentalism on our campus. Learn how you can become involved from the individual level to activism in the greater Geneseo community. The workshop is a panel discussion in which several members from the EcoHouse community speak about their involvement in the House and how others can get involved as well. The presenters use a PowerPoint presentation to aid in their discussion.

LEARNING OUTCOMES

Upon completion of the workshop, participants will:

- Be able to locate opportunities at SUNY Geneseo to take part in environmental and sustainability activities.
- Have an understanding of the activities of the Geneseo Environmental Organization and EcoHouse (Putnam Residence Hall).
- Understand the connections that EcoHouse has made with the broader community to be leaders in sustainability.

WORKSHOP ACTIVITIES

- The presenters ask participants the question, "What does sustainability mean to you?"
- Participants learn about individual initiatives they can become involved in as well as on-campus clubs and organizations, such as the community garden or the environmental organizations on campus.
- The origins of EcoHouse are discussed as well as what EcoHouse does to promote sustainability on campus and in the greater Geneseo community.
- Each panel member discusses success stories of their activism.
- The workshop ends with a question-and-answer session.

RESOURCES USED

Clark, K. (2011). *Sustainability Practices in EcoHouse and at Geneseo PowerPoint.*

"We won't have a society if we destroy the environment." –Margaret Mead

EFFECTIVE PUBLICITY AND PROMOTION

CERTIFICATE: Bronze | **INSTRUCTOR:** Tom Rodgers, Director of Campus Life, St. John Fisher College

"It is easy to come up with unique and affordable ideas, when enough time is spent during the actual planning process."

Jennifer, sophomore, 2011

WORKSHOP DESCRIPTION

The success of any event or program is often determined by how it is publicized. In this session, open your creative mind and gain tools that will assist you in promoting events. The room is decorated with various forms of promotion and publicity like T-shirts, cups, pens, and rulers in order to create a stimulating environment. By completing an interactive group activity, participants are encouraged to think outside the box to come up with creative promotional solutions that they can then use in their own organizations.

LEARNING OUTCOMES

Upon completion of the workshop, participants will:

- Understand how to avoid being trapped in the same strategies for promoting events, and know the importance of brainstorming new ideas.
- Know strategies for brainstorming unconventional ways to promote events.

WORKSHOP ACTIVITIES

- The instructor shows a Power Point presentation. One slide is labeled "standard items we can use," and the instructor asks students to share their ideas of standard promotion items, so they can be written on the board. The instructor then provides his own ideas of standard items.
- Participants are split into four groups with equal numbers of participants. Each group is given a sheet of paper and a bag containing either a cowbell, juggling balls, a barrel of monkeys, or an Etch-a-Sketch®. They are given 3–5 minutes to open the bag and think of a campus activity associated with their object.
- The instructor asks, "Knowing that money is not an object, how will you promote this idea to the Geneseo campus without using the standard items identified earlier?" Participants are asked to write these ideas on their sheet of paper.
- The financial resources available for the event become limited and students must pick their top three ideas.
- Each group puts these ideas on their piece of poster paper and presents their ideas to everyone in the workshop.
- The instructor provides some information on campus resources that could be helpful for advertising events. After passing out the handouts, the instructor lets the participants take home one of the promotional items that he brought with him.

RESOURCES USED

Rodgers, T. (2010). *Handout on Promo Gumbo.*
Rodgers, T. (2010). *Effective Publicity and Promotion PowerPoint.*

"Assign roles and responsibilities early in the process. There are many areas to cover, details to attend to, decisions to be made, and someone needs to do them." –Shannon Kilkenny, event planner with over 25 years of experience

EMOTIONAL INTELLIGENCE AND ITS IMPACT ON LEADERSHIP

CERTIFICATE: Silver | **INSTRUCTOR:** Dr. Avan Jassawalla, Professor, School of Business, SUNY Geneseo

"I see myself using the benefits of this workshop at many points in my future. I will definitely use it for interviews and future job endeavors, but I feel like it is also useful for everyday life. We should be able to help one another, and emotional intelligence allows us to understand and interpret how others are feeling."

Bianca, junior, 2010

WORKSHOP DESCRIPTION

IQ and technical skills are entry-level qualifications, but it is emotional intelligence (EQ) that leaders must possess to be successful. This session will familiarize you with the five dimensions of emotional intelligence, drawing from Daniel Goleman's book on the topic. His research indicates that the most effective leaders have one important thing in common: they have a high degree of emotional intelligence. This session will include a video and substantive discussion on emotional intelligence and its impact on the practice of leadership.

LEARNING OUTCOMES

Upon completion of this workshop, participants will:

- Be able to identify the five dimensions of EQ and how it differs from IQ.
- Be able to explain the link between EQ and effective leadership.
- Have formulated at least two job interview questions that a manager can use to select a new employee with high EQ for a leadership position.

WORKSHOP ACTIVITIES

- The instructor asks participants to identify their favorite leaders and what qualities make them good leaders. Workshop participants provide answers and the instructor writes them on the whiteboard. The instructor leads a group discussion about which qualities are related specifically to emotional intelligence.
- The instructor shows a video clip related to emotional intelligence.
- The instructor explains the basics of EQ and provides information about Daniel Goleman, an author who popularized EQ in the business world.
- The instructor provides a handout that offers participants a "snapshot" of the different areas of Emotionally Intelligent Leadership.
- The instructor provides a small group exercise in which students develop two job interview questions that a manager can ask to test the interviewee's EQ.

RESOURCES USED

Goleman, D. (2004). What makes a leader? *Harvard Business Review*, 82(1), 82–91.

Jassawalla, A. (2011). *Handout on Emotionally Intelligent Leadership.*

Jassawalla, A. (2011). *Emotional Intelligence PowerPoint.*

Stossel, J., Sloan, D., LeFosse, J., Esner, A. J., & Coleman, D. (1995). ABC News, New York. Retrieved from http://www.worldcat.org/title/2020-emotional-intelligence/oclc/079405547 on March 7, 2012.

"Good leadership consists of doing less and being more." –Lao-Tse

FAIR USE? YOUR RIGHTS AS A USER AND CREATOR OF DIGITAL CONTENT

CERTIFICATE: Ruby (Required) | **INSTRUCTOR:** Sue Ann Brainard, Reference and Instruction Librarian, Milne Library

"In a world where everything is just a click away and all you have to do to get information is copy and paste, it becomes difficult to remember to cite your sources."

Caitlyn, junior, 2012

WORKSHOP DESCRIPTION

Can you be sued for using an image you found online? Is writing fan fiction legal? When you get inspired by something you read online and create something new from it, do you own it? After discussing scenarios, attendees will appreciate the fine line between fair use and copyright infringement, and will recognize the difference between student and professional behavior.

LEARNING OUTCOMES

Upon completion of this workshop, participants will:

* Understand the definition of Fair Use and Copyright-related issues.
* Have real-world examples to follow as they consider how they use digital content.
* Be prepared to transition from appropriate student-use behavior to acceptable professional use of ideas and images.

WORKSHOP ACTIVITIES

* The instructor provides an overview of some of the legal and moral issues that are involved with ethical use of information.
* Participants are divided into pairs and provided with several scenarios. Each pair develops an opinion on whether the scenario depicts an ethical and/or legal use of information and shares their views with the other attendees.
* After each scenario is presented and discussed among the participants, the instructor points out existing laws and regulations, as well as ethical issues involved, citing experts when possible.
* As the scenarios are addressed, the instructor answers questions that arise in regard to particular issues.
* The instructor provides and explains the laws that pertain to information ethics, as well as defines certain terms and exceptions.

RESOURCES USED

Brainard, S. A. (2012). *Fair Use PowerPoint.*
Brainard, S. A. (2012). *Handout on Fair Use.* Milne Library, SUNY Geneseo.
Brainard, S. A. (2012). *Handout on Fair Use Scenarios.* Milne Library, SUNY Geneseo.

"The copyright bargain: a balance between protection for the artist and rights for the consumer." –Robin Gross, founder and Executive Director of IP Justice, an international civil liberties organization that promotes balanced intellectual property law and defends freedom of expression

FINDING ARTICLES EFFICIENTLY

CERTIFICATE: Ruby | **INSTRUCTOR:** Michelle Costello, Education and Instructional Design Librarian

"I have been able to use my knowledge from this workshop with great success. As a history major I am constantly doing research. Most recently I have been doing research on the German Holocaust during World War II. In just 20 minutes I was able to find numerous articles that are of immense value to my topic."

Luke, junior, 2011

WORKSHOP DESCRIPTION

In this introductory workshop, students will learn the basic mechanics of a database, which could include web engines like Google, the databases subscribed to by Milne Library, or a free database on the web. Participants will discover helpful tips and strategies that are used in any kind of database to help improve their searches, find better resources, and save time. This required workshop for the Ruby Certificate serves as an introduction to finding resources through a variety of research databases online. This workshop is discussion-based with many hands-on activities to allow the participants to explore a variety of resources. This workshop intends for the participants to use a current research topic as a model to explore and use the various sources discussed in this workshop.

LEARNING OUTCOMES

Upon completion of this workshop, participants will:
* Know the mechanics of a database.
* Be familiar with helpful tips and strategies to find better resources in any database.
* Be able to critically examine different types of databases when deciding which is best for their research projects.

WORKSHOP ACTIVITIES

* The instructor goes over the learning outcomes of the workshop and asks the participants if they know what a database is. After several minutes of talking with their neighbor, the participants share their responses to the question. After all of the participants discuss their answers to the question, the instructor discusses her analysis of a database as a collection of easily accessible material. The instructor then asks the participants to list different forms of databases as they share their responses.
* The instructor goes to the Internet Movie Database and explains why most people do not consider it to be a database. The instructor shows the participants how the titles on the left are the fields of the database and explains that the website creators put the most relevant and searchable information on the left.
* The instructor shows the participants how to access the school's library website and the guide full of usable databases for research projects.
* The instructor discusses what a catalog record is and how the presentation of a catalog record is different than the Internet Movie Database.
* The instructor distributes the handout on *Finding Articles Efficiently* and asks participants to write down a potential research topic they are interested in investigating. The instructor explains that the first thing to do when starting a research project is to pick a database. Participants are advised to assess the different databases offered.
* The participants are given time to try to find sources by subject for their topic.
* The instructor talks about key words to use in the search engine, stressing that it is important to think of the main concepts of their topic. The instructor explains the way database searches work. Participants are directed to go to a database, find the main concepts of their topic, and put those concepts into a search engine to get results.

RESOURCES USED

Costello, M. (2011). *Handout on Finding Articles Efficiently.*

Laptops are required for this workshop.

FINDING MAPS ONLINE

CERTIFICATE: Ruby | **INSTRUCTOR:** Tom Ottaviano, Reference and Instruction Librarian

"Before taking this workshop I often saw maps in strictly the standard physical geography manner. Now I see that maps can be extremely helpful to individuals of all disciplines to map trends, demographic information, and historical information."

Kate, sophomore, 2009

WORKSHOP DESCRIPTION

Maps convey intriguing and valuable information, from hints for locating the illusive pot of gold to finding driving directions to a restaurant to providing visualization of voting trends. Learn how the Internet now enables us to access a treasure trove of historic (i.e., primary source) maps, utilize color-coded census data, and even create your own Google-based mashups. This highly interactive and hands-on workshop integrates direct instruction, individual activities, and large-group discussion.

LEARNING OUTCOMES

Upon completion of this workshop, participants will:

- Have exposure to and awareness of the vast number of maps available online.
- Know how to use maps for purposes other than weather or directions.
- Be capable of using the library website resources and links.

WORKSHOP ACTIVITIES

- Students discuss the many different potential uses of maps, both historically and today, and answer several questions that are better understood when looking at a map.
- Workshop participants create their own maps to visualize data using freely available tools.
- Students are able to practice using Google Earth, a general map site with political and historical maps, innovative sites, statistical maps, interactive maps, and satellite imagery.

RESOURCES USED

Maps.

"A good plan is like a road map: it shows the final destination and usually the best way to get there." –H. Stanley Judd

FIRST YEAR ON THE JOB

CERTIFICATE: Emerald | **INSTRUCTOR:** Kerrie Bondi, Career Counselor

"I believe the tips I learned on what employers expect, which areas need improvement, and how to be the most professional will help me be successful in my first year. I feel that I will be at an advantage knowing this information, because I know what employers are looking for, and I can assess my strengths and weaknesses in order to be more successful."

Amanda, senior, 2011

WORKSHOP DESCRIPTION

This workshop is designed for juniors and seniors planning to enter the workforce upon graduation. The first year on the job can have a significant impact on the progress of a career. What actions will people take to make a strong impression on their co-workers and supervisors? Come and learn about goal setting, soft skills, presenting a professional image, office etiquette, and developing a positive relationship with the most important person during that first year—the supervisor.

LEARNING OUTCOMES

Upon completion of this workshop the participant will:
- Understand work culture and how it impacts a first-year employee.
- Have created a list of individual goals for the first year on the job.
- Have the ability to plan the types of behaviors and mindset required to reach stated goals.

WORKSHOP ACTIVITIES

- The instructor asks the participants to introduce themselves and state their major and reason for taking workshop.
- The handout of *Your First Year on the Job PowerPoint* slides are distributed and the instructor presents the PowerPoint, taking time to initiate discussion about the material. Participants are encouraged to ask questions throughout the lecture.
- Participants are asked to list a few characteristics employers may be looking for and to discuss the top 10 skills according to the National Association of Colleges and Employers.
- Participants are asked to write down objectives and goals for their first year out of college. The instructor asks if anyone is comfortable sharing his/her goals. Participants converse about common goals and aspirations among college students.
- Further discussion includes expectations, office politics, having a new boss, making an impression, personal image, etiquette, and tips for success in a person's first year in a job.

RESOURCES USED

Bondi, K. (2011). *Your First Year on the Job PowerPoint.*

"The best way to appreciate your job is to imagine yourself without one."–Oscar Wilde

FISH!®

CERTIFICATE: Silver | **INSTRUCTOR:** Chip Matthews, Director, College Union & Activities

"After taking this workshop, I realized that I am not there for my friends as much as I could be and that I rarely ever make their day. When you live with the same people every day, it is easy to get annoyed with them. I need to make it my choice to remember that they have stress in their lives, and to have a more positive attitude myself. I can use the principles I learned in this workshop to be more positive and make it my choice to be energetic and excited about what's going on in my life."

Chelsea, sophomore, 2010

WORKSHOP DESCRIPTION

FISH!® Catch the energy and release the potential. This interactive and fun workshop will review the four simple principles of the national bestseller FISH: Choose to make today a great day; Play—be serious about work but make it fun; Be there—take the time to be present in interactions with others; Make another's day by offering a helping hand or a word of encouragement. The format of this workshop is a short movie presentation and a group discussion afterwards.

LEARNING OUTCOMES

Upon completion of this workshop, participants will:

- Know about the philosophy of management and the shaping of organizational culture that is related to the FISH!® video.
- Understand how the morale of organization members has a direct correlation with their production, success, and team cohesion.

WORKSHOP ACTIVITIES

- A short movie is shown documenting the energetic fish shop whose business practices have become a focus of study.
- Participants perform activities in which they rate themselves in the categories related to FISH!® The instructor leads discussion on the ratings and which specific categories need improvement.
- A reflection piece is conducted and participants are asked how following the FISH!® philosophy could improve an organization that they are involved with.
- Participants are asked to brainstorm ways in which they will use FISH!® principles in the upcoming week.

RESOURCE USED

FISH!® video, which can be purchased at www.charthouse.com.

"He who has great power should use it lightly." –Seneca

FOOD, GLORIOUS FOOD: WORKING PERSONAL INTERESTS INTO YOUR RESEARCH PROJECTS

CERTIFICATE: Ruby | **INSTRUCTORS:** Kim Hoffman, Coordinator of Instruction & Reference Services, and Jim Aimers, Professor of Anthropology

> *"I plan on using this methodology as often as possible because research is not something I enjoy and I believe this will make it far more enjoyable, and possibly improve the quality of my papers."*
>
> *Robert, sophomore, 2010*

WORKSHOP DESCRIPTION

The first step to any successful research project is finding a topic that is both of personal interest to the researcher and workable in terms of scope. Food is a topic with broad appeal which can be studied from a range of perspectives in many disciplines at varying levels of specificity. The broad topic of food is relevant to everyday life, but can contribute to scholarly discourse where students can build a deeper understanding of issues and create synergy among studies across disciplines. In this workshop, a librarian, an anthropology professor, and a student will lead you on a successful path to topic construction that will whet your appetite. Discussion is strongly encouraged during this workshop.

LEARNING OUTCOMES

Upon completion of the workshop, participants will:
- Have a model of how to brainstorm for research projects.
- Understand the importance of incorporating creativity and passion into research.
- Be able to utilize database search engines to find supporting information for these ideas.

WORKSHOP ACTIVITIES

- The workshop begins with a brainstorming session on crosscutting research topics (topics that a person is interested in that can be incorporated into multiple classes).
    - If there is a particularly large group, participants can break out into groups to brainstorm.
    - Some examples may include:
        - Food: a topic that can be incorporated into chemistry classes, sociology, history, etc.
        - Performing arts: history, dress, themes, influence diffusion of art, class, propaganda, etc.
    - The instructor works with the group to incorporate culture into research.
        - Listen to the radio, conversations, etc.
        - Is there anything unique that could turn into a research topic?
- The instructor then gives each participant a piece of wrapped chocolate and participants are asked to use their senses and think deeply about a topic and deriving a thesis for a research paper based on chocolate.
    - For example, topics may include geography, economic benefits to a specific country, chemicals in chocolate that affect the human brain, etc.
- After the chocolate activity, the instructor summarizes what has been discussed and emphasizes the following:
    - This chocolate activity, for instance, takes one "off the beaten path" and leads to creative, well-thought-out theses! Thinking outside the box and allowing creativity to stem from passion creates an interesting form of critical thought.
- The instructor assures the class that there are enough sources (especially scholarly and peer-reviewed articles) to support the topic and demonstrates this by searching library resources.

RESOURCES USED

https://wiki.geneseo.edu:8443/display/food/Geneseo+Food+Researchhttps://wiki.geneseo.edu:8443/display/food/Food%2C+Glorious+Food

FOSTERING CREATIVITY

CERTIFICATE: Silver | **INSTRUCTOR:** Joe Van Remmen, Inspector, University Police

"I took this workshop because I think that I am not an extremely artistic person and I've always wondered how I could improve my creativity without improving my artistic ability. I didn't realize that creativity is more than just artistic ability. The workshop defined what it means to be creative, which helped me realize that I am creative, but in different ways than other people."

Katherine, sophomore, 2009

WORKSHOP DESCRIPTION

Vibrant and successful organizations and leaders encourage and foster creativity. Participants will find out what creativity is and how they can use it to bring out the best in the members of their groups. In this workshop, participants learn how to enrich their creative minds and use creativity every day. Participants will also focus on how to work with others to develop creative and effective solutions to problems.

LEARNING OUTCOMES

Upon completion of this workshop, participants will:

- Understand and be able to use the COPS (Challenges Options Planning Solutions) thinking process for problem solving, decision making, and conflict management.
- Understand how diverging and converging can be used to solve and resolve problems.
- Have new methods of brainstorming and how they can be implemented in everyday life.

WORKSHOP ACTIVITIES

- The instructor provides an example of how he creatively solved a problem in his personal life.
- Participants are asked to share their own examples and experiences.
- The instructor asks why we use creativity. One answer is that it makes life easier and more interesting. The instructor starts a discussion about the necessity of creativity.
- Participants are asked to provide answers to the question of what makes something creative. Possible answers include innovation, efficiency, and originality.
- Another question is, "Do we need creativity to solve problems?" Participants again provide answers and participate in discussion.
- Some key elements to successful brainstorming are introduced and discussed. The instructor stresses the importance of creating and maintaining a supportive environment. The principles of convergent and divergent thinking and how they are applied to brainstorming are explained.
- Participants are given a problem to solve and split into small groups to practice brainstorming creative solutions to the problem. The instructor gives out the handout on Fostering Creativity.
- Students are asked to utilize divergent and convergent thinking and focus on the five Ws and H (Who, What, Where, When, Why, and How).
- The instructor brings everyone back together and leads a discussion about the solutions that each group produced.

RESOURCES USED

Van Remmen, J. (2009). *Handout on Fostering Creativity.*

FROM PAGE TO PRESS TO PEER REVIEW

CERTIFICATE: Ruby | **INSTRUCTOR:** Tom Ottaviano, Reference & Instruction Librarian

> *"I now know how difficult it is to have your work published after being peer reviewed and the underlying significance to using peer reviewed/scholarly articles when performing your own research."*
>
> *Bohdan, freshman, 2009*

WORKSHOP DESCRIPTION

All information is not created equal. During the publishing cycle, scholarly information goes through intense scrutiny. Understanding the ins and outs of scholarly publishing allows the researcher to select appropriate material for university-level work. Learn what constitutes scholarliness, what is meant by "peer reviewed/refereed," and how to find scholarly sources. This required workshop introduces participants to the different types of publications that can be found through online databases and in libraries.

LEARNING OUTCOMES

Upon completion of this workshop, participants will:

- Know how to recognize the difference between scholarly and non-scholarly publications for research purposes.
- Be able to quickly and efficiently find scholarly information online and in the library.
- Have an understanding of the peer-review process.

WORKSHOP ACTIVITIES

- Participants are welcomed and checked into the workshop. The instructor gives a brief introduction outlining the purpose of the workshop.
- The instructor splits the participants into three groups and provides each group with six resources of varying level of scholarliness. Participants are asked to complete the *Handout on Comparing Publications* by comparing and contrasting characteristics of the six different resources. They are also asked to rank the most scholarly to least scholarly publication based on those characteristics.
- After completing the worksheet, each group reports their rankings to the rest of the groups and explains their reasoning behind the order. The goal is to distinguish between scholarly and popular publications and promote discussion about credentials and opinion pieces.
- The instructor leads the participants through a PowerPoint on Page to Press to Peer Review describing the information cycle and the distinguishing characteristics of scholarly, popular, and trade publications.

RESOURCES USED

Ottaviano, T. (2010). *Handout on Comparing Publications.*
Ottaviano, T. (2010). *Page to Press to Peer Review PowerPoint.*

> *"I was brought up to believe that the only thing worth doing was to add to the sum of accurate information in the world."*
> *—Margaret Mead*

FROM PRESERVATION TO CONSERVATION TO SUSTAINABILITY AND INTERGENERATIONAL EQUITY

CERTIFICATE: Jade (Required) | **INSTRUCTOR:** Dr. Chris Annala, Associate Professor of Economics

"Concepts of sustainability have been in my mind a lot recently, and it is really terrifying to think of what the future might look like in 50 or 100 years if things do not change. Sustainability, though not perfectly defined, seems an admirable and necessary action if we are going to prevent the degeneration of the Earth, and mankind with it."

Ryan, sophomore, 2012

WORKSHOP DESCRIPTION

This workshop will help participants better understand the terms and concepts surrounding environmental issues in general and sustainability specifically. In order to be a successful leader in sustainability, it is critical to have working definitions of the important terms that are used by academics, politicians, and the media. Discussed are the differences between preservation, conservation, and sustainability. Particular attention will be given to different definitions and concepts of sustainability with a discussion of intergenerational equity and intragenerational equity.

LEARNING OUTCOMES

Upon completion of the workshop, participants will:
- Be able to define preservation, conservation, sustainability, and intergenerational and intragenerational equity.
- Demonstrate understanding of sustainability and sustainable development as demonstrated by John Hartwick (1977) and John Rawls (1971).
- Be able to compare and contrast the definition of sustainability from the United Nations with the definition given by Robert Solow (1991).

WORKSHOP ACTIVITIES

- The instructor provides a basic overview of sustainability and explanation of why issues regarding sustainability are important.
- The instructor gives a brief explanation of the categories of environmental values (direct-use values, indirect-use values, non-use values, and intrinsic value).
- Participants are asked for their understanding of "preservation," then given the correct definition. This is repeated with other terms: conservation, sustainability, intergenerational and intragenerational equity, etc.
- The instructor also asks several discussion-prompting questions, such as "Do you think preservation is a reasonable goal for the environment and environmental amenities? Why or why not? When should conservation supersede preservation?"
- The instructor discusses the history of conservation, comparing Gifford Pinchot and John Muir.
- The instructor leads a short activity that demonstrates the "Veil of Ignorance."

RESOURCES USED

Annala, C. (2011). *From Preservation to Conservation to Sustainability and Intergenerational Equity PowerPoint*.

Rawls, J. (1971). *A theory of justice*. Boston: Harvard University Press.

Solow, R. (1991). Sustainability: An economist's perspective. In R. Dorfman & N. S. Dorfman (Eds.), *Economics of the environment: Selected readings* (pp. 179–187). (1993). New York: Norton.

"Earth provides enough to satisfy every man's needs, but not every man's greed." –Mahatma Gandhi

FUNDRAISING 101

CERTIFICATE: Bronze | **INSTRUCTOR:** Lauren Dougherty, Assistant Director, College Union & Activities

"I am the Recognition Coordinator for Jones Hall, and part of my duty includes planning campus-wide as well as building-wide events. Some of these events will include fundraisers, and I plan to integrate trips and ideas from this workshop. I will also pass along ideas to other members who may be planning a fundraiser."

Katherine, freshman, 2009

WORKSHOP DESCRIPTION

Are you looking for fresh ideas of how to successfully fundraise for your student organization or for a charity? This session will provide an opportunity for you to think "outside the box" for new, innovative fundraising ideas, as well as how to effectively publicize them. Bring your enthusiasm! This workshop utilizes small- and large-group discussions in order to encourage the exchange of creative and novel fundraising ideas. Participants will also learn how to utilize campus resources to make their fundraising plans a reality.

LEARNING OUTCOMES

Upon completion of the workshop, participants will:

- Begin to think outside of the box when it comes to fundraisers.
- Understand how to publicize fundraisers and have an awareness of environmentally friendly forms of publicity.
- Know how to access resources available from the College and on the Internet to assist them in the fundraising process.

WORKSHOP ACTIVITIES

- As a large group, participants share past experiences with fundraisers, both good and bad. They are also asked to share the advertising methods they employed during their events.
- The group brainstorms methods of fundraising and ideas for publicity. The instructor adds her own ideas as well as ideas found on the Internet. Ideas for "green" publicity are encouraged.
- The workshop breaks into small groups. Each group plans one fundraiser and how they will publicize it. The groups are also asked to identify their target audience, goals, and needed resources, and a time of year that they would perform their fundraiser.
- After the individual groups have been given sufficient time, they share their result with the rest of the group.
- The instructor discusses resources that are available to students. This includes websites that have ideas for fundraisers, as well as resources from College staff. The College's and student government's rules and regulations of fundraisers are also discussed.

RESOURCES USED

No additional resources.

"You make a living by what you get. You make a life by what you give." —Winston Churchill

GAME ON! PLANNING PROGRAMS AND MAJOR EVENTS

CERTIFICATE: Bronze | **INSTRUCTOR:** Carey Backman, Associate Director, College Union & Activities, and Andrea Klein, Director, Campus Scheduling & Events

"In the future I will be looking to get more involved on campus by taking on more leadership roles and by doing so, myself and a team of others will be responsible for planning programs and major events."

Krista, sophomore, 2010

WORKSHOP DESCRIPTION

King Kandy is hosting a grand celebration and everyone's invited to his castle for a concert! You are in charge of making all of the arrangements for the concert and you will need to travel the Rainbow Path to put all the details in order. Along the way, you'll encounter challenges and tasks that will help you prepare, and travel the ups and downs of event preparation. But watch out for those pitfalls in planning—they are everywhere and you will need to learn ways to avoid unexpected roadblocks and keep moving forward to bring everything together! The first to reach the castle with a good event plan in place wins the treats!

LEARNING OUTCOMES

Upon completion of this workshop, participants will:
- Have a better understanding of the complexity of programming.
- Know the logistics of programming at Geneseo.

WORKSHOP ACTIVITIES

- Workshop attendees play a game built around the different concepts of programming, such as creating a budget, reserving space, evaluating programs, and other event-planning basics.
- As attendees move through the game, the instructors explain the different aspects of programming in more detail and use specific and detailed examples of events they have planned in the past.
- The instructors also move through the room offering one-on-one instruction to the different teams to allow for more in-depth conversation about programming.
- At the end of the workshop, there is an opportunity for group discussion and questions and answers.

RESOURCES USED

Duell, J., Klein, A., & Backman, C. (2010). *Original Game Board and Playing Pieces.*

Klein, A., & Backman, C. (2010). *Electronic Presentation: Game On! Planning Programs and Major Events.*

Klein, A., & Backman, C. (2010). *Handout on Budget Bakery.*

Klein, A., & Backman, C. (2010). *Handout on Candy Apple Checklist.*

Klein, A., & Backman, C. (2010). *Handout on Concert Confirmation.*

Klein, A., & Backman, C. (2010). *Handout on Double Bubble Delegation Deadline.*

Klein, A., & Backman, C. (2010). *Handout on Easy Bake Evaluation.*

Klein, A., & Backman, C. (2010). *Peanut Butter Pie Publicity.*

Klein, A., & Backman, C. (2010). *Handout on Peppermint Network.*

Klein, A., & Backman, C. (2010). *Handout on Reservation Rainbow.*

Klein, A., & Backman, C. (2010). *Resource Sheet.*

Klein, A., & Backman, C. (2010). *Handout on Unpleasant Pitfalls/Stuck on Bubblegum.*

Klein, A., & Backman, C. (2010). *Moore's Career Planning PowerPoint.*

GETTING REAL ABOUT RACE IN EDUCATION

CERTIFICATE: Opal | **INSTRUCTOR:** Susan Norman, Director, Xerox Center for Multicultural Teacher Education

"Since I am an international student and being in the foreign country, I often think of racism unconsciously but through this workshop, I could understand cultural preferences and socialization. Discrimination and racism exist not only in the United States, but all over the world. I think that people should be aware of not perceiving people just by appearance and colors."

Renee, sophomore, 2011

WORKSHOP DESCRIPTION

This workshop is an introduction to becoming more culturally responsive in diverse professional settings, as well as about understanding how to cross cultural boundaries in a sensitive manner. The instructor provides samples of conversations with colleagues who are working in the community using current media examples. Participants will be able to use the strategies in the seminar and apply them to K-12 classroom situations or in training environments where urban professionals are working with diverse populations.

LEARNING OUTCOMES

Upon completion of this workshop, participants will:

- Know whether race affects their personal interactions with people/clients/children.
- Have a better understanding of cultural preferences and the effects of socialization.
- Be equipped with strategies to effectively cross cultural boundaries.
- Understand the necessity of being culturally responsive/sensitive.

WORKSHOP ACTIVITIES

- The workshop begins with a preliminary poll of the participants: Does race matter in your interactions with people? The instructor provides background statistics on this question, exploring whether race is believed to affect, for example, career advancement, job opportunities, educational opportunities, prison rates, and medical care. The statistics are divided by the race of the responders and participants' opinions are compared to the statistical evidence.
- The instructor addresses whether racism and reverse racism exist in America today. Statistics and video clips ("Shopping while Black") are used to explore this query.
- Participants learn about a Harvard study that measured, through a visual test, the implicit bias certain people have toward specific races. After learning about the study, participants engage in a discussion about how implicit bias may reveal important insidious aspects about American society and the effects of socialization toward racism. Additional topics are discussed, such as whether implicit bias can be changed, how does this manifest in the educational system, do teachers have implicit bias toward or against certain races, and can this contribute to the failure of inner city schools with predominately white teachers.
- The instructor and participants discuss whether cultural boundaries should be crossed, and if so, how one might effectively do so.
- An example of a culturally insensitive event is given, and participants reflect upon and discuss the importance of awareness and sensitivity when interacting with and talking about people from different cultures.

RESOURCES USED

Norman, S. (2010). *Getting Real About Race in Education PowerPoint.*

GIVE 'EM THE PICKLE™!

CERTIFICATE: Emerald | **INSTRUCTOR:** Chip Matthews, Director, College Union & Activities

> *"I plan to employ the techniques of good customer service presented in this workshop in the future, because one's attitudes and manner of service in work represents the establishment that one is working for and may positively or negatively reflect how business is conducted."*
>
> *Kimberly, sophomore, 2011*

WORKSHOP DESCRIPTION

PICKLES are those special or extra things you do to make people happy. This session will cover the most important thing a business or service can do...take care of the customer by giving them a "pickle." This workshop is designed to teach participants the basic foundations of the "Give 'em the Pickle™" campaign before learning how it applies to their lives. The workshop is split equally between a brief DVD, small-group discussions, and a large-group conversation.

LEARNING OUTCOMES

Upon completion of this workshop students will:

- Understand the foundational thinking behind "Give 'em the Pickle™" through an informational DVD.
- Think of themselves as customer service employees regardless of their role or position on campus.
- Discover basic methods of providing quality service to others.

WORKSHOP ACTIVITIES

- Participants watch the informational DVD of "Give 'em the Pickle™."
- The instructor splits the participants into small groups. Each group discusses their own experiences with negative customer service, positive service, and suggestions for future efforts to serve others.
- The instructor brings everyone back together and leads a large group discussion.

RESOURCES USED

This workshop requires the purchase of materials from Give 'em the Pickle™. To purchase these materials, please visit www.givveemthepickle.com.

Farrell, B. (2011). *Give 'em the Pickle™.* [DVD]. United States. (Can be purchased online at http://www.giveemthepickle. com).

> *"The goal as a company is to have customer service that is not just the best but legendary."* –Sam Walton, founder of Wal-Mart

GLOBAL LEADERSHIP: WHAT HAPPENS THERE, MATTERS HERE

CERTIFICATE: Silver or Opal | **INSTRUCTORS:** International Panel of Faculty, Staff and Students

"I intend to study abroad while in college, and intend to use the knowledge I gained in this workshop to be aware of different cultural ideas surrounding leadership. This will allow me to interact with diverse groups of people without experiencing conflicts."

Molly, freshman, 2012

WORKSHOP DESCRIPTION

Globalization is a reality and it is essential to understand leadership in other parts of the world. In this session, participants will learn about how leadership is practiced in several other countries and cultures. Whether students want to enrich their leadership knowledge, prepare to work in a multinational enterprise, develop their life awareness, or prepare to study abroad, this workshop is for them.

LEARNING OUTCOMES

Upon completion of this workshop, participants will:

- Learn how the decision-making process works in panel members' native countries.
- Learn about gender differences in leadership abroad.
- Learn about different ethnic groups and minorities in panel members' native countries and their approaches to leadership.
- Learn about the effects of globalization and modernization and whether or not they have had an effect on leadership development.
- Learn how panel members personally define leadership.

WORKSHOP ACTIVITIES

- Panelists introduce themselves and describe the current situation in their native countries.
- Panelists answer questions from students and GOLD mentors.

RESOURCES USED

No additional resources.

"We must ensure that the global market is embedded in broadly shared values and practices that reflect global social needs, and that all the world's people share the benefits of globalization." –Kofi Annan

GOOGLE ALTERNATIVES

CERTIFICATE: Ruby | **INSTRUCTOR:** Rich Dreifuss, Coordinator of Reference & Instruction, Milne Library

"I am a big Google fan, and I use that search engine all the time. After attending the Google Alternatives workshop I now see the issues with that and know of more options to help me find what I am looking for."

Samantha, sophomore, 2011

WORKSHOP DESCRIPTION

While Google does a terrific job of searching the web, there are many other specialized search engines that participants should know about. There are search engines that focus on particular content, those that present results in novel ways, and others that offer alternative means of ranking. And, of course, there are sites whose aim is simply to develop a search algorithm superior to Google's. Come learn about Yippy, Dogpile, Exalead, Infomine, and more.

LEARNING OUTCOMES

Upon completion of this workshop participants will:

- Understand search engines rationale, history, and future.
- Know alternative searching options.
- Know alternative results display options.
- Know alternative ways to refine search results.

WORKSHOP ACTIVITIES

- The instructor explains the following:
  - Why we use search engines
  - The history of search engines
  - Popularity and background of Google's consumer profiling
  - The "Long Tail"
  - Why there are so many search engines
  - What makes one search engine better than another (e.g., user interface, display results, efficiency, ordering)
- Participants are split up and each group spends five minutes looking at a different search engine, comparing why it is unique, and why they'd use or not use (Usa.gov, Yippy, etc.).
- Participants go to the front of the room and share their results.
- The instructor explains other search engines to take advantage of:
  - http://www.goby.com/
  - http://tenbyten.org/10x10.html
  - http://newseum.org/

RESOURCES USED

Dreifuss, R. (2011). *Non-Google Search Engines PowerPoint.*

"Our mission is to organize the world's information. Clearly, the more information we have when we do a search, the better it's going to work." Larry Page, co-founder of Google

GOOGLE—MORE THAN JUST AN INTERNET SEARCH ENGINE

CERTIFICATE: Ruby | **INSTRUCTOR:** Rich Dreifuss, Coordinator of Reference & Instruction, Milne Library

"Becoming an adolescent educator, I am constantly looking for ways to pique the teenage mind to continue learning. Putting science terms into Google is an avenue I can utilize in my classroom. The information about the Google resources was vast. I felt as if I needed another hour to appreciate all the extras and to explore some more on the site— something I plan on doing as a self study."

Lorie, senior, 2011

WORKSHOP DESCRIPTION

This workshop will examine three Google products that extend web searching to include full textbooks, news sources, and scholarly publications. Also, we'll look at Google applications that enable participants to work collaboratively with their classmates, to engage in cloud computing so that their work is available from any location, and to receive updates on current research and developments in areas of their interest. This workshop is lecture-based with the instructor using a PowerPoint. Participants need to have laptops or have access to computers to practice the Google techniques during the workshop.

LEARNING OUTCOMES:

Upon completion of this workshop, participants will:

- Know about the many Google applications, including document sharing, Google books, Google desktop, and up-and-coming applications such as Google health.
- Understand how to efficiently and accurately use Google's search function.

WORKSHOP ACTIVITIES:

- The instructor has students Google their names and shows participants how to refine results by using quotation marks.
- Students are shown how to use the library guides available on the Milne website to search for particular subjects.
    - Participants learn how to find information on Google and the guide for how to use Google more effectively.
    - Google Doc with direct link to Milne LibGuide on Google: http://tinyurl.com/34b6qq5
- The basic history of Google is described, such as:
    - The founders are Larry Page & Sergey Brin
    - The history of the word "googol" (1 followed by 100 0s)
    - Other miscellaneous history
- The instructor demonstrates how to use Advanced Search and quotation marks in Google to narrow down results, especially when searching for a phrase.
- The instructor shows participants how to find an article for an object when we do not know the name of the object.
- Participants are shown how to use the following Google applications:
    - Google Docs
    - Google Books
    - Google Scholar
    - Google Desktop
    - Google News
- The workshop concludes with a group discussion on whether Google is too dominant.

RESOURCES USED

Dreifuss, R. (2010). *The Google Search Engine PowerPoint* (available online at http://tinyurl.com/2fl8yr7)

GOT TALENT?

CERTIFICATE: Emerald | **INSTRUCTOR:** Kerrie Bondi, Career Counselor

"Knowing what my strengths are now, I don't have to second-guess myself as much. Now I can more effectively target job searches and consciously be on the lookout for positions, even if they are just summer jobs or roles in a group project/ activity that utilizes my strengths."

Eric, junior, 2011

WORKSHOP DESCRIPTION

StrengthsQuest, Gallup's® strengths development program for college-age students, will give you the opportunity to understand your strengths and build on your greatest talents—the way in which you most naturally think, feel, and behave as a unique individual. Maximize your potential by building on your talents rather than focusing on your weaknesses. This is an introductory workshop to StrengthsQuest. Prior to the workshop, you will be assigned an access code for completion of the instrument. Class size is limited to 25.

LEARNING OUTCOMES

Upon completion of the workshops, participants will:

- Understand individual strengths and how they help in academic, professional, and daily life.
- Be able to analyze the strengths of others and how differing strengths can complement one another in the formation of effective teams.
- Have ideas for maximizing individual strengths in school, business, and team settings.

WORKSHOP ACTIVITIES

- Participants are required to take a StrengthsQuest test prior to the workshop and are asked to bring their top five strengths on the day of the workshop.
- The instructor asks participants to use their dominant hand to sign lines 1–5 of the handout on the left-hand side and to use their non-dominant hand to sign the lines on the right-hand side.
- The instructor facilitates a discussion about weaknesses vs. strengths. With practice and training, weaknesses may become adequate talents, but use that same practice and training on your strengths and you can go from good to great.
- The instructor presents a PowerPoint and discusses several topics:
    - Characteristics of the highest achievers
    - Definition and characteristics of "talents"
    - Turning talents into strengths
    - How people differ in relation to their strengths
- Participants receive a handout that describes the four different domains of strengths.
- The instructor distributes a Reference Card on the 34 strengths and leads a discussion about individual strengths. The participants are asked to provide personal examples of how they demonstrate their strengths.
- Each participant receives a copy of how to use the StrengthsQuest website before leaving.

RESOURCES USED

Bondi, K. (2011). *Got Talent? PowerPoint.*
Rath, T., & Conchie, B. (2008). *Strengths domains from strengths based leadership.* New York: Gallup, Inc.
The Gallup Organization (2006). *StrengthsQuest Writing Challenge.* Gallup, Inc.
The Gallup Organization (2000). *StrengthsQuest Reference Card.* Gallup, Inc.

GRADUATE SCHOOL APPLICATION PROCESS

CERTIFICATE: Emerald | **INSTRUCTORS:** Kerrie Bondi, Career Counselor, and Elizabeth Seager, Associate Director of Career Development

"In this session I learned about the importance of figuring out what graduate program I want to do before even thinking about the application process. This first statement led me to a serious reflection of my interests and capabilities. I am looking forward to using this information in the immediate future."

Maria, sophomore, 2011

WORKSHOP DESCRIPTION

Each year over 40% of Geneseo's new graduates enroll in graduate school full-time the following fall. (The national rate is about 25%.) This general session will provide strategies on how to identify schools and programs as well as present an overview of the numerous components of the application process.

LEARNING OUTCOMES

Upon completion of this workshop, participants will:

- Have an understanding of the resources that Career Development offers students who are thinking about applying to graduate school.
- Understand how to research graduate schools and what steps are needed to apply to graduate school.
- Be able to think critically about what they want in the future and the necessity for graduate school.

WORKSHOP ACTIVITIES

- The instructor asks about each student's plan for graduate studies.
- The participants are given the opportunity to ask themselves, "Are you academically/physically/mentally prepared to go to school for another 1–8 years? What do you want to get out of it?"
- The instructor shares a variety of resources, including books and websites that can be used to help with the application process and some that rate grad schools.
- The participants are given advice to apply to the best programs that meet their needs and not just the best programs.
- The instructor explains the visitation process and provides information about the standardized tests that could be required by certain schools. Participants are advised to start the entire application process early!
- The instructor explains additional components of the application process, such as how to properly ask people to provide a recommendation, what an official transcript means, how to write thank-you letters, how to write a personal statement essay, how to choose the schools to apply to, and how to navigate financial aid.
- Participants are given the *Graduate School Guide*.

RESOURCES USED

Bondi, K. (2011). *Graduate School PowerPoint*.
SUNY Geneseo Office of Career Development. (2011). *Handout on Graduate School Guide*.

"Graduation is only a concept. In real life every day you graduate. Graduation is a process that goes on until the last day of your life. If you can grasp that, you'll make a difference." –Arie Pencovici

GRANT WRITING: SHOW ME THE MONEY!

CERTIFICATE: Diamond | **INSTRUCTOR:** Helen Thomas, SUNY Geneseo Grants Writer

"I learned how to write grants, how to search for them, and what they are used for. I now realize the possibilities are really limitless, and grants are an amazing resource."

Iwona, sophomore, 2010

WORKSHOP DESCRIPTION

Agencies and foundations give away billions of dollars each year from donations or legacies that are held as endowments. The money is allocated to support a huge variety of causes and activities, but you have to know where to look and how to ask for it. Whether you are thinking about writing a proposal now, are planning to go to grad school, or work for an NGO or a public institution, knowing the basics of grant writing will help you along the way. This workshop provides information about the types of grants available and how to pursue them.

LEARNING OUTCOMES

Upon completion of the workshop, participants will:

- Understand the need to write the right proposal to the right funding source.
- Know the importance of a careful and thorough response.
- Appreciate the realities of reviewer expectations and proper writing style.

WORKSHOP ACTIVITIES

- The instructor introduces herself and discusses some of the areas where grants are useful.
- Participants introduce themselves by providing their name, major/job, and which area discussed relates most to why they are attending this grant writing workshop.
- The instructor uses a PowerPoint presentation to explain funding sources, how to find them, and why proposals need to be matched to the appropriate source.
- The group is divided into small groups for 5–7 minutes to look at samples of Requests for Proposals. They are asked to identify the major components of a response.
- The major components of a proposal are reviewed along with a PowerPoint slide.
- The instructor distributes copies of the application forms for internal funding for student work and asks the group who can find which of the standard components that are there.
- Using the PowerPoint Presentation, the instructor emphasizes writing as the most critical concern in responding to proposals.

RESOURCES USED

Thomas, H. (2012). *PowerPoint on Grant Writing: Show Me the Money.*

SUNY Geneseo Sponsored Research Office. (2012). Applications for student funding. Retrieved from http://www.geneseo. edu/sponsored_research/forms_page, March 19, 2012.

"Good sense is both the first principal and the parent source of good writing." –Horace, Roman lyric poet, satirist, and critic

GRIMM LESSONS ON LEADERSHIP

CERTIFICATE: Bronze | **INSTRUCTOR:** Carey Backman, Associate Director, College Union & Activities

"I hope that by recognizing the talents of individuals in a group and by finding ways for members of that group to work together, I will be able to serve as an effective leader and help my group to achieve their goals."

Nick, sophomore, 2011

WORKSHOP DESCRIPTION

Long before you'd ever heard the word "leader," you were learning about leadership from the stories in children's books or that had been passed down in fairy-tale form. This workshop uses the Grimms' fairy tales to facilitate a dialogue among students on what it means to be a good leader and the potential pitfalls that a person may encounter on their leadership path.

LEARNING OUTCOMES

Upon completion of the workshop participants will:
- More clearly define what it means to be a good leader.
- Identify potential pitfalls leaders may encounter.
- Communicate how storytelling can enhance their own leadership.

WORKSHOP ACTIVITIES

- After reviewing the format of the workshop with attendees, the instructor gives a brief talk on why fairy tales are used, the tradition of storytelling, and how it connects to today.
- A short history of the Grimm Brothers is given and copies of the fairy tales are handed out.
- Attendees are divided into groups and asked to review their assigned fairy tale. Specifically, they should pull out some different leadership lessons and prepare to share these with the larger group.
- After a group shares, the larger group discusses the leadership lessons outlined and adds to comments on the list. The instructor also shares a list of related leadership lessons.
- This same process is followed for each of the stories.
- After each group has shared, the larger group works to put together a list of other characteristics, attributes, and behaviors that make a good leader.
- As a wrap-up, the larger group talks about the role of storytelling itself and how it can be a useful tool for leaders.

RESOURCES USED

Backman, C. (2011). *A Grimm Perspective on Leadership PowerPoint.*
Backman, C. (2011). *Handout on Various Fairy Tales.* Adapted from: http://en.wikipedia.org/wiki/List_of_fairy_tales
http://en.wikipedia.org/wiki/Grimm_brothers
http://en.wikipedia.org/wiki/Storytelling
Grimm, J., & Grimm, W. (1972). *The complete Grimm's fairy tales.* New York: Random House.

"Leadership and learning are indispensable to each other." –John F. Kennedy

GROUP DYNAMICS

CERTIFICATE: Bronze | **INSTRUCTOR:** Kimberly Harvey, Director of New Student Programs

"I realize now that I can be a crucial part in helping my group pass the steps of forming, storming, norming, and performing to help my group reach their goal."

Corinne, junior, 2011

WORKSHOP DESCRIPTION

This session will help participants understand how groups interact and work with each other. The session will focus on the group process, roles that people play, strategies for interacting effectively in any group situation, and resolving problems to become a high-achieving organization. This lecture-style workshop also includes interactive components where participation and discussion are encouraged.

LEARNING OUTCOMES

Upon completion of the workshop, participants will:
- Understand the four stages of group development: forming, storming, norming, and performing.
- Understand the common roles taken by individuals in groups, and the importance of maintaining a balance of these roles.
- Realize the difference between groups and teams, and the importance of different perspectives.

WORKSHOP ACTIVITIES

- The workshop begins with a definition of the word group: "A group is three or more people who are interacting and communicating interpersonally over time in order to reach a goal" (Cathcart, Samovar, & Hennam, 1996, p. 1).
- The participants think about some of the purposes, timing, and structure of some of the groups that they are involved with. The instructor discusses the importance of understanding the development of a group through four phases: "forming," "storming," "norming," and "performing."
- The instructor facilitates the following discussion:
  - Participants think of a group of which they are an active member and describe what it was like to be a member of the group in each of the four stages.
  - Did the group experience any problems? In which stage?
  - What did you do to resolve the problems?
  - Have you ever known a group to dissolve itself?
- Participants discuss why groups are formed and purposes they serve. As a group, the five basic elements of group learning are analyzed: positive interdependence, individual accountability, promote interaction (face-to-face), use of teamwork skills, and group processing.

- The instructor breaks down the nine common roles that individuals play in a group setting (information seeker, opinion seeker, opinion giver, summarizer, clarifier, gatekeeper, encourager, mediator, and follower) and facilitates a discussion.
- Participants are given the Perfect Star activity handout and are asked to find the perfect five-point star in mixed geometric shapes. Once one person in each group has found the star, they should help others in their group to find it. This activity is to show how individuals work together for one common goal (finding the star).
- The workshop ends with a discussion about the similarities and differences between groups and teams.

RESOURCES USED

Harvey, K. (2010). *Group Dynamics: Helping Groups to Work Effectively PowerPoint.*

Harvey, K. (2010). *Handout on Perfect Star Activity.* Adapted from Mohan, M., & La Spada, S. (1979). Mind-stimulating activities. Buffalo, NY: D.O.K. Publishers, Inc.

Komives, S. R., Lucas, N., & McMahon, T. R. (2007). *Exploring leadership for college students who want to make a difference.* San Francisco, CA: Jossey-Bass.

Mohan, M., & La Spada, S. (1979). *Mind-stimulating activities.* Buffalo, NY: D.O.K. Publishers, Inc.

"Coming together is a beginning. Keeping together is progress. Working together is success." –Henry Ford

HIDDEN MEANINGS…DECIPHERING BODY LANGUAGE

CERTIFICATE: Bronze | **INSTRUCTOR:** Caroline Whelan, Residence Life Area Coordinator

"This skill can be very useful in everyday life as part of social networking, leadership positions, and talking to authority figures."

Shona, sophomore, 2011

WORKSHOP DESCRIPTION

How do you know people are saying what they mean? Come learn a few body language "tells" and tips for interviews, meetings, relationships, and daily interactions. This workshop will help you prepare for job interviews, graduate school interviews, and give you general tips for day-to-day life. This workshop is designed to help students improve their communications in everyday scenarios. Body language is not just what you say, and this interactive workshop helps reinforce this concept. Students will learn how to make sure their interactions are culturally and contextually relevant.

LEARNING OUTCOMES

Upon completion of this workshop, participants will:

- Have an awareness of the messages they are sending through body language.
- Know about situations where body language can be inappropriate.
- Realize that body language is culture-specific and an important component to successfully adapting to new cultures and situations.

WORKSHOP ACTIVITIES

- The *Hidden Meanings…Deciphering Body Language PowerPoint* is presented and participants watch a comical YouTube video entitled "*Learn to Speak Body: Tape 5.*"
- Follows the video there is a discussion about important gestures and how specific movements can send positive and negative messages.
- An explanation of the 2 + 2 = 5 concept is given: when there is a disconnect between what you're saying and what your body language is saying.
- A "Whose line is it…?" exercise is conducted, where student volunteers improvise to act out a scenario; examples include a close-talker, someone who doesn't make eye contact, someone who speaks in a monotone, and someone with a disconnect between speaking and body language.
- A list of helpful hints is provided to conclude the workshop.

RESOURCES USED

Morgan, G., & Pennello, C. (2010). *PowerPoint on Hidden Meanings…Deciphering Body Language.*

Morgan, G. (2010). *Hidden Meanings…Deciphering Body Language PowerPoint.*

Zarefsky, D. (2008). *Public speaking: Strategies for success.* Boston, MA: Pearson.

"What you do speaks so loud that I cannot hear what you say." –Ralph Waldo Emerson

HISTORICAL ORIGINS OF THE CURRENT ENVIRONMENTAL CRISIS

CERTIFICATE: Jade (Required) | **INSTRUCTOR:** Dr. Paul McLaughlin, Professor of Sociology

"The environmental crisis is one of the most pressing issues that my generation has to face, and many other pressing issues are either contribute to or are caused by environmental concerns."

Jessica, sophomore, 2012

WORKSHOP DESCRIPTION

This workshop traces the historical roots of the current environmental crisis to the ideology of Manifest Destiny. Participants will come to understand that the latter is an amalgam of: (1) an anti-environmental interpretation of Christianity (White, 1967); (2) the idea of progress which, beginning with Aristotle, defines "the Good" as independence from external forces (Lovejoy, 1936; Nisbet, 1969); and (3) Francis Bacon's conceptualization of science as the masculine domination of female nature (Keller, 1985). We will discuss how these closely interrelated ideas were used to legitimize environmentally destructive technologies and organizational practices over the last three hundred years. The workshop consists of a PowerPoint lecture with breaks for student discussion.

LEARNING OUTCOMES

Upon completion of the workshop, participants will:

- Have a better understanding of the Bible creation story in the book of Genesis and how it relates to the current environmental crisis.
- Understand the tentative classification of environmental frames.

WORKSHOP ACTIVITIES

- The instructor hands out a copy of the first three chapters of Genesis and participants look for any pro-environmental (e.g., the notion that the natural order is a moral order, a positive valuation of diversity, the idea of stewardship, and an implied balance of nature) and anti-environmental (e.g., a static view of nature, an anthropocentric worldview, the concept of human dominion over other species, the encouragement of overpopulation, androcentrism, the notion that nature is man's enemy, and a despiritualization of nature) attitudes or sentiments.
- The instructor summarizes the pro-environmental and anti-environmental attitudes and discusses Lynn White's (1967) classic argument that anti-environmental sentiments have dominated Christianity since the 7th century. The instructor also traces the origins of the idea of progress to Aristotle, and briefly discusses its subsequent history.
- Participants are also asked to identify instances where the idea of progress has been used to justify environmentally destructive technological choices and practices.
- In the final section of the workshop, the instructor discusses how Francis Bacon's patriarchal model of science (Keller, 1985) became embedded in early scientific institutions such as the Royal Society in Britain and how Bacon's assumption that nature is feminine, passive, and simple and thus easily dominated by masculine science distorted the Industrial Revolution by reinforcing the anti-environment tendencies of Christianity and the idea of progress. Students are asked to consider the implications of Bacon's model for various fields of endeavor—e.g., medicine, agriculture, the environment, household management, and the war on terror.

RESOURCES USED

(2002). Book of Genesis, chapters 1–3. In K. L. Barker (Ed.), *New international version Bible* (rev.), Grand Rapids, MI: Zondervan.

McLaughlin, P. (2011). *Handout on the Tentative Classification of Environmental Frames.*

HISTORY OF LEADERSHIP

CERTIFICATE: Gold (Required) | **INSTRUCTOR:** Dr. Tom Matthews, Associate Dean of Leadership and Service

"Hearing different people's insights to the theory they were assigned was fascinating and I was surprised by the amount of knowledge people had and how well they connected these theories to events in their lives."

Annemarie, junior, 2010

WORKSHOP DESCRIPTION

This required workshop for the Gold level of the Leadership Certificate Program will provide participants with a review of the history of leadership theories and concepts. This session is limited to students planning to complete the Gold Certificate in the current semester. This required workshop is crucial to the overall Gold Certificate because it provides basic knowledge that will be useful when participants prepare their final papers. Participants learn about 16 different historical perspectives on leadership during the workshop. Participants will also be encouraged to attend workshops that focus on individual theories of leadership in the future.

LEARNING OUTCOMES

Upon completion of this workshop, participants will:
- Gain a general knowledge of the concepts, theories, and approaches to leadership.
- Be able to use the PowerPoint handout as a reference tool for further reading and research in preparing an analysis of leadership theories for document # 2 of the Personal Leadership Model required to earn the Gold Leadership Certificate.

WORKSHOP ACTIVITIES

- After a brief introduction explaining the purpose of the workshop to help students prepare their Personal Development Model paper, the instructor distributes a copy of the PowerPoint presentation that will be reviewed in the workshop. The instructor reviews the first several historical images of leadership, beginning with the animal kingdom and ending with the first scholarly studies of leadership.
- The instructor assigns each person, either individually or in pairs, depending on the number of participants, one or more slides that represent key components of each of 16 different theories/approaches to leadership. Authors, names, and dates associated with each theory are included as references. The students are given several minutes to review their images and to connect, if possible, any examples they might cite that could help illustrate their leadership theory.
- Students are asked to come to the front of the room and review their assigned theory using the words on the images and any additional thoughts or examples they wish to add. Additional comments and personal stories from the other participants are also encouraged. The instructor also adds comments as appropriate to reinforce key points or illustrate the theory.
- The workshop concludes with the instructor holding up some of the key books and resources recommended for reading and citing in the Personal Leadership Model paper.

RESOURCES USED

The History of Leadership workshop provides a short review of the major leadership theories. Although the instructor provides a short list of recommended books as a handout with the Personal Leadership Model workshops, the following sources were used in the creation of the History of Leadership workshop (the PowerPoint and books are reviewed and updated every year).

Astin, A. W., & Helen, S. A. (2006). *Leadership reconsidered: Engaging higher education in social change.* Greenville, NC: East Carolina University.

Astin, H. S., & Alexander, W. A. (1996). *A social change model of leadership development: Guidebook : Version III.* Los Angeles, CA: Higher Education Research Institute, University of California.

Bass, B. M., & Ralph, M. S. (1990). *Bass & Stogdill's handbook of leadership: Theory, research, and managerial applications.* New York, NY: Free Press.

Burns, J. M. (1978). *Leadership.* New York, NY: Harper & Row.

Chrislip, D. D., & Carl, E. L. (1994). *Collaborative leadership: How citizens and civic leaders can make a difference.* San Francisco, CA: Jossey-Bass.

Covey, R. S. (1990). *The seven habits of highly effective people: Restoring the character ethic.* New York, NY: Fireside Books.

Crawford, C. B., Curtis, L. B., & Micol, M. (2000). *Understanding leadership: Theories & concepts.* Longmont, CO: Rocky Mountain.

Dansereau, F., Graen, G. B., & Haga, W. J. (1975). A vertical dyad linkage approach to leadership within formal organizations. *Organizational Behavior and Human Performance,* 13, 46-78.

Fleishman, A. E. (1955). *Leadership and supervision in industry: An evaluation of a supervisory training program.* Columbus, OH: Ohio State University.

Fiedler, F. E. (1967). *A theory of leadership effectiveness.* New York, NY: McGraw-Hill.

French, J. R. P., & Raven, B. (1959). The bases of social power. In D. Cartwright and A. Zander, *Group dynamics.* New York: Harper & Row.

Goleman, D. (2006). *Emotional intelligence.* New York: Bantam Books.

Graen, B. G., & Uhl-Bien, M. (1991). The transformation of professionals into self-managing and partially self-designing contributors: Toward a theory of leadership-making. *Journal of Management Systems,* 3(3), 25-39.

Greenleaf, R. K. (1977). *Servant leadership: A journey into the nature of legitimate power and greatness.* New York: Paulist.

Hersey, P., & Kennet, B. (1969). *Management of organizational behavior: Utilizing human resources.* Englewood Cliffs, NJ: Prentice-Hall.

House, R. J. (1971). A path-goal theory of leader effectiveness. *Administrative Science Quarterly,* 16: 321–339.

Huber, S. N. (1998). *Leading from within: Developing personal direction.* Malabar, FL: Krieger Pub.

Katz, L. R. (1955). *Skills of an effective administrator.* Boston, MA: Harvard Business Review.

Komives, S., Nance, L., & Timothy, M. (2007). *Exploring leadership: For college students who want to make a difference.* San Francisco, CA: Jossey-Bass.

Kouzes, J. M., & Barry, Z. P. (1995). *The leadership challenge: How to keep getting extraordinary things done in organizations.* San Francisco, CA: Jossey-Bass.

Lewin, K., Lippitt, R., & White, R. K. (1939). Patterns of aggressive behavior in experimentally created social climates. *Journal of Social Psychology,* 10: 271–301.

Likert, R. (1961). *New patterns of management.* New York: McGraw-Hill.

Matthews, T. (2011). *PowerPoint on Historical Perspectives on Leadership.*

McGregor, D. (1960). *The human side of enterprise.* New York: McGraw-Hill.

Mumford, M. D., Marks, M. A., Connelly, M. S., Zaccaro, S. J., & Reiter-Palmon, R. (2000). Development of leadership skills: Experience and timing. *Leadership Quarterly,* 11, 87-114.

Northouse, P. G. (2011). *Leadership: Theory and practice.* Thousand Oaks, CA: SAGE Publications.

Rost, C. J. (1991). *Leadership for the twenty-first century.* New York: Praeger.

"If your actions inspire others to dream more, learn more, do more and become more, you are a leader." –John Quincy Adams

HOW TO GROW ORGANIC HERBS FOR CULINARY PURPOSES FOR A CAMPUS DINING HALL

CERTIFICATE: Jade | **INSTRUCTOR:** Darlene Necaster, Environmental Health & Safety Officer

"I will definitely use all of the information I collected in this workshop because it is applicable to everyone, not just avid gardeners. My herbs currently look great and I am very excited to use them in my future cooking."

Lindsay, junior, 2012

WORKSHOP DESCRIPTION

In order to emphasize the need to support local food production, proponents of the Community Supported Agriculture (CSA) movement have long used this example: A tomato usually travels about 1,500 miles from where it is grown to your salad bowl. Yet few contemplate how many miles herbs have traveled. The vast majority of herbs that American companies are using and selling do not come from within the United States. Most are imported (some estimates range over 95%) from Eastern Europe, India, China, Mexico, and many third-world countries. Many herbs are grown using pesticides and are fumigated when they are brought into the United States. Given these facts, it is critical to ask questions about where our herbs come from and whether or not our choices are sustainable.

LEARNING OUTCOMES

Upon completion of this workshop participants will:

- Understand how importing herbs from other countries contributes to the carbon footprint.
- Understand the health benefits of growing herbs organically.
- Learn how to grow herbs from seed.

WORKSHOP ACTIVITIES

- Participants will select one herb to grow from seed using an egg carton for the container.
- The growing medium will include a mix of compost from dining center food waste.
- Participants will learn how to organically cultivate the herb from seed to seedling to transplanting into single containers or a community garden.

RESOURCES USED

No additional resources.

"Where you have a plot of land, however small, plant a garden. Staying close to the soil is good for the soul."
—Spencer W. Kimball

HOW TO SWOT YOUR WAY TO SUCCESS

CERTIFICATE: Bronze | **INSTRUCTOR:** Gabe Iturbides, T.O.P. Counselor, Access Opportunity Programs

"I noticed that using a variation of SWOT helped me get an A in logic, and I feel that if I could use it in one course that I love why not apply it to courses that I have no particular interest in."

Stiylord, freshman, 2010

DESCRIPTION OF WORKSHOP

Learn how to develop a strategic planning method, called a SWOT analysis, that one can apply to anything he/she wants to succeed in. It's a planning vehicle that actually shows what needs to be worked on in order to succeed at anything, ranging from that tough exam you have next week to beating the next level of a video game.

LEARNING OUTCOMES

Upon completion of this workshop, participants will:

* Know how to become more successful and effective decision-makers through the use of SWOT analysis.

WORKSHOP ACTIVITIES

* The instructor introduces himself and provides a general background about his experience with SWOT analysis and discusses how he has used SWOT in situations in his own life.
  * Possible uses of SWOT include finding a job, interviewing, and maintaining one's own happiness.
* The instructor uses the *SWOT PowerPoint* to explain the history of the SWOT method and talks about the founder, Albert Humphrey. During the presentation the major parts of the SWOT method are discussed:
  * Having a set objective helps identify the issue.
  * Looking at/analyzing the issue in four aspects: Strengths, Weaknesses, Opportunities, Threats.
* The group is presented with many different examples of situations highlighting SWOT and its components.
* Following the *SWOT PowerPoint* presentation, the instructor goes around the room and has each participant shares a current issue in their lives.
  * Examples of issues may include studying for a big exam or organizing/doing homework.
* The instructor and group use active discussions with the SWOT method to find solutions to the issues. Depending on the size of the group, participants can be broken into sub-groups and each sub-group assigned one of the following areas to focus on and discuss (strengths, weaknesses, opportunities, and threats). After the sub-groups discuss their area of SWOT, they then share their insights with the entire group.
* The instructor summarizes what has been covered about SWOT and how the technique is a very effective way to approach everyday situations, mentioning that in some situations SWOT may not provide immediate solutions but is a tool to provide direction in addressing the issue.

RESOURCES USED

Iturbides, G. (2010). *Handout on SWOT Analysis Worksheet.*
Iturbides, G. (2010). *SWOT PowerPoint.*

"Success is liking yourself, liking what you do, and liking how you do it." –Maya Angelou

IDENTITY EXPRESSION

CERTIFICATE: Opal (Required) | **INSTRUCTOR:** Fatima Rodriguez-Johnson, Coordinator, Multicultural Programs & Services

"Personally, I was most surprised by the socioeconomic aspect of my identity. I've also thought of myself as very average and middle class. However, the bean activity revealed that I am relatively extremely fortunate in comparison to other income brackets."

Russell, sophomore, 2011

WORKSHOP DESCRIPTION

Everyone has multiple identities. This session will demonstrate how people express their different identities and provide a new understanding of the wide range of diversity that exists in our daily interactions with other people. This is a required workshop for the Opal Diversity and Cultural Competency Certificate. As the foundation of the Opal Certificate, Identity Expression introduces participants to an interactive analysis of diversity. They will learn what aspects go into creating an identity. Using their own lives as examples, participants will take a look at how they express that identity.

LEARNING OUTCOMES

Upon completion of this workshop, participants will:

- Reflect upon how they express their own identity in their daily lives.
- Identify the wide range of diversity that is present within different peoples' identity expressions.
- Understand how their identity expression affects their lives and the people around them.

WORKSHOP ACTIVITIES

- The participants are asked to think about the question "Who are you?" The instructor explains how identities can be broken into two categories: primary and secondary. Participants should note that primary and secondary identity categories may vary depending upon the individual.
- After thinking about this question, participants are asked to use a marker to divide a sheet of paper into two halves. The left side of the paper is to be labeled "Identity," while the right side of the paper is labeled "Expression." Participants are asked to write down all of their identities on the left side of the paper, both primary and secondary. On the right side, they write down how they express those individual identities. Identities can be expressed through mannerisms, appearances, traditions, activities, etc. Students also discuss which identities are affected by laws.
- Workshop participants take turns sharing their various identities and expressions. By breaking down their identities, they are able to see the similarities and differences they have with each other. The instructor asks, "What if you were put in a situation where you could not express your identity?" Participants provide personal examples of such a situation, and these situations are discussed as a large group.
- Students learn about the Social Identity Development Model, which shows the stages of identity. Students also learn about the progression from naïve to acceptance, resistance, redefinition, and internalization.
- Students discuss self-evaluation and why knowledge about other people's identity is an important aspect to leadership. Students learn that understanding their own identities influences their view of others' identities, in turn affecting their leadership.
- As a closing activity, a handout on Cultural Competency is provided.

RESOURCES USED

Clark, K. (2002). *Handout on Cultural Competence*. Adapted from Strategic Diversity & Inclusion Management magazine.

Clark, K. (2002). *Handout on Ethnicity and Class Worksheet*.

Clark, K. (2002). *Handout on Identity Worksheet*.

Mercedes, M., & Vaughn, B. (2007). Strategic Diversity & Inclusion Management magazine, 31–36.

IF SUSTAINABILITY IS THE SOLUTION, WHAT IS THE PROBLEM?

CERTIFICATE: Jade (Required) | **INSTRUCTOR:** Dr. Kristina Hannam, Professor of Biology

> *"By making the suggestion that Starbucks on campus make the transition to reusable cups, I can apply the ideas of this workshop and make a change for the better in my society."*
>
> *Juliana, freshman, 2012*

WORKSHOP DESCRIPTION

All people on the planet participate in activities that impact the environment through use of power sources and water, heat, transportation, food consumption, and waste production. The impacts of these activities differ depending on the technologies used and the number of people involved. This seminar will help participants better understand environmental issues related to overpopulation, consumption, pollution, climate change, etc., that result from human activities, and that have led to the rise of sustainability as a mindset/strategy to mitigate these problems. The workshop will follow the theme of "Think Globally, Act Locally" by examining the issues from a global perspective, considering the campus community's carbon footprint, and helping participants understand their individual contributions to the problems through the use of an ecological footprint calculator.

LEARNING OUTCOMES

Upon completion of this workshop, participants will:

- Be able to explain how issues like overpopulation and consumption patterns contribute to environmental problems globally and locally.
- Be able to identify the aspects of the campus community's activities that contribute most to environmental impacts.
- Recognize areas in which their individual contributions to the environmental problems are largest (relative to other Americans and other people around the globe), and potential areas to minimize their impact.

WORKSHOP ACTIVITIES

- The workshop starts with a PowerPoint presentation about sustainability. The PowerPoint shows data from the campus' carbon footprint calculation in addition to areas of significant environmental impact.
- After the PowerPoint, students use the website footprintnetwork.org to complete a personal ecological footprint calculation.
- The workshop concludes with participants comparing their ecological footprint score to scores of typical Americans, and people from other parts of the globe.

RESOURCES USED

Hannam, K. (2011). *Sustainability PowerPoint.*
Laptops are required for this workshop.

"The fate of the living planet is the most important issue facing mankind." —Gaylord Nelson

INTRODUCTION TO DESIGN FOR FLIERS & PROMOTIONAL MATERIALS

CERTIFICATE: Bronze | **INSTRUCTOR:** Kristen Fuest, Student Association Graphics Coordinator

"I will use the ideas of rhythm, repetition, and unity in fliers because I realized how it gives a sense of wholeness and movement throughout a poster."

Abigail, sophomore, 2009

WORKSHOP DESCRIPTION

Ever needed a quick flier for an event or project and didn't have the budget for a professional designer? Learn about basic design principles to make publicity a success no matter what software is used!

LEARNING OUTCOMES

Upon completion of this workshop, participants will:

- Have a clear understanding of basic design concepts.
- Be able to recognize the difference between a weak design and a strong design.
- Feel comfortable creating effective designs.

WORKSHOP ACTIVITIES

- The instructor provides a brief overview of three to five design concepts using a PowerPoint presentation. The presentation will contain a bad example and a good example (or two!) of each design concept.
- Participants are broken into groups to critique a magazine ad. Each group chooses an ad from a collection at the front of the room. They have approximately 15 minutes to critique the ad using the design principles learned at the beginning of the workshop.
- After 15 minutes, everyone comes back together and each group takes turns presenting their ad, and their thoughts on what is strong and what is weak. Participants have a chance to learn from the feedback of other groups as it pertains to each ad.
- Before the end of the workshop, participants are given an opportunity to ask questions. The presenter also stresses that the design concepts learned can be applied to any design created using any software. The students are reminded that there are often design templates in programs such as Microsoft Word that can get them started on the right track.

RESOURCES USED

Fuerst, K. (2010). *Electronic Presentation: 3 Design Basics.*
Fuerst, K. (2010). *Handout on File Types, Fonts, and Design Principles.*
Magazine ads.

"Design is a plan for arranging elements in such a way as best to accomplish a particular purpose." –Charles Eames

IS IT YOUR JOB OR YOUR PASSION? VISIONING YOUR FUTURE

CERTIFICATE: Silver or Emerald | **INSTRUCTOR:** Marilyn Moore, Emeriti Director, Intercollegiate Athletics

"My story connected to this workshop is about my job this summer. I was a camp counselor for four-year-old girls. When I first got the job, I thought that it would be awful and I would dread going to work every day. However, once I started working, I realized that I loved my job and that it was more of a passion rather than a job."

Melissa, sophomore, 2010

WORKSHOP DESCRIPTION

Is it possible to create a job that meets all of your interests and makes you want to come to work every day? Learn how to take your vision and map your future. This workshop is intended to help participants realize that when exploring career options these options should involve content that the participants are passionate about.

LEARNING OUTCOMES

Upon completion of this workshop, participants will:

- Know how to create job opportunities that they feel passionate about.
- Understand the importance of networking and taking advantage of opportunities.
- Evaluate their career paths to determine if they fulfill expectations and are in congruence with their attitudes, values, and beliefs.

WORKSHOP ACTIVITIES

- The instructor asks the students about their summer jobs and they discuss the following questions: Do you like your job? Is it something you want to do for the rest of your life? Do you have this job because the pay is good? Would you have a different job if you had the choice?
- Participants are asked to define "passion" and the answers are discussed.
- The instructor asks the participants to write down what they wanted to be when they were younger. Volunteers share their answers with the group, and the instructor shares her personal journey for reaching her current career.
- The instructor stresses the importance of being willing to create the opportunity that you want, even if it means creating a brand-new job in a company.
- The instructor highlights the importance of "becoming one's own best friend," meaning that students should capitalize on their strengths and be aware of their weaknesses.
- Participants are asked to finish the sentence, "I feel strong when…" and share their answers with the group.
- The instructor shows a PowerPoint presentation that consists of:
  - Job statistics
  - The well-roundedness of job candidates that employers are searching for
  - Clarifying, situational, and value questions
  - The importance of networking

RESOURCES USED

Moore, M. (2010). *Visioning Your Future PowerPoint.*

"We don't get a chance to do that many things, and every one should be very excellent. Because this is our life." –Steve Jobs

JOB INTERVIEWING SKILLS

CERTIFICATE: Emerald (Required) | **INSTRUCTOR:** Elizabeth Seager, Associate Director of Career Development

"My past experience has been intense. I have attended many job interviews and have learned my personal style of getting through the interview. I realize that my potential employers have limited information about me and it is up to me to give them an honest history of my skills and background."

Lori, junior, 2011

WORKSHOP DESCRIPTION

Nearly every interview format today includes behavioral-based interview questions (BBI). BBIs require a thorough analysis of one's skills and examples to support those skills. This type of analysis also helps you in other areas of the interview, such as answering open-ended and opinion questions. Be prepared to learn and practice these types of very important questions that will help you get the job offer.

LEARNING OUTCOMES

Upon completion of this workshop, participants will:
- Be able to answer an open-ended question such as "Tell me about yourself."
- Identify a strength and weakness and explain why they chose those examples to an employer.
- Answer a behavioral-based interview question, citing a specific example and utilizing the STAR (Situation, Task, Action, and Result).

WORKSHOP ACTIVITIES

- The instructor presents the behavioral-based interviewing technique with examples and a description on how to identify skills through use of specific examples. Students are given a practice sheet with four exercises. Students are paired up and instructed to select and practice behavioral-based interview questions using the STAR method with each other.
- A discussion on answering open-ended questions is addressed. Students are instructed on how to break down the "Tell me about yourself" question. The practice session for the open-ended question involves students taking a moment to formulate and write down the answer to this question, then practice with a partner.
- Students are instructed on the importance of answering opinion questions addressing strengths and weaknesses. In their pairs, students practice each question.
- During the practice sessions, the instructor listens to students' responses and offers feedback and answers questions.

RESOURCES USED

Bondi, K., & Seager, E. (2010). *Interviewing Skills PowerPoint.*
Office of Career Development. (2011). *Handout on the Interview.* Office of Career Development, SUNY Geneseo.
Seager, E. (2009). *Handout on How Would You Handle These Questions? Practice, Practice, Practice.*
    Office of Career Development, SUNY Geneseo.
Seager, E. (2009). *Handout on Behavioral-Based Interview Questions.* Office of Career Development, SUNY Geneseo.

"Believe in yourself and all that you are. Know that there is something inside you that is greater than any obstacle."
—Christian D. Larson

JOB SEARCH LETTERS

CERTIFICATE: Emerald | **INSTRUCTOR:** Elizabeth Seager, Associate Director of Career Development

"I immediately felt personally connected to this workshop because just the week before, I was asked to submit a cover letter while applying for summer positions. I had no idea where to begin so I just tried frantically Googling 'how to's.' I do plan to use this information in the future. In fact I emailed a thank-you note to the presenter within 24 hours of the workshop because I enjoyed it so much, and also wanted to practice my email etiquette as well as thank-you note procedures."

Marlee, freshman, 2012

WORKSHOP DESCRIPTION

I have to write a cover letter. Where do I begin? Job searching is an exciting and overwhelming process. Whether you're starting a full-time job search, seeking an internship, or looking for a part-time job, at some point you'll need to write a cover letter and a thank-you letter. This session covers the practical guidelines for writing professional cover letters that will help you secure an interview. In addition, thank-you letters and handling these issues in the electronic age will be discussed.

LEARNING OUTCOMES

Upon completion of this workshop, participants will:
- Gain an understanding of the importance of proper business communication.
- Gain an understanding of how to write an effective cover letter in order to market one's skills.
- Learn the impact that thank-you letters have, both during the job search process and throughout one's career.

WORKSHOP ACTIVITIES

- The instructor asks students to share their experiences writing cover letters and the challenges and successes they have experienced. A discussion is held on the importance of cover letters in the job search process.
- A PowerPoint presentation is utilized to highlight the proper format of cover letters. A detailed discussion is conducted on the components needed for the opening and closing paragraphs of the cover letter and then the body, which consists of highlighting skills related to the job description.
- Students are separated into five groups. Each group is given a cover letter to evaluate, and students are asked to rate the letters from excellent to very poor and explain why. The cover letters are shown to all participants and each group shares their ratings and evaluations.
- A discussion is held using thank-you letter examples highlighting the importance, use of, and format of thank-you letters.

RESOURCES USED

Office of Career Development. (2010). *Resume and Cover Letter Guide—Business, Education, or Liberal Arts & Sciences.* Office of Career Development, SUNY Geneseo.

Seager, E. (2008). *Thank You Letter Examples.* Office of Career Development, SUNY Geneseo.

Seager, E. (2009). *Job Search Letters PowerPoint Presentation.*

"Do something for somebody every day for which you do not get paid." –Albert Schweitzer

KEYS TO EFFECTIVE MENTORING

CERTIFICATE: Sapphire | **INSTRUCTOR:** Student Coordinators of the HEROS Program

"I have worked as a peer tutor for students at Geneseo, and most recently I began volunteering as a mentor through the HEROS program. I am able to use the information and the experience I have gained from this workshop to be more effective at my jobs and in my relationships with others."

Toby, junior, 2011

WORKSHOP DESCRIPTION

Successful volunteers and leaders often cite a mentor who helped guide them in their leadership journey. In this session, students will learn the 10 principles of effective mentoring. This workshop is designed to have students learn about mentoring, become more comfortable as mentors, and be more prepared to go out and serve as a mentor.

LEARNING OUTCOMES

Upon completion of this workshop, participants will:

- Understand the 10 principles of effective mentoring.
- Be more comfortable with various situations that can arise in a mentoring session.
- Know different options and activities one can do with their mentee.
- Be more prepared to go out and be a mentor.

WORKSHOP ACTIVITIES

- The participants are broken up into groups of six and given "problems/situations" to try to solve:
  - You are mentoring a session and your mentee says, "I think I might be pregnant."
  - You are in a mentoring session and your mentee asks the following: do you have a boyfriend, what do you do on the weekends, and where do you live?
  - You are in a mentoring session and your mentee states, "I hate school, I can't wait to turn 16, get my GED, and get out of here!"
  - Your mentee told you, "I went to a party this weekend and tried _____." How do you respond and why?
  - You and your mentee have worked together for a long time and you have seen them grow. However, it is time to end the school year. How do you leave on a good note and maintain a good relationship?
  - You are in a mentoring session and you notice that your mentee has bruises and marks on his/her body. How would you respond?
- The booklet handout entitled *The 10 Principles of Effective Mentoring* is distributed to participants. The group as a whole discusses the key points. Participants are instructed to read further.
- The instructor talks about the importance of confidentiality, especially in the workplace.
- The instructor discusses what motivates the HEROS Program: To mentor students to try to break the cycle of poverty by giving students positive role models.

RESOURCES USED

Garringer, M., & Jucovy, L. (2008). *Building relationships: A guide for new mentors*. Washington, DC: National Mentoring Center.

Montenarello, T., & Taveniere, A. (2010). *Handout on the 10 principles of effective mentoring*. Adapted from *Building relationships: A guide for new mentors*.

Montenarello, T., & Taveniere, A. (2010). *Handout on Scenarios*.

LEADERSHIP CONCEPTS

CERTIFICATE: Bronze (Required) | **INSTRUCTOR:** Dr. Tom Matthews, Associate Dean of Leadership and Service

"Sometimes, the most charismatic and popular people are not always the most efficient leaders. I do not necessarily have to fill all of the stereotypes of leadership to lead effectively. The most important quality of leadership is to take into account the opinions and feelings of those whom you are leading."

Amanda, junior, 2011

WORKSHOP DESCRIPTION

Everyone has an opinion about leaders and what constitutes effective leadership. Everyone can be a leader and most of us will be called upon to lead at one time or another. Start or continue your leadership journey with this introductory session to the GOLD program and to the fascinating world of leadership concepts, myths, and possibilities. This required program serves as both an introduction and foundation to the leadership programs within the GOLD program. Within this highly interactive workshop, participants are asked to engage in a variety of activities. The activities range from self-reflection on what leadership means from a personal perspective, to identifying with leadership philosophies of a great number of leaders from both history and the present. The instructor explains to the participants the nature and purpose of the GOLD program and the requirements for completion of the various certificates, and guides participants through a foundational understanding of what leadership is and what role everyone has to play as leaders.

LEARNING OUTCOMES

Upon completion of this workshop, participants will:

- Demonstrate an understanding of the breadth and depth of leadership concepts.
- Be able to critically analyze myths regarding leadership.
- Have begun thinking about leadership from multiple perspectives and viewpoints.

WORKSHOP ACTIVITIES

- Prior to the workshop, the instructor posts a dozen leadership quotes, with attribution blocked out by a Post-it® note, around the room at eye level in 11–12 point size so they cannot be read except at close range (see *Quotes on Leadership With Instructions* for quotations used in the workshop).
- After a brief introduction to the workshop, each individual is given the handout *Characteristics of an Influential Person in My Life* that requests participants to "Describe the characteristics of an influential person in your life."
- Participants are asked to write as many words as possible to describe their choice and after a few minutes everyone is paired with the person next to them and asked to share the characteristics with that partner. The instructor asks participants about the categories of people they admired and described. Common traits are discussed and the instructor asks the question, "Why would I have you do this?" The end goal is to work toward a broad and flexible understanding of the various types, styles, and admirable traits of leadership. Participants are guided through an analysis of leadership that illustrates the point that we admire and aspire to the positive traits of other leaders.
- Transitioning from the discussion of leadership traits, participants are asked to individually turn over the handout *Characteristics of an Influential Person in My Life* and draw a picture of leadership. Individuals are given three to four minutes for this task with the instructor surveying the room. Once the drawings are done, the instructor asks for volunteers to share completed drawings with their partner. The instructor asks a few participants to briefly share their drawings and concludes with one or two creative examples from previous workshops, such as an anchor. This is often a time for good-natured laughs with the analysis. Typically, most participants draw leaders rather than leadership. The distinction between the two is examined briefly in the discussion.

- Upon completion of the drawing exercise, participants are asked to tour the room and take time to read all the quotes posted on the wall. After everyone has had a few minutes to do so, the individuals are asked to pick a quote they identify with and stand near it. (Facilitation note: If more than three or four participants are by one quote, participants are encouraged to pick a second choice to avoid overcrowding.) The instructor calls on every person in the room to share why s/he picked the quote or what it says to him/her, and these insights quickly begin to demonstrate and highlight differing views and perceptions on leadership. The underlying goal of this segment is to focus on the fact that leadership is about more than being in charge. At the end, the facilitator suggests that they lift the Post-it® notes to see the name of the author of the quote. The reactions to the quotes from Attila the Hun and Lenin are often interesting to observe.

- Participants return to their seats and are given the handout *Thoughts About Leadership* with 10 statements on frequently heard myths of leadership. The instructor does not label them myths during the discussion. The instructor assigns all 10 statements to pairs of students to discuss and determine if they agree or disagree with the statements. After a few minutes, the instructor leads a discussion by asking each pair of students to report on their conclusions. The instructor solicits other opinions from the audience and adds a few comments, as appropriate, as each pair reports on their conclusions.

- Upon completion of this discussion, each participant is given a booklet containing a summary of the myths of leadership as a means of wrapping up the conversation.

- The handout also contains a historical chart on the major approaches and studies of leadership. The instructor points out that these approaches will be described in more detail when students reach the Gold level of the program.

- The handout also includes the guidelines for writing journal reflections and two examples of good journals. The instructor explains the requirements for earning leadership certificates and offers suggestions and tips on how to proceed through the GOLD Leadership Certificate Program.

RESOURCES USED

Crawford, C. B., Brungardt, C., & Maughan, M. (2000). *Understanding leadership: Theories & concepts*. Longmont, CO: Rocky Mountain.

Matthews, T. (2008). *Reflection Journal Guidelines*.

Matthews, T. (2009). *Handout on Characteristics of an Influential Person in My Life*.

Matthews, T. (2009). *Handout on Thoughts About Leadership*. Adapted from *Understanding leadership: Theories & concepts*.

Matthews, T. (2010). *Quotes on Leadership With Instructions*.

Matthews, T. (2011). *Handout on Leadership Approaches, Myths of Leadership, Journal Guidelines, and Sample Journals*.

"A leader is one who knows the way, goes the way, and shows the way."–John C. Maxwell

LEADERSHIP IDENTITY DEVELOPMENT

CERTIFICATE: Gold (Required) | **INSTRUCTOR:** Dr. Tom Matthews, Associate Dean of Leadership and Service

"In the future, I hope to further develop my skills and ultimately reach the integration/synthesis stage of the Leadership Identity Development Model."

Krista, junior, 2010

WORKSHOP DESCRIPTION

When did you first discover that there was such a thing as a leader? When did you decide that you could be a leader? When did you first experience leading? Can you remember what you did? Where do you think you are in the developmental process of leading? This session is based on the recent research on leadership identity development by the American College Personnel Association. Participants will critically evaluate the development of their personal leadership identity by connecting their own experiences and stages of development to this important theory. The workshop will also assist students in preparing their Personal Leadership Model.

LEARNING OUTCOMES

Upon completion of this workshop, participants will:

- Understand the six developmental stages of leadership that an individual progresses through as they engage in leadership experiences.
- Have an awareness of the leadership stage(s) they are currently at.
- Be able to critically evaluate their past leadership experience and stages of development.

WORKSHOP ACTIVITIES

- The instructor poses a simple question: Who are you? Students are asked to jot down a list of words that describe their multiple identities, such as big brother, oldest son, biology student, senior, employee, athlete, artist, gamer, political junkie, etc. The instructor asks participants to share their identities in a triad. After the groups have time to converse, a few volunteers are asked to share a few identities with the entire group.
- The instructor asks the participants, "When was the first time you can remember that you witnessed or observed the concept of leadership or leaders?" Students share their answers with the same triad and the instructor asks a few people to share their brief stories with the entire group.
- The instructor briefly explains the Leadership Identity Development Model (LID) research project and then distributes a four-page handout of the LID model that includes a graphic of the six stages of leadership. He also distributes reprinted sections of the ACPA article on the research to six students and indicates he will call on them in the order marked on the handouts to read aloud highlighted descriptions of each stage and quotes from student participants in the study. Workshop participants are asked to listen to the narrative and look at the stage being described and to think about which stage they might currently be in on the continuum.
- The participants analyze the chart and share and explain to their triad their thoughts and reactions to the leadership identity stages. The instructor moves his chair around the room to listen to the discussions and ask questions or offer comments as appropriate.
- The instructor concludes the workshop by posing questions to the entire group about their experiences and asks for a show of hands about what stage participants think they are in at the time of the workshop. It is not unusual to have a range of students from freshman to seniors in the workshop and that diversity is usually very helpful to the discussion. Although some students are on occasion very unrealistic in their self-assessment, most participants are able to connect their past experiences and envision moving to the higher stages of development.
- The instructor reminds the participants that this workshop is directly related to the Personal Leadership Model workshop and paper required to complete the Gold Leadership Certificate.

RESOURCES USED

Two resources are used in this workshop. Selected descriptions of the six stages of development and quotes from the participants in the study are read during the workshop. The four-page handout that includes a graphic representation of the theory is given to the participants to help them connect their leadership experiences to the developmental stages in the theory.

Komives, S. R., Owen, J. E., Longerbeam, S. D., Maniella, F. C., & Osteen, L. (2005). Developing a leadership identity: A grounded theory. *Journal of College Student Development, 46,* 593–611.

Komives, S. R., Owen, J. E., Longerbeam, S. D., Maniella, F. C., & Osteen, L. (2006). A leadership identity development model: Applications from a grounded theory. *Journal of College Student Development, 47*(4), 401–418.

"A good leader inspires people to have confidence in the leader; a great leader inspires people to have confidence in themselves."
—Eleanor Roosevelt

LEADERSHIP IN ENERGY SUSTAINABILITY

CERTIFICATE: Bronze or Diamond or Jade | **INSTRUCTOR:** Dr. Dennis Showers, Professor, School of Education

"As leaders, we must be able to work around roadblocks to find cleaner, more efficient energy sources that will benefit both our community and our environment without costing a fortune."

Gina, freshman, 2011

WORKSHOP DESCRIPTION

Civic engagement in modern times often requires addressing issues involving technology. Using energy sustainability as a case study, we will examine how we can understand the limits of technological solutions to social problems and possible ways this thinking might influence leadership for social change.

LEARNING OUTCOMES

Upon completion of this workshop, participants will:

- Realize how energy is used up so quickly in our everyday lives.
- Become more aware of why certain appliances use more energy than others.
- Be able to begin identifying ways in which to act more sustainably.

WORKSHOP ACTIVITIES

- The instructor introduces himself and reviews his career and experience at SUNY Geneseo. He talks about badges for Girl Scouts and Boy Scouts that will relate to the content of the workshop and shares that he actually wrote the merit badge book for the Boy Scouts.
- The instructor discusses making decisions both individually and in groups and how to use science and technology sustainably, stressing the point that it is important to understand science in order to understand technology and vice versa.
- The instructor shows a YouTube video called "Salt Water Fuel," about a man who is looking for a way to cure cancer, but stumbles upon a machine that could burn salt water and create a flame, as it conducts electricity. After the movie, the instructor reviews and discusses it with the participants, asking, "Who would say no to this discovery?"
- The instructor discusses energy in appliances. Many people buy the cheaper fridge, but the more expensive fridge costs less in the long run because it runs on less energy. Why does it cost more? It costs more to produce because of newer technology and more expensive parts.
- The instructor talks about the Corporate Average Fuel Economy (CAFE) standards and the CAFE failure.
- The instructor raises the point that if the coal firing electric plants is collected and put into one place, the pollution can be controlled. Challenges are the costs of cleaning up the air and of the filters that lower the pollution concentrations.

RESOURCES USED

Tang, C. (2007, June 27). *Salt Water Fuel*. Retrieved from: www.youtube.com/watch?v=Tf4gOS8aoFkA.

National Highway Traffic Safety Administration. http://www.nhtsa.gov/fuel-economy/

"Consume less; share better." –Hervé Kempf

LEADERSHIP IN HEALTH CARE: BEING AN ADVOCATE FOR A HEALTHY PERSONAL & COMMUNITY LIFESTYLE

CERTIFICATE: Bronze | **INSTRUCTOR:** Dr. Steven A. Radi, Medical Director, Student Health & Counseling

"This presentation taught me valuable healthcare facts that I can actually use to help keep my family, my friends, and myself healthy."

Melissa, freshman, 2012

WORKSHOP DESCRIPTION

This session will explore ways in which individuals can impact the lives of their families, friends, and community by promoting healthy life habits.

LEARNING OUTCOMES

Upon completion of this workshop, participants will:

- Understand why is important to be an advocate for good health.
- Know how to be an advocate for good health.
- Describe what is required to be an advocate for good health.

WORKSHOP ACTIVITIES

- The instructor asks participants what they are studying in order to tailor his presentation to fit their interests.
- The instructor provides background information on leadership and explains what to do to be an advocate for good health. The handout "Leadership in Health: Advocating for Good Health" is distributed and read as a group.
- By referring to the handout, the instructor discusses the specifics of prevention and screening and information regarding screening for specific diseases.
- Participants engage in a brief discussion about tobacco on campus prompted by the handout "Position Statement on Tobacco on College and University Campuses."
- The workshop concludes by discussing how to pass the information learned in the workshop on to family, friends, and peers.

RESOURCES USED

American College Health Association (2009). Position statement on tobacco on college and university campuses. *Journal of American College Health,* 58(3), 291–292.

Radi, S. R. (2012). *Handout on Leadership in Health: Advocating for Good Health.*

"Let us be the ones who say we do not accept that a child dies every three seconds simply because he does not have the drugs you and I have. Let us be the ones to say we are not satisfied that your place of birth determines your right for life. Let us be outraged, let us be loud, let us be bold." –Brad Pitt

LEADERSHIP STYLES

CERTIFICATE: Silver (Required) | **INSTRUCTOR:** Chip Matthews, Director, College Union & Activities

"It is much easier to gain respect and work hard for someone who is being respectful and working just as hard."

Paige, freshman, 2012

WORKSHOP DESCRIPTION

Each individual has a leadership style that s/he prefers to use and to follow. It is valuable to recognize that different situations call for different leadership styles. In this interactive workshop, participants will learn about different leadership styles and will review some of the effective uses of these leadership styles.

LEARNING OUTCOMES

Upon completion of this workshop, participants will:
- Know about three styles of leadership: autocratic, laissez-faire, and democratic.
- Understand that a successful leader utilizes all three styles of leadership.
- Be able to apply the appropriate style of leadership to each situation they are faced with as a leader.

WORKSHOP ACTIVITIES

- Participants take the Leadership Styles Survey to find out whether they are naturally an autocratic, democratic, or laissez-faire leader.
- The instructor breaks the participants into groups of four or five. Each group consists of people who share a leadership style.
- Each group works together to generate a list of adjectives that describe their leadership style. They share the list with the rest of the workshop.
- The instructor leads a discussion about the situations in which each style is most effective.
- In small groups, participants think of examples of current leaders with each style. These examples are shared and discussed with all of the workshop participants.
- Participants then take the Style Questionnaire to find out whether they are task- or relationship-oriented.
- As a large group, participants discuss whether their leadership styles are consistent with their orientation (e.g., relationship-oriented and democratic style together).

RESOURCES USED

Matthews, C. (2000). *Handout on Leadership Styles Chart.*
Matthews, C. (2000). *Handout on Leadership Styles Survey.*
Matthews, C. (2000). *Handout on Style Questionnaire.*

"Leadership…the art of mobilizing others to want to struggle for shared aspirations."
—Jim Kouzes & Barry Posner, authors of The Leadership Challenge

LEADING WITH INTEGRITY

CERTIFICATE: Silver | **INSTRUCTOR:** Karen Duerr-Clark, Residence Life Area Coordinator

"After taking this workshop, I realized that I need to take the time to reflect on my values and actions, and my integrity more often and to be happy with the choices I make and uphold the integrity that keeps me feeling good about myself."
Samantha, sophomore, 2011

WORKSHOP DESCRIPTION

How can you earn respect as a leader? This interactive session will offer creative and personalized ways to make decisions that allow you to lead with integrity to increase your credibility among colleagues, professionals, and friends. Using the Teamwork Integrity Model, we will explore the many beliefs and values that are most important to you and how they affect your leadership style.

LEARNING OUTCOMES

Upon completion of this workshop, participants will:
- Know the definition of integrity and understand how integrity is applicable in leadership.
- Have explored their core values and how these values translate into actions.

WORKSHOP ACTIVITIES

- The instructors ask participants what integrity means to them and explain how integrity is applicable to leadership because a leader's values and beliefs translate into their actions and priorities.
- The instructors show the PowerPoint presentation, the Core Value Inventory.
- Using the Core Values Inventory and the "Do You Walk the Talk?" worksheet, participants list their personal values and beliefs and any corresponding actions and priorities.
- Additionally, using the Core Values Inventory and the "Do You Walk the Talk?" worksheet, participants list values and beliefs and any corresponding actions and priorities that they believe would be congruent with an employee at a company.
- Participants are asked whether they think it is easier to pick personal values and beliefs or values and beliefs for the employee of a company.
- Participants break into small groups and are given scenarios to discuss in which certain core values were in conflict. Participants are asked to solve the dilemmas.
- The answers from the small-group work are discussed with all participants.

RESOURCES USED

Duerr-Clark, K., & Smaak, Z. (2010). *Handout on Scenarios.*
Duerr-Clark, K., & Smaak, Z. (2010). *Leading With Integrity PowerPoint.*
Smaak, Z. (2010). *Handout on "Do You Walk the Talk?" Worksheet.*

"As we look ahead into the next century, leaders will be those who empower others." —Bill Gates

LEARN TO FACILITATE DELIBERATIVE DIALOGUES

CERTIFICATE: Opal | **INSTRUCTOR:** Joe Van Remmen, Inspector, University Police

"I believe that deliberative dialogues are a lot more productive than debates because they force the parties to find a common ground and work on resolving the issues."

Alyssa, junior, 2011

WORKSHOP DESCRIPTION

Deliberative Dialogue is a conversation strategy that allows people with differing viewpoints to share those views with an opportunity to work together on a problem in the hope of reaching common ground; i.e., to find those points on which they agree without trying to persuade or coerce each other to change their basic stances and then take some action. Deliberative Dialogues (DDs) use a specific structure and a trained facilitator to keep discussions on track. DDs are successful as one-time events, for class discussions on controversial topics, and for organizations making decisions.

LEARNING OUTCOMES

Upon completion of this workshop, participants will:

- Have compared and contrasted deliberative dialogues and debates.
- Be able to list all of the steps that comprise a deliberative dialogue.
- Understand and be able to explain the roles of a facilitator and of a recorder.

WORKSHOP ACTIVITIES

- The workshop requires 90 minutes and a minimum of eight participants.
- The instructor spends approximately 30 minutes explaining the differences between debate and dialogue.
- Participants are divided into groups and given a topic to discuss. Participants are given an opportunity to practice facilitating and recording the deliberative dialogue session in order to gain a better understanding of the process that takes place.

RESOURCES USED

National Issues Forum. Retrieved from http://nifi.org/

Franklin Pierce College. FAQs on Deliberative Democracy. Retrieved from http://franklinpierce.edu/institutes/neccl/nec_deliberative.htm

"It is understanding that gives us an ability to have peace. When we understand the other fellow's viewpoint, and he understands ours, then we can sit down and work out our differences." –Harry S Truman

LEARNING TO LIVE WITH CONFLICT

CERTIFICATE: Silver or Sapphire | **INSTRUCTOR:** Bob Hall, President of Learning to Live With Conflict, Inc.

"As an RA, if I can get residents to understand that fighting is not productive, but talking about things is what will solve their problem, then mediations would go much more smoothly."

Alix, junior, 2008

WORKSHOP DESCRIPTION

Life and leadership involve conflict, and getting people to work together effectively involves learning to live with conflict. Conflict is often seen as a negative phenomenon to be ignored, avoided, or eliminated as quickly as possible. Perception shapes reality, and the way we think about conflict matters! In line with Peter Senge's notion of the learning organization, this session will explore the perception of conflict as a lesson and our capacity to learn and grow from the experience of conflict. This elective workshop introduces the five-step process of dealing with conflict. It is discussion-based and focuses on the difficult and often unsafe and unforgiving environment American culture has created to deal with conflict.

LEARNING OUTCOMES

Upon completion of this workshop, participants will:

- Be able to recognize and act on the five steps of conflict.
- Recognize that communication, trust, and respect are the key ingredients in dealing with conflict successfully.

WORKSHOP ACTIVITIES

- The instructor discusses the five steps of dealing with conflict (Affirm the Relationship, Seek to Understand, Seek to Be Understood, Own Responsibility by Apologizing, and Seek Agreement). He compares conflicts to fires because they spread easily and quickly, and notes that trust and respect are necessary to facilitate communication.
- The instructor reflects upon American culture and points out that our culture is the wealthiest per capita in human history, yet it has the highest rates of homicide, suicide, addiction, domestic violence, arms production, and trade in the developed world. While violence is an effective strategy in the short run, but it always destabilizes and undermines trust and respect in the long run.
- The participants learn that there are two ways at looking at conflict. It can be viewed as a disease (external) or as a battle with each other (internal).
- The instructor ends the workshop by pointing out that companies that learn how to deal with problems the fastest earn the most money and are generally the most successful.

RESOURCES USED

For more information, go to Learning to Live With Conflict, Inc., www.conflictaslesson.com/

"Peace is not absence of conflict, it is the ability to handle conflict by peaceful means." –Ronald Reagan

LISTENING SKILLS (VERSION A)

CERTIFICATE: Bronze (Required) | **INSTRUCTORS:** Dr. Beth Cholette, Clinical Director for Counseling Services, and Melinda DuBois, Administrative Director, Health & Counseling

"As a teacher, I may not be able to relate to my students in the future, but I am determined to earn their trust and listen to them effectively no matter what they need to talk about."

Kristina, junior, 2010

WORKSHOP DESCRIPTION

What makes someone a good listener? Think of their characteristics. What can prevent someone from listening carefully? This workshop will examine listening skills and offer ways to improve them.

LEARNING OUTCOMES

Upon completion of this workshop, participants will:

- Demonstrate an understanding of basic negotiating and listening skills, including leading, reflecting, informing, summarizing, and problem solving.
- Be able to identify at least two components of active listening behavior.
- Be able to ask an open-ended question.
- Be able to engage in paraphrasing and/or reflection of a simple statement.

WORKSHOP ACTIVITIES

- The instructor begins the workshop by asking students why they think listening skills are important.
- The instructor explains that it is important to pay attention to what is not stated just as much as what is stated, and highlights the importance of repeating a paraphrased version of what is said in order to avoid miscommunication.
- Students are taught about breathing techniques and meditation as ways to focus.
- The differences between empathy and sympathy are discussed.
- The instructor asks participants to pair up and dialogue specific listening scenarios of useful and not-so-useful ways of dealing with problems. The instructor switches the participants' roles in order to get different opinions. The workshop ends with a group discussion about the activity.

RESOURCES USED

Brammer, L. M. (1988). *The helping relationship: Process and skills* (4th ed.). Englewood Cliffs, NJ: Prentice Hall.

Cholette, B. (2011). Handout on Examples of Listening Skills. Adapted from Brammer, L. M. (1988). *The helping relationship: Process and skills* (4th ed.). Englewood Cliffs, NJ: Prentice Hall.

Cholette, B. (2011). *Handout on Conversational Dos and Don'ts: A Guide for Helper/Helpee Relationships.* Adapted from Kanfer, F. H., and Goldstein, A. P. (1991). *Helping people change: A textbook of methods* (4th ed.). New York: Pergamon Press.

Cholette, B. (2011). *Handout on Active Listening.*

Cholette, B. (2011). *Active Listening PowerPoint.*

"Silence is a source of great strength." –Lao Tzu

LISTENING SKILLS (VERSION B)

CERTIFICATE: Bronze (Required) | **INSTRUCTOR:** Sandy Glantz, Nurse Practitioner, Health and Counseling

"Being a good listener is a great tool to use to further yourself as a family member, friend, boss, or even as a stranger. "
Alyssa, junior, 2011

WORKSHOP DESCRIPTION

What makes someone a good listener? Think of their characteristics. What can prevent someone from listening carefully? This workshop will examine listening skills and offer ways to improve them.

LEARNING OUTCOMES

Upon completion of this workshop, participants will:
- Be able to describe two communication skills that foster better listening behavior.
- Be able to give examples of three barriers to good listening behavior.

WORKSHOP ACTIVITIES

- Each participant is provided with three documents: (A) examples of listening skills, (B) listening quotes, and (C) summary sheet of eight barriers to effective listening.
- Chairs are arranged in a circle, or in two concentric circles, so each person can see and hear others in the room.
- The instructor introduces herself and explains the purpose of workshop.
- Participants are asked to introduce themselves by name.
- The instructor polls students to see what majors are represented and what types of student groups they are leading this year. The instructor uses this information to give several brief examples of when effective listening skills are useful for these majors and student leaders in real-life scenarios.
- The instructor asks for Listening Quotes #1–3 to be read aloud.
- The instructor briefly discusses the handout on basic types of listening skills and the handout on things to avoid when serving as a listener.
- The instructor asks for Listening Quotes #4–6 to be read aloud.
- The instructor divides the group into eight subgroups and gives each subgroup one page of the eight-page handout on barriers to effective listening, pointing out that each participant also received a two-page summary of these as a handout. Subgroups read and discuss their given barrier, and prepare a short "lesson" or role play about it for the entire class.
- Each subgroup gets three minutes to teach the class about their barrier.
- The instructor asks for Listening Quotes #11–12 to be read aloud.
- The workshop concludes with a question-and-answer session.

RESOURCES USED

Eight Barriers to Effective Listening. From *Better communication through better listening*. Retrieved from http/://sklatch.net/ thoughtlesslisten/html.

Glantz, S. (2011). Handout on Examples of Listening Skills. Adapted from Brammer, L. M. (1988). *The helping relationship: Process and skills* (4th ed.). Englewood Cliffs, NJ: Prentice Hall.

Glantz, S. (2011). *Handouts of Listening Quotes.*

LOCATING INTERNSHIPS

CERTIFICATE: Emerald | **INSTRUCTOR:** Andrea DiGiorgio, Coordinator, Student Employment Service

"In the future, I hope to obtain an internship to gain real-life experience, and I think having an internship in the psychology field would open up a lot of opportunities for me. This workshop helped me to get started with this process."
Krista, junior, 2011

WORKSHOP DESCRIPTION

Internships are becoming increasingly important when competing for positions after graduation. This workshop is designed to help participants get started on the search for an internship. The session will cover locating and applying for internships, including a brief overview of resumes and cover letters. Applying for college credit from an internship will also be discussed. Come and get an overview of launching a successful search.

LEARNING OUTCOMES

Upon completion of this workshop, participants will:

- Demonstrate an understanding of the value of internships.
- Know how to navigate SUNY Geneseo's Student Employment Services website.
- Gain an awareness of the most effective, reliable ways to search for internships.
- Have an introductory understanding of resumes, cover letters, and interviews.

WORKSHOP ACTIVITIES

- Using a PowerPoint presentation, the instructor introduces and discusses the following topics and questions:
    - What is an internship?
    - What types of internships are available?
    - Who should complete an internship?
    - Benefits of internships
    - Factors in choosing an internship
    - Finding an internship—research
    - Developing your own internship
    - Resume advice
    - Cover letter advice
    - Interviewing
    - When to look for internships
    - Academic credit
    - "While at your internship…"
- The instructor guides the participants through SUNY Geneseo's Student Employment Services website resources, such as:
    - Knight Jobs online system
    - Other links on the website that would help students locate internships

RESOURCES USED

SUNY Geneseo Office of Career Development. (2011). *Handout on Internships.*
SUNY Geneseo Office of Career Development. (2011). *Handout on Resumes and Cover Letters Guide.*
SUNY Geneseo Office of Career Development. (2011). *Locating Internships PowerPoint.*

MASS IMPRISONMENT IN THE UNITED STATES

CERTIFICATE: Opal or Diamond | **INSTRUCTOR:** Dr. William Lofquist, Professor of Sociology

"The idea that I simultaneously took for granted our country's criminal justice system while never having been a part of it myself is in some ways more troubling than any personal story I could tell."

Calla, sophomore, 2011

WORKSHOP DESCRIPTION

Over the past four decades, the imprisonment rate in the United States has increased by more than 500%, leading to the highest rate of imprisonment in our history and in the world. This workshop explores why U.S. imprisonment rates are so high, the financial costs of mass imprisonment, and its effects on families, communities, and democracy.

LEARNING OUTCOMES

Upon completion of this workshop, students will:

- Be able to identify issues in our social justice system.
- Have knowledge of U.S. imprisonment rates and financial costs of mass imprisonment.
- Understand how mass imprisonment affects families, communities, and democracy.

WORKSHOP ACTIVITIES

- After a brief introduction, the facilitator displays several graphs using an overhead projector and explains how mass imprisonment in the United States developed and transitioned through history.
- Students are encouraged to ask questions throughout the workshop.

RESOURCES USED

Lofquist, W. (2010). *Overhead Slides of Development of Mass Imprisonment.*

"In matters of truth and justice, there is no difference between large and small problems, for issues concerning the treatment of people are all the same." –Albert Einstein

MERGER INTEGRATION AND BUSINESS TRANSFORMATION: LEADERSHIP PRACTICES FOR PROCESS IMPROVEMENT—USING SIX SIGMA AND KANRI PRINCIPLES

CERTIFICATE: Gold | **INSTRUCTOR:** Daniel Ward, Geneseo Graduate Class of '87, Senior Vice President of Bank of America

> *"It is always important to consider what your target audience desires and also to have results that are repeatable within certain strict parameters."*
>
> *Cory, sophomore, 2011*

WORKSHOP DESCRIPTION

Daniel Ward introduces students to the mathematical principles of Six Sigma and the organizational skills of Hoshin Planning and Kanri Principles. He applies these to business, but also shows how they can be applied to everything in life. He uses a combination of personal experience with Bank of America and business and math theory.

LEARNING OUTCOMES

Upon completion of this workshop, participants will:

- Have a fundamental understanding of Six Sigma principles.
- Have a fundamental understanding of Hoshin and Kanri principles.

WORKSHOP ACTIVITIES

- The instructor introduces himself and his career achievements in the banking industry.
- The instructor presents a basic definition of Six Sigma as a "methodology...to systematically work towards managing variation to eliminate...defects. The objective of Six Sigma is to deliver world-class performance, reliability, and value to the end customer" (Wikipedia). The instructor compares this to the "miracle on the Hudson," when no one was injured in a plane crash.
- A large focus of the seminar is the importance of precision and accuracy and the difference between the two. Precision is being able to repeat results many times very regularly, and accuracy is being able to generate results that are desired.
- Six Sigma uses a system of Champions/Master Black Belts, Black Belts, and Green Belts to facilitate change in a corporation. These are different levels of proficiency in a non-command-controlled system. It is focused on core business and customer needs, and is a systematic method for process and product improvement.
- The instructor discusses Hoshin Planning. Hoshin means "compass," and Hoshin Planning is an organizational tool that also plans for the future.
- The instructor quizzes participants on the basics of Six Sigma and its importance in all careers and open discussion follows. The instructor shares his idea of "chewable chunks," which breaks things down for all levels of workers to be able to work with.

RESOURCES USED

Ward, D. (2011). *Six Sigma and Kanri Principles PowerPoint.*

> *"The achievements of an organization are the results of the combined effort of each individual."* –Vince Lombardi

MICROSOFT POWERPOINT: CREATE MULTIMEDIA & HYPERMEDIA PRESENTATIONS

CERTIFICATE: Ruby | **INSTRUCTOR:** Steve Dresbach, Technology Instructor

"In Microsoft PowerPoint, there are a myriad of features and tools that go unused by the average presenter."

Jennifer, junior, 2007

WORKSHOP DESCRIPTION

Bring MS PowerPoint presentations to life by replacing bullet slides with graphic-rich slides. Learn how to create graphically enhanced slides with complementing animation to emphasize points, links, and buttons in presentations.

LEARNING OUTCOMES

Upon completion of this workshop, participants will:

- Be able to identify components and features of a good PowerPoint presentation.
- Have practiced creating multimedia and hypermedia presentations.

WORKSHOP ACTIVITIES

- Each participants takes a seat at a computer, logs on, and opens up Microsoft PowerPoint.
- Once everyone is set up on a computer, the instructor asks participants to discuss the purposes of visual aids with each other. After a few minutes, the participants share and discuss their answers with all of the participants.
- Following the discussion, the instructor displays a slide that is a bad example of a visual aid and asks the participants to explain what is wrong with it. A better version of that same slide is shown and participants are asked to explain what makes the second slide a better visual aid. This is repeated with a few more examples.
- The instructor speaks about the best way to structure a PowerPoint presentation.
- A brief overview of how to design a PowerPoint slide is given by the instructor. It begins with an explanation of the provided templates and the "Background Styles" feature in the program to create the background for each slide. The importance of the "Insert" tab is explained as well as a tour of the different features under it. Different elements of design are talked about and demonstrated, including picture effects, layering, rotating, shapes, grouping, WordArt, images in shapes, and Smart Art. Participants are encouraged to explore and sample each of the features as they are discussed.
- The next section of this workshop addresses the hypermedia aspects of Microsoft PowerPoint. A hypermedia presentation is defined as a link-driven presentation and instructions on how to create one are provided. Buttons, action setting, and jumping slides are all features discussed with creating a hypermedia presentation and participants are given an opportunity to sample each of these tools.
- The instructor stresses the importance of avoiding the overuse of animations, and provides tips about timing, custom animation, and motion path settings.
- The use of multimedia in PowerPoint presentations is discussed. Participants learn how to insert sounds and movies into their slides. The developer tab is discussed along with each of its features.
- Participants are asked to find a YouTube video and insert it into their PowerPoint slide. The instructor provides assistance and answers questions as needed.

RESOURCES USED

Laptops are required for this workshop.

MICROSOFT WORD: CREATE PROFESSIONAL RESUMES & PAPERS

CERTIFICATE: Ruby | **INSTRUCTOR:** Steve Dresbach, Technology Instructor, Milne Library

"This workshop showed me some easy tricks and tips to spruce up my resume and make it look very appealing to potential employers."

Carolyn, junior, 2011

WORKSHOP DESCRIPTION

How does one line up text? How can paragraphs look the same throughout a document? Is there a way to line up decimals? Successful document layout requires a proper understanding of how and when to use the assortment of Microsoft Word's paragraph formatting tools. Come and learn how to effectively use tabs, indents, tables, and styles.

LEARNING OUTCOMES

Upon completion of this workshop, participants will:

- Know how to easily and efficiently create a resume on Microsoft Word.
- Understand the differences between tabs, indents, and styles.
- Become familiarized with other formatting features in Microsoft Word.

WORKSHOP ACTIVITIES

- Participants are checked in to the workshop and asked to take a seat at a personal computer and open Microsoft Word. The instructor passes out a sample resume to participants and has them open up a document on Microsoft Word with all the information on the resume already typed but not yet formatted.
- The instructor leads the participants through step-by-step instructions on how to turn the resume information into the fully formatted resume as they follow along on their own computers. Participants are shown how to center the name on the resume and how to separate each section with a line across the page.
- Each subsection of the resume (Profile, Professional Experience, Education, Interests, and References) is formatted by introducing the paragraph marker button. The instructor explains how the paragraph marker shows paragraph marks as well as hidden formatting symbols. Once participants are comfortable with that, the small caps feature and indents are shown, which should finish the set-up for the Profile heading.
- After the participants have the first heading formatted, the instructor introduces styles to the participants and how to create styles of their own. Using this feature, participants are shown how to create a style from the first subsection of their resume and then apply that style to the remaining headings.
- Participants finish with a fully formatted resume that resembles the sample resume passed out at the beginning of the workshop. The instructor asks the participants if they have any questions and as they leave, passes out a Microsoft Word instruction packet for future reference.

RESOURCES USED

Dresbach, S. (2009). *Handout of Microsoft Word Instruction Packet.*
Dresbach, S. (2009). *Handout on Sample Resume.*
Laptops with Microsoft Word are required for this workshop.

MOTIVATING OTHERS: A KEY TO SUCCESSFUL LEADERSHIP

CERTIFICATE: Silver | **INSTRUCTOR:** Dr. Daniel Repinski, Associate Professor of Psychology

"True leaders motivate not by treats or threats, but rather by example."

Sean, junior, 2005

WORKSHOP DESCRIPTION

Leaders and members of organizations are frequently faced with challenges relating to motivation and achievement. During this session, the issue of deciding whether one takes on or avoids a challenging task will be explored, as well as how leaders can facilitate achievement for themselves and members of their organizations.

LEARNING OUTCOMES

Upon completion of this workshop, participants will:
- Understand the importance of setting and achieving realistic goals when motivating others.
- Have an awareness of the degree to which their own attitudes and level of commitment affect those around them.
- Know why supportive leadership is a key to motivation.

WORKSHOP ACTIVITIES

- The instructor asks the participants to share personal experiences with problems in a leadership position. For example, a student may discuss a student organization that s/he is a part of and what challenges that have occurred for the group's leadership. This gives the instructor an opportunity to form connections between the ideas being taught in this workshop and how they are relevant to the participants' daily lives.
- The instructor splits the workshop into small groups to resolve the discussion questions on the handout. The first question addresses brainstorming and prompts small groups to generate ideas for new approaches to motivation. The second question allows participants to practice action planning. Participants outline steps they can take to become better leaders using skills they learned during this workshop.

RESOURCES USED

Repinski, D. (2011). *Handout on Motivating Others.*

"Motivation is the art of getting people to do what you want them to do because they want to do it." –Dwight D. Eisenhower

NETWORKING/INFORMATIONAL INTERVIEWING STRATEGIES

CERTIFICATE: Emerald (Required) | **INSTRUCTOR:** Kerrie Bondi, Career Counselor

"I plan to use this skill all my life, especially in searching for my first job next year when I graduate, and it will be a very efficient tool in looking for jobs when I want to switch jobs in the future."

Nazir, junior, 2010

WORKSHOP DESCRIPTION

Nearly every day of your life you have an opportunity to make connections and build relationships. The people you know and even people you don't know can influence the direction your life may take. If you don't know how to talk to people about your future, then this workshop is for you. Come and learn how to introduce yourself (even to those you know), what questions to ask to help you in your career decision making, and how to use social media in this process.

LEARNING OUTCOMES

Upon completion of this workshop, participants will:

- Demonstrate understanding of the differences between networking and informational interviewing.
- Be able to apply interpersonal conversational skills when talking about themselves and their career directions.
- Be able to assess opportunities for networking and informational interviewing.
- Appreciate the value of both online and in-person networking.

WORKSHOP ACTIVITIES

- The presenter breaks students into six groups and asks them to find three to five things that they have in common. This exercise teaches how easy it is to start conversations with people they may not know.
- After distributing the *Networking Handout,* the instructor provides a clear definition and examples of networking. An online example would be LinkedIn, a professional networking community. She then distributes a worksheet that provides information on LinkedIn accounts. There are five golden rules to LinkedIn: have a photo of you alone, a headline with area(s) of study and/or ambitions, a keyword-rich summary, activities, and recommendations. Facebook is discussed as a social networking site that may also be a source of contacts for networking or gathering career information. The instructor discusses why online networking is so important and strongly encourages participants to create a LinkedIn account.
- Participants speak for about five minutes with another person. They are told that when they introduce themselves to a new person they must say their first and last names. They should talk about why they are networking and include information about themselves.
- The next topic is informational interviewing, which is defined as collecting information about potential career fields and occupations. Upon completion of this discussion, the instructor addresses and elaborates on how to build a list of contacts. A person must start with those he or she knows, such as family, friends, and coworkers, and then move to those whom they do not know. The last handout, the *Networking Chart,* allows participants to think of contacts and begin their list of those they can talk to in the next couple of months to get information about a career.

RESOURCES USED

Bondi, K. (2011). *Networking/Informational Interviewing PowerPoint.*

LinkedIn™. (2011). *How to Build a Professional Student LinkedIn Profile.*

LinkedIn™. (2011). *How to Network Professionally Online.*

SUNY Geneseo Office of Career Development. (2011). *Handout on Networking.*

SUNY Geneseo Office of Career Development. (2011). *Handout on Informational Interviewing Fact Sheet.*

SUNY Geneseo Office of Career Development. (2011). *Handout on Networking Chart.*

OFFICE ETIQUETTE

CERTIFICATE: Emerald | **INSTRUCTOR:** Julie Briggs, Assistant Vice President for Human Resources

"I learned how to correctly act, dress, and succeed in an office setting. Also, the competitive aspect of the workshop kept my attention the entire time and encouraged me to participate."

Kate, sophomore, 2012

WORKSHOP DESCRIPTION

Working in an office requires employees to meet performance and behavior standards. Learn the survival skills needed to become a high-performing, valued, and trusted employee.

LEARNING OUTCOMES

Upon completion of this workshop, participants will:

- Know the skills and behaviors necessary to become a successful employee.
- Be able to apply techniques and proper behaviors to the job setting.
- Have an understanding of general and specific job behavioral standards.

WORKSHOP ACTIVITIES

- The instructor describes the workshop as being modeled after the TV show "Survivor." Participants are divided into four teams. The instructor explains that the goal is to vote everyone on your team into the office. During the activities, the presenter awards points to your team based on the information provided.
- The ground rules for the workshop are to show respect, stay involved/participate, be open to ideas, and use teamwork. There are Five Survivor Rules: adaptation, teamwork, creativity, interaction, and quality. Participants are guided through an analysis of these five survivor rules. Points are given to teams who effectively model the Survivor Rules.
- Before introducing the first activity, the instructor asks the question, "In general, what is office etiquette?" Common responses are "being professional when interacting with others" and "wearing professional dress."
- The instructor introduces the activity called "the fortune cookie." Each participant introduces him- or herself to other team members. They are asked to relate fortunes to positive office behavior. For example, "every friend rejoices in your success" is one fortune. This relates to a work environment because when an employee does something successful all the employees of the organization can benefit from that success. Teams take turns sharing information.
- The next activity is the "longest list competition." Each group receives a sheet that says "Do's and Don'ts" and is assigned a topic such as communication (electronic and otherwise) in the work environment or positive customer interactions. Teams are given five minutes to fill out the worksheet. Points are awarded for the number of facts that each team records. Teams take turns sharing information and record it on the handout on Office Survival/Etiquette for the Workplace. The instructor then gives the participants the same handout but with the instructor's answers already listed.
- The instructor reads conversation excerpts deemed "jargon." Participants are asked to guess what profession the excerpts are from.
- A prize is awarded at the end of the program to the team with the most points.

RESOURCES USED

Briggs, J. (2011). *Handout on Longest List Competition.*
Briggs, J. (2011). *Handout on Office Survival/Etiquette for the Workplace: (Blank worksheet).*
Briggs, J. (2011). *Handout on Office Survival/Etiquette for the Workplace: (Presenter's answer worksheet).*
Briggs, J. (2011). *Handout on Do's and Don'ts—Tips for Student Employees.*
Briggs, J. (2011). *Office Etiquette Survival Skills PowerPoint.*

ORGANIZE YOUR WEB RESEARCH WITH DIIGO

CERTIFICATE: Ruby | **INSTRUCTOR:** Tracy Paradis, Reference & Instruction Librarian

> *"I will try to use Diigo with the other members in my group for projects as a means of sharing information, with key points highlighted and multiple Post-it® notes to indicate important information."*
>
> *Aaron, sophomore, 2011*

WORKSHOP DESCRIPTION

Diigo is a powerful research and collaboration tool that can help you save, organize, and share what you discover on the web. Don't do research twice! Learn how to save, annotate, tag, and share websites while creating your own personal archive.

LEARNING OUTCOMES

Upon completion of this workshop, participants will:
- Have been introduced to the Diigo bookmarking tool.
- Understand how to use Diigo to more efficiently organize research.
- Be able to download and install Diigo onto personal laptops OR use Diigolet on library-provided laptops in order to experience hands-on learning.
- Have explored the highlighter, sticky note, capture, bookmarking, tagging, and library tools.

WORKSHOP ACTIVITIES

- The instructor asks participants to describe their current methods of organizing research.
- The instructor provides a brief description of the Diigo tool and its updated features.
- Participants then either download Diigo onto their personal laptops or use the Diigolet application on the library-provided computers.
- The instructor demonstrates how to use the various features.
- The instructor asks the participants to find two or three websites and tag, bookmark, capture, and add notes to them. Participants are encouraged to ask questions and seek help throughout the exercise.

RESOURCES USED

Laptops are required for this workshop.

> *"Don't agonize. Organize."* –Florence Kennedy

PEARLS OF WISDOM FROM SUCCESSFUL LEADERS: DOING THE RIGHT THING

CERTIFICATE: Gold | **INSTRUCTOR:** Cynthia Oswald, President, Livingston County Chamber of Commerce

"Oswald's inspiring presentation taught me to surround myself with good people, do the right thing, and to make bad days into learning days."

Krista, senior, 2012

WORKSHOP DESCRIPTION

Cynthia Oswald is the president of the Livingston County Chamber of Commerce and has a distinguished record of transformational and ethical leadership throughout her career. Oswald will share her experiences and leadership stories and inspire participants to make a difference in the world by "doing the right thing."

LEARNING OUTCOMES

Upon completion of this workshop, participants will:
- Understand what it means to "do the right thing."
- Be able to think about ethical leadership from multiple perspectives and viewpoints.

WORKSHOP ACTIVITIES

- After a brief introduction, the instructor explains her background. She serves on 18 boards, one of which is the United States Chamber of Commerce where she is a member of the Council on Small Business. The instructor points out that she did not always lead a naturally successful life; it took her 25 years to obtain her bachelor's degree after having two children at a young age.
- The instructor states that participants should "surround yourself with good people" and to "know what kind of leader you want to be."
- The instructor discusses the following points with participants:
    - Knowledge is only wisdom if it is shared.
    - It is hard to teach others without a relationship.
    - A bad day is actually a learning day.
    - It should not be "lonely at the top"; instead, bring people to the top with you.
    - Be who you think you should be.
    - We all make mistakes—it is up to you to use your mistakes to learn and grow.
    - Life and leadership is not always easy, good things come from hard work.
- The instructor concludes the workshop with a short question-and-answer period and provides her contact information.

RESOURCES USED

No additional resources.

PEARLS OF WISDOM FROM SUCCESSFUL LEADERS: FROM SA PRESIDENT TO FEDERAL PROSECUTOR TO CORPORATE MANAGER

CERTIFICATE: Silver | **INSTRUCTOR:** Jeffrey Cramer, Esq., Class of '86, Managing Director, Kroll

"Mr. Cramer had invaluable experience to teach the students, and I feel better personally after his lecture because I know that landing the dream job right out of college is highly unlikely."

Aaron, senior, 2011

WORKSHOP DESCRIPTION

The special guest speaker, Jeffrey Cramer, was an active student leader and a former Assistant United States Attorney at the U.S. Department of Justice in Chicago. He is now a managing director and Midwest head of Kroll, a 3,000-person international investigations and risk management company. In addition to a law degree, Jeff holds an MBA and worked for American Express and a large international bank. Jeff discusses how his career progressed from leading high-profile financial transactions and criminal/civil legal cases to managing teams of people across the world, and how the same set of skills helped him succeed at each step.

LEARNING OUTCOMES

Upon completion of this workshop, participants will:

- Have a better understanding of the skills needed to succeed as a leader in the workforce.

WORKSHOP ACTIVITIES

- After a brief introduction, the instructor discusses his college career, specifically the leadership roles he held and the goals he was hoping to achieve. The instructor talks about his role as Student Association President and fraternity president, as well as his goal to attend law school.
- The instructor discusses his post-undergraduate ambitions as a young law student at Temple Law School and as an employee of American Express.
- After speaking about his education, the instructor begins describing his career path to his current position as managing director at Kroll. He discusses in detail how his role as a prosecutor for the Manhattan District Attorney led him to a position in the U.S. Attorney's office under the tutelage of Pat Fitzgerald and then to his current position as a corporate manager. The instructor highlights some of his most memorable experiences, including the prominent cases he has tried and investigated, the places he has traveled, and the dignitaries he has had the privilege of meeting.
- The instructor focuses the remaining part of the workshop on the lessons and advice that he has acquired to become a successful leader in the workforce. The instructor illustrates the importance of each lesson through an example he has experienced in his career.
- The instructor concludes the workshop with a short question-and-answer period.

RESOURCES USED

No additional resources.

PEARLS OF WISDOM FROM SUCCESSFUL LEADERS: FROM THE WADSWORTH STAGE TO THE WORLD STAGE

CERTIFICATE: Diamond or Emerald | **INSTRUCTOR:** Bruce Jordan, Class of '66; adaptor, actor, producer, and Broadway director

"Bruce's story was a really good illustration of the process that people must go through before reaching their goals."

Mary, senior, 2011

WORKSHOP DESCRIPTION

Shear Madness is not only the longest-running play in the history of the American theater, it is also the second- and third-longest running play. Adaptor, actor, producer, and director Bruce Jordan, a member of the founding company of Geva, was instrumental in changing this German crime investigation into a shoot-from-the-hip, interactive comedy whodunit that plays around the world. Jordan and his partner, Marilyn Abrams, own the world rights to this popular play, which recently started a very successful run in Paris. Jordan will recount the *Shear Madness* journey from his work with Professor Pop Sinclair on the Wadsworth stage to the Geva stage to an internationally produced hit on stages all over the world.

LEARNING OUTCOMES

Upon completion of this workshop, participants will:

- Have a better understanding of the skills needed to succeed as a leader in the performing arts, production, and management fields.

WORKSHOP ACTIVITIES

- The instructor describes his career path to his current position as producer of *Shear Madness*, discussing in detail the importance of his experience at Geneseo, specifically with the Theater Department, and how it prepared him for his future endeavors. The instructor highlighted plays he acted in, professors and people that were instrumental in building his foundation of acting, and specific events that proved to be turning points in his life.
- The instructor discusses his post-graduate career working as a schoolteacher at Glens Falls High School and the development of a summer theatre in Lake George. He explains the importance the summer theater had on his career and specific shows in which he has starred and produced.
- The instructor discusses how *Shear Madness* became the sensational play it is currently, going into detail about the people who made the play possible, the events that led up to the production, and tips that helped him achieve such a high level of success.
- The instructor concludes the workshop with a short question-and-answer period.

RESOURCES USED

No additional resources.

PEARLS OF WISDOM FROM SUCCESSFUL LEADERS: REBUILDING COMMUNITIES FROM BROOKLYN TO MOUNT MORRIS

CERTIFICATE: Gold | **INSTRUCTOR:** Greg O'Connell, Class of '64, CEO, Red Hook Waterfront Properties

"I have tried to apply Greg's words to life in general, such as getting to know the people and businesses around you, so you can better work with and utilize them to advance your own career and those of the people you work with."

David, junior, 2011

WORKSHOP DESCRIPTION

Greg O'Connell, the son of a Queens teacher and police officer, spent four memorable years in Geneseo majoring in education. He returned to New York City to live, teach, and work as a detective in Brooklyn and Harlem. He watched the Red Hook area of Brooklyn, cut off by the Robert Moses parkway, fall into decay and ruin. Inspired by Jane Jacob's seminal work and book, *The Death and Life of Great American Cities,* O'Connell started investing in Red Hook waterfront properties and rebuilding commercial sites and apartments. His efforts paid off and Red Hook is now a thriving urban community. Most recently, he returned to the Genesee Valley and started investing in run-down properties in Mt. Morris. Another success story is unfolding as O'Connell's work is impacting people and families and communities in upstate New York. One person can make an amazing difference.

LEARNING OUTCOMES

Upon completion of this workshop, participants will:

- Have a better understanding of the skills needed to succeed as a leader in the workforce.

WORKSHOP ACTIVITIES

- After a brief introduction, the instructor begins by describing his career path to his current position as CEO of Red Hook Waterfront Properties. He specifically discusses how his jobs as a UPS worker, a part-time teacher, and an NYPD detective, prepared him for his future position. The instructor highlights specific lessons he learned in each career that helped him become a successful leader.
- The instructor focuses the remaining workshop time on discussing his future endeavors of entering the agricultural business in the Genesee Valley, his current vision for Livingston County towns, specifically Mount Morris and Dansville, and his work developing the Red Hook properties.
- The instructor concludes the workshop with a short question-and-answer period.

RESOURCES USED

No additional resources.

PEARLS OF WISDOM FROM SUCCESSFUL LEADERS: SELLING YOURSELF IN THE CAREER MARKETPLACE—HOW TO BUILD YOUR "BRAND"

CERTIFICATE: Emerald | **INSTRUCTOR:** Terry Bernat, Group Manager, Sun Life Financial

"I am planning to build my resume in new and creative ways by looking at all my assets and experiences and using them to put a positive spin on my work ethic and personality."

Akshara, freshman, 2012

WORKSHOP DESCRIPTION

This discussion focuses on how to package yourself as you navigate the career marketplace, market your assets, and develop and implement a business plan. Learn how the relationship-buildings skills you've acquired both in and outside of the classroom, coupled with a well-developed business plan, can provide the foundation for a successful career. The instructor will discuss life lessons and how a BA in economics and finance and participation in college athletics have led to a successful 20-plus–year career in the insurance wholesale industry.

LEARNING OUTCOMES

Upon completion of the workshop, participants will:
- Be able to develop one's personal brand and sell oneself in resumes and interviews.

WORKSHOP ACTIVITIES

- The instructor gives his PowerPoint presentation, which relates the concepts of personal branding to his own experience. After using himself as an example of personal branding, he asks the audience to relate personal branding to themselves.
- The instructor asks participants to consider the question "Who are you?" Examples from his own life are provided and the qualities and characteristics these examples demonstrate. He then asks the audience to relate their own experience and the qualities and the characteristics they demonstrate.
- The instructor asks participants if they have a mission statement and defines what a mission statement means to him and the importance of developing one and writing it out. He then has the audience develop their own personal mission statements.
- The instructor discusses the importance of developing and writing goals to direct oneself in one's profession, and asks participants to create their own professional goals.
- The instructor asks participants to think about what do they want to do and provides his own example of what he wanted to do and how he accomplished it, with an example of a SUNY Geneseo graduate who successfully sold himself through personal branding to Sun Life Financial and received a job offer.
- The instructor summarizes the main points: Who are you? What's your mission? Who do you want to be? What are your long-term goals? What do you want to do? Participants are asked to remember these points after the workshop.
- The workshop ends with a question-and-answer session.

RESOURCES USED

Bernat, T. (2011). *Selling Yourself in the Career Marketplace—How to Build Your "Brand" PowerPoint.*

PERSONAL DEVELOPMENT SESSION

CERTIFICATE: Bronze (Required) | **INSTRUCTOR:** GOLD Leader Mentors

"This development session helped me because the GOLD mentor showed me the certificates in the program that would be most beneficial for me to develop professionally. I also had the ability to reflect on past leadership experience and realize where I wanted to go next."

Alyssa, junior, 2010

WORKSHOP DESCRIPTION

This session is one of the four required workshops for the Bronze Leadership Certificate. The GOLD Leader Mentor volunteers have been trained to assist participants in developing a personal plan for successfully completing the GOLD Certificate Program. Interested participants need to register for the session and schedule a specific individual appointment time with a mentor. This required workshop is unique because it is formatted as a one-on-one meeting between the participant and a GOLD Leader Mentor that may take between 20–40 minutes, depending on the experience of the individual. It serves as an important, personal, and friendly introduction to the program, and is most effective if it is one of the first workshops the participant completes. The workshop is especially helpful for freshmen. Each participant receives advice on how to proceed through the GOLD program based on their previous and current leadership experience, strengths, weaknesses, interests, and career goals. This workshop is also a useful way to increase interaction between participants and leader mentors, and provides an opportunity for mentors to share advice based on their own experiences with GOLD.

LEARNING OUTCOMES

Upon completion of this workshop, participants will:
- Have an understanding of the structure of the certificate program.
- Have created a plan for earning certificates and deciding which workshops to attend.
- Know about extracurricular activities they can consider. This includes specific student organizations and volunteer opportunities.
- Have been encouraged to create a cocurricular involvement transcript.

WORKSHOP ACTIVITIES

- The session is structured around a worksheet that both the mentor and student are given at the beginning of the session. The worksheet serves as a guide to the session as the mentor and student have a dialogue about each section of the worksheet. The sections build upon each other as the session starts with a discussion about what the student did in high school and leads to what the student could do in college or later.
- The mentor takes the student to the GOLD website and Knightlink to illustrate the options that students have to join student organizations. The mentor also brings up their own Cocurricular Involvement Transcript on the computer to demonstrate how it may be established and used during college.

RESOURCES USED

Matthews, T. (2010). *Personal Development Session Worksheet.*

PERSONAL FINANCE SERIES: BASICS OF MONEY MANAGEMENT

CERTIFICATE: Bronze | **INSTRUCTOR:** Dr. Michael Schinski, Dean and Professor, Jones School of Business

"This workshop showed me that if I can put just a little money away every year, I can hope to be more comfortable when it comes to retirement."

Amy, sophomore, 2012

WORKSHOP DESCRIPTION

In today's economic environment, keeping your financial house in order can be a challenge. Through this workshop, participants learn the basics of money management and personal finance. Find out about the key do's and don'ts when it comes to achieving financial success. The session will address budgeting, debt management, saving and investing, and the power of compound interest.

LEARNING OUTCOMES

Upon completion of the workshop, participants will:
- Understand the time/value of money concept.
- Know how to build long-term wealth and security.
- Understand the key concepts of money management.
- Understand and be able to practice the three principles of financial planning.

WORKSHOP ACTIVITIES

- This workshop is presented in a lecture format.
- The instructor provides information about financial consequences and feelings of financial safety and security.
- Using the handout on the three principles of financial planning, the instructor offers several real-life examples related to each of the principles.
- Using the handout on the magic of compound interest, the instructor contrasts the experiences of two hypothetical individuals.

RESOURCES USED

Miller, M. (2012). Yahoo Finance: 6 Retirement Moves for the Young. Retrieved from
       http://finance.yahoo.com/news/the-6-most-important-retirement-moves-for-the-young.html.
Schinski, M. (2011). *Handout on Three Basic Principles of Financial Planning.*
Schinski, M. (2011). *Handout on the Magic of Compound Interest.*

"Beware of little expenses; a small leak will sink a great ship." —Benjamin Franklin

PERSONAL FINANCE SERIES: BUILDING PERSONAL WEALTH

CERTIFICATE: Bronze | **INSTRUCTOR:** Kevin Gavagan, Owner, QCI Asset Management

"This workshop opened my eyes and has encouraged me to start thinking about saving money for my future. I now know how to invest my money and how to save my money by setting up a retirement plan."

Alexandra, freshman, 2012

WORKSHOP DESCRIPTION

Learn from an independent financial planner the tools and techniques to start you on the road to a more secure financial future. Learn how planners interact with clients to achieve goals through saving, asset allocation strategies, and managing income streams. Common terminology and the types of decisions you may need to make for your own future such as 401(k)s, 403(b)s, and Roth IRAs will be discussed.

LEARNING OUTCOMES

Upon completion of this workshop, participants will:

* Have a basic understanding of what financial planning is and how to sustain one's lifestyle in retirement.

WORKSHOP ACTIVITIES

* The instructor introduces himself and his background in financial planning.
* Financial planning and the importance of savings are described.
* The instructor shares ways to start saving for retirement and possible deterrents to savings.
* Effects of compound interest and taxes on various retirement savings methods are explained along with an investor profile questionnaire.
* Graphs are presented that compare returns on stocks, bonds, Treasury bills, and money market funds. The effects of inflation and taxes on these investments is shown.
* The importance of maintaining discipline despite the market's emotional roller-coaster impact is emphasized.
* Participants have an opportunity to take part in a question-and-answer period.

RESOURCES USED

Gavagan, K. (2012). *Handout on Financial Planning Packet.*

"It requires a great deal of boldness and a great deal of caution to make a great fortune, and when you have it, it requires ten times as much skill to keep it." –Ralph Waldo Emerson

PERSONAL FINANCE SERIES: DEALING WITH DEBT COLLECTORS

CERTIFICATE: Bronze | **INSTRUCTOR:** Chad Reflin, Director Credit Education Bureau of Rochester

"I have never 'officially' had to deal with a debt collector but as a college student with varying amounts of spare cash I have borrowed from friends and eventually paid them off. I feel though it is bound to happen at some time, especially by the time I am done with all of my schooling. I feel prepared to handle these situations, should they occur, and help out others that may be experiencing the same problem."

Katelyn, sophomore, 2011

WORKSHOP DESCRIPTION

This workshop is the perfect way to gain the knowledge and confidence to tackle old collection debts with skill and ease. The class covers what collectors can and cannot do, how debt collectors get paid, options for responding to a debt collector, record keeping, enlisting the help of an attorney, and options when a debt collector violates the law. The workshop is designed to include a presentation followed by group participation from workshop participants.

LEARNING OUTCOMES

Upon completion of this workshop, participants will:
- Know the rights of collection agencies when trying to recover payments.
- Be able to identify and react accordingly when a collection agency is illegally attempting to recover debts.

WORKSHOP ACTIVITIES

- The instructor presents a PowerPoint with printed copies as handouts. Participants are able follow along and take notes if they care to do so.
- After the presentation, the instructor has two participants read *You Make the Call* and play the roles of debt collector and debtor.
- Participants are broken into groups and asked to discuss what illegal actions the debt collector was making, what the debtor was doing incorrectly, and how the debtor should respond.
- After some time, the presenter facilitates a dialogue between all groups and participants covering what the groups had discussed: what illegal actions the debt collector was making, what the debtor was doing incorrectly, and how the debtor should response.
- The workshop ends with the instructor providing time for participants to ask questions and gives participants two worksheets, *Statute of Limitations* and *Account Type and Debt Collection Worksheet*.

RESOURCES USED

Credit Education Bureau. (2010). *Dealing With Debt Collectors.*
Reflin, C. (2010). *Handout on You Make the Call.*
Reflin, C. (2010). *Handout on Account Type and Debt Collection Worksheet.* Adapted from the Credit Education Bureau.
Reflin, C. (2010). *Handout on Debt Collection Contacts.* Adapted from the Credit Education Bureau.
Reflin, C. (2010). *Handout on Statute of Limitations PowerPoint.*

PERSONAL FINANCE SERIES: FINANCING GRAD SCHOOL AND MANAGING STUDENT LOANS

CERTIFICATE: Bronze | **INSTRUCTOR:** Archie Cureton, Director, Financial Aid

"My story connected to this workshop involves my interest in attending a veterinary school after college. This subject had always made me a bit fearful because I had my first job this past summer, and I will be solely responsible for any education after my undergraduate studies. This workshop helped me to see that there are ways that I can afford the education I need to receive the job I envision myself having."

Breanne, freshman, 2011

WORKSHOP DESCRIPTION

Are you concerned about financing graduate school or what you need to do to manage paying off existing college loans? This session will help participants prepare for managing their loans and other financial commitments after graduation. This lecture-based workshop uses a reference guide to offer participants information about finding funding for graduate school and provides tips on how to manage existing student loans upon graduation.

LEARNING OUTCOMES

Upon completion of this workshop, participants will:
- Understand the different methods of funding graduate school (fellowships, grants, federal aid, etc.).
- Have explored different aspects of managing student loans, including the grace periods, repayment plans, and loan consolidation.
- Know how to manage a budget and become credit-card savvy.

WORKSHOP ACTIVITIES

- The instructor discusses the following topics while referencing the EXIT Counseling Guide for Direct Loan Borrowers:
  - When to apply for financial aid
  - Eligibility for financial aid
  - Assistantships, teaching grants, fellowships, etc.
  - Different types of loans
  - Consolidation of loans and grace periods
  - Repayment plans and interest rates
  - How to budget expenses
  - Credit card caution
  - How to start saving early
  - How to properly communicate with lenders and negotiation techniques

RESOURCES USED

Cureton, A. (2011). *Handout on EXIT Counseling Guide for Direct Loan Borrowers.*
Cureton, A. (2011). *Handout on Managing Your Student Loan Debt.*

PERSONAL FINANCE SERIES: FINANCING YOUR LIFE

CERTIFICATE: Bronze | **INSTRUCTOR:** Bonnie Swanson, Branch Manager, Key Bank of Geneseo

"This workshop encouraged me to plan diligently now and invest diligently now in many areas so that I can experience the benefits later on in life."

Nathanael, sophomore, 2012

WORKSHOP DESCRIPTION

In this day and age, knowing your FICO score is imperative to living a comfortable life. Don't understand what FICO is? Come and learn from a professional who is well-versed in the financial world. It is important that money is well managed and monitored and that people take charge of their lives and bank accounts. The instructor will explain how to interpret the FICO score and how the FICO score can be used to obtain car loans, mortgages, etc. The focus of this workshop is to encourage students to responsibly establish credit. Participants are encouraged to be proactive about building credit.

LEARNING OUTCOMES

Upon completion of the workshop, participants will:
- Be able to articulate how credit scores can affect loan rates.
- Demonstrate an understanding of how to responsibly build credit.
- Be able to differentiate myths and facts concerning credit.

WORKSHOP ACTIVITIES

- This workshop starts with a basic overview of the FICO score and how it affects personal finances throughout life. There are many opportunities for participants to ask questions, and the workshop goes in the direction of the questions asked.
- The instructor covers the following basic information:
  - The FICO score is the most common credit score and has a range of 300 to 850.
  - Individuals who have a higher score are considered to be a lower risk for banks. Therefore, individuals with a higher score get a better loan rate.
  - A credit score is made up of many factors, of which the most important is the individual's payment history. This is a review of what transactions show up on a person's credit history. For example, student loan and credit card payments will show up on a credit history. Cable bills and energy bills do not show up in a regular credit history. However, if the utility bill goes unpaid and ends up in a collection account, that will lower the individual's credit score.
  - There is a breakdown of how the credit score is determined.
  - Debit cards vs. credit cards are discussed.
- Participants fill out the *Real World Math* worksheet, with discussion on the answers following.

RESOURCES USED

Swanson, B. (2012). *Handout on Hypothetical Example of Compounding Interest and the Power of Starting Early.*
Swanson, B. (2012). *Handout on Real World Math.*
Financial Education Center. www.key.com/moneymadeeasy
https://www.key.com/business/resources/understanding-credit-scoring.jsp

PERSONAL FINANCE SERIES: INVESTING IN THE STOCK MARKET

CERTIFICATE: Bronze | **INSTRUCTOR:** Zubair Dawood, Student Managed Investment Fund (SMIF) Manager

"When I was younger, my dad used some of my money to invest in the stock of the Corning Glass Company. I followed the stock market closely, watching as the price of my stock fluctuated, plummeting after the September 11th terrorist attacks and subsequent collapse of Wall Street, and then rebounding slowly afterwards. My stocks performed terribly and I was very curious on why this was and how I could have been more knowledgeable in choosing the stocks. I now know that it is important to look at the individual company's business plan and account balances to see if the company is trustworthy."

Toby, junior, 2011

WORKSHOP DESCRIPTION

Student managers of the Student Managed Investment Fund (SMIF) at Geneseo share their recent experience buying and selling stocks. Learn from their School of Business training and hands-on experience with financial analysis, searching for opportunities, and managing a portfolio. This session will provide tips and tools you will need to get started with investing in the stock market. The lecture-style workshop helps students realize the power of the stock market and how to access resources that may assist them with their personal investments.

LEARNING OUTCOMES

Upon completion of this workshop, participants will:
- Understand what stocks are and how the market works.
- Know the functions of exchange.
- Know how to begin investing in the stock market.
- Gain awareness of the opportunities available through SMIF.

WORKSHOP ACTIVITIES

- Using a PowerPoint presentation, the instructor introduces the concepts of stock and the stock market.
- The instructor outlines the logistics of stock trading and lists several major stock exchanges as well as a brief description of the New York Stock Exchange. He also explains how stock markets work, the determinants of a stock's price, anticipated futures of stocks, the economics of stocks, and personal investing.
- The instructor explains the opportunities SMIF brings to the Geneseo campus: bottom up/bottom down analyses of markets, identifying long-term trends, understanding industry dynamics, and establishing buy/sell targets.

RESOURCES USED

Dawood, Z. (2010). *Investing in the Stock Market PowerPoint.*

"Rule No.1: Never lose money. Rule No.2: Never forget Rule No.1." –Warren Buffett

PERSONAL FINANCE SERIES: NAVIGATING THE CREDIT ROAD

CERTIFICATE: Bronze | **INSTRUCTOR:** Chad Reflin, Director, Credit Education Bureau of Rochester

"Most young adults don't know the first thing about credit and how to handle it, but I can now say that I will not have that problem."

Jessica, sophomore, 2011

WORKSHOP DESCRIPTION

Understanding the ins and outs of credit can be like trying to fight through a treacherous maze. One wrong move or turn can lead to disastrous consequences with long-lasting effects. Navigating the Credit Road leads students through the process of establishing and maintaining good credit without becoming burdened by debt. Participants will learn how to order their credit report for free from the annual credit reporting service, read and understand the information in the credit file, how credit scores work, what things affect their credit score, how to establish and maintain good credit without going into debt, and how to live a lifestyle that uses good debt instead of bad debt.

LEARNING OUTCOMES

Upon completion of the workshop, participants will:

- Be able to interpret a credit report.
- Know how to effectively write a credit report dispute letter.
- Demonstrate understanding of different types of credit scores.
- Be able to differentiate between myths and facts concerning credit.

WORKSHOP ACTIVITIES

- The instructor briefly outlines the handouts and asks who has already checked their credit scores and/or requested a credit report.
- Participants are encouraged to use annualcreditreport.com (a secure, government-endorsed website) and not freecreditreport.com (which actually charges a fee, despite the name of the website). When using annualcreditreport.com, be sure to check the box that masks the social security number.
- Annualcreditreport.com will give the option for three credit report venues: Experian, Equifax, and TransUnion. Experian is the easiest to use, but they are all legitimate options.
- Throughout a PowerPoint presentation, the instructor provides the following credit advice:
  - If there are errors on the credit report, one may write a dispute letter and send it directly to their preferred credit report venue. (See the sample letter of dispute.) Up to 70% of all credit reports have errors. Sending one dispute letter will correct the information in all three credit report venues. The company will contact the individual if changes are made. Although it is relatively safe to make changes online, the law only protects changes that are made in writing and sent via certified mail.
  - Not all credit scores are equivalent. The FICO score is the most common (this is the credit score that Suze Orman uses) and has a range of 300 to 850. One can obtain a FICO score from myfico.com (this costs about $15) or annualcreditreport.com (this costs about $8).
  - The Vantage credit score evaluates "thinner" credit files and has a range of 501 to 990. The Vantage score also gives a letter grade and costs about $5.
  - Two other forms of credit score are the Plus Score and the Trans Risk score.
  - Bankrate.com is a free website to use for estimating one's credit score and has a 25-point range. On this website, one may change certain variables to see what will happen.
  - Responsible use of student loans and a credit card will positively affect the credit score.

- A secured credit card may be a good option for college students. A secure credit card requires that the holder make a security deposit on the card. In this scenario, the credit limit is equal to the amount of the security deposit. Once the cardholder establishes credit, they get their deposit back.

RESOURCES USED

Reflin, C. (2011). *Handout on Sample Dispute Letter.*

Reflin, C. (2011). *Handout on Community Resources.*

Reflin, C. (2011). *Handout on Sample Credit Report.*

Reflin, C. (2011). *Navigating the Credit Road PowerPoint.*

"The more credit you give away, the more will come back to you. The more you help others, the more they will want to help you."
—Brian Tracy

PLANNING AND LEADING SERVICE TRIPS

CERTIFICATE: Diamond or Sapphire | **INSTRUCTOR:** Kay Fly, Coordinator, Volunteerism & Service Learning, and Dr. Tom Matthews, Director, Associate Dean of Leadership and Service

"I may find myself in a leadership position as I gain experience and this has provided me with a good base to begin considering or planning a trip."

Emily, freshman, 2012

WORKSHOP DESCRIPTION

If an individual's passion is service work and s/he would like to further develop his/her service and leadership skills, this workshop is designed for him/her! Learn what is involved in planning a successful service event or in leading a group of peers on a service-related activity. This workshop will cover the do's and don'ts and help prepare participants to step into the role of a team leader or trip coordinator.

LEARNING OUTCOMES

Upon completion of the workshop, participants will:
- Have an understanding of the mechanics of running a service trip.
- Know the leadership responsibilities and roles associated with leading trips.
- Have reflected on what motivates participants.

WORKSHOP ACTIVITIES

- Participants find a partner and tell each other why they want to be a part of service trips or become a service leader. After a few minutes, the participants share their responses with the rest of the workshop.
- The participants receive *The Continuum Exercise* and fill it out. Participants are then asked to discuss their responses.
- The definitions of the three leadership styles (autocrat, democrat, and laisséz faire) are discussed. Participants are asked if they considered themselves democratic leaders. After they share their responses, the instructor asks them to imagine themselves in a situation where they had to be the leader. Would the participants then still remain democratic? The participants discuss their responses, and the instructor emphasizes the importance of being a good listener.
- A hypothetical situation is given where a group of volunteers is on a service trip, and it is close to noon. The group wants to take their lunch break and go to the beach. However, the site leader wants the project finished that day and there is still 45 minutes of work to do. As the project leader, what would you do? Participants discuss this situation.
- Another hypothetical situation is described that involves the whole service group on their lunch break at the beach where there is an ice chest full of beer bottles. Some of the participants with the service project are being tempted to drink the beer. When making the decision, one must keep in mind that the organization has a zero tolerance policy for alcohol on school-sponsored activities and trips. Participants discuss their responses.
- Participants brainstorm as many components of a service trip as they can.
- The handout on *Planning a Service Trip* is distributed and the importance of being flexible and having a high tolerance for ambiguity is emphasized. The instructors share some more personal stories about previous service trips and then the handout on *Planning and Leading Service Trips* is distributed.

RESOURCES USED

Arneson, E. (2009). *Handout on Livingston CARES, Questions to Think About, Reflect On, and Write in Your Journals.*
Axt, D. (Ed.) (2004). *The Continuum Exercise in Break Away Site Leader Survival Manual*, p. 11.
Matthews, T. (2010). *Handout on GOLD Workshop on Planning a Service Trip.*
Rogers, K. (2010). *Handout on Planning and Leading Service Trips.*

POWER COUPLES

CERTIFICATE: Bronze | **INSTRUCTORS:** Various couples, including:
- Tracie Lopardi Brown, Class of '95 & Attorney, Harris Beach PLLC, and Chris Brown, Class of '94 & Editor, *Bills Media Digest*
- Michele DeLass, Class of '85, Sr. Account Executive, Eagle Production Solutions, and JC DeLass, Class of '85, Station Manager at WYSL
- Stephanie Dickman, Assembly & Integration COE Manager, Geospatial Systems, ITT Exelis, and Doug Dickman, Manager of Information Systems, ITT Geospatial Systems, ITT Exelis
- Mark S. Kane, Class of '80, Partner, Kane & Sabo CPAs PC; President, Column of Hope Foundation, and Barbara Kane, Class of '80, Special Education Teacher, Co-founder, Column of Hope

"This couple proved that anything is possible with good planning and there is always more than one way to solve a problem."

Bianca, sophomore, 2010

WORKSHOP DESCRIPTION

Want to marry someone as driven as you are? In this session, we will take a look at the daily lives of two very busy married people. This workshop will provide participants with answers to questions such as "Can I have a family and still be successful?" Participants will learn how this couple balances personal life and work. While success is great, wouldn't people want to share it with another person?

LEARNING OUTCOMES

Upon completion of this workshop, participants will:
- Understand that it is possible to have a successful career and family at the same time.
- Have discussed the challenges faced by a couple who both have full-time jobs.
- Have learned tips on how to best balance personal life and work.

WORKSHOP ACTIVITIES

- The instructors introduce themselves and give a quick summary of the schedule for the workshop and what they hope to teach to the participants through the workshop.
- The instructors alternate telling their life stories and experience from college through graduate school, job searching, working full-time, buying a house, adopting a child, to where they are today. As they tell these stories, they point out both good and bad decisions they made along the way and answer any questions from participants.
- The instructors discuss how they currently keep their balance between personal and work life and give tips on how participants can do the same.
- To conclude the workshop, the instructors answer any remaining questions and offer to speak with anyone who would like further advice or to hear more of their story.

RESOURCES USED

No additional resources.

PREPARING YOUR RESUME

CERTIFICATE: Emerald | **INSTRUCTOR:** Kerrie Bondi, Career Counseling, Elizabeth Seager, Associate Director of Career Development, and Stacey Wiley, Director of Office of Career Development

> *"I learned the 'ins and outs' of preparing a quality resume. I learned about the characteristics of a good resume, including being skill- and accomplishment-oriented, and meeting the requirements of the potential employer or job. A resume is a living document that should be constantly changing."*
>
> *Lauren, sophomore, 2012*

WORKSHOP DESCRIPTION

Got a resume? If not, this workshop will help you get started. A review of resume content and structure will be followed by a question-and answer period to address any questions concerning how to write and produce a professional resume.

LEARNING OUTCOMES

Upon completion of this workshop, participants will:
- Understand the purpose of a resume.
- Know the basic definition, purpose, and proper components of a resume.
- Have an awareness of the resources offered by Career Development to produce a quality resume.

WORKSHOP ACTIVITIES

- The instructor asks the participants to introduce themselves, including name, major, school year, and whether or not they currently have a resume. This helps the instructor see if the focus of the workshop should be on basic resume concepts (if a majority of participants do not have a resume at all) or on details that help fine-tune an existing resume (if a majority of participants do have a resume).
- The majority of the workshop is a PowerPoint presentation that outlines each part of a resume, starting with the contact information and ending with references.
- The instructor stops at various points throughout the workshop to answer questions about resumes in general or questions related to a participant's major and/or career.
- The workshop concludes with an open question-and-answer session and a major-specific handout that outlines resume tips for students.

RESOURCES USED

Bondi, K., & Seager, E. (2011). *Resume Writing PowerPoint.*
SUNY Geneseo Office of Career Development. (2011). *Handouts on Major-Specific Resumes:*
- *Resume and Cover Letter Guide for Educators*
- *Resume and Cover Letter Guide—Business*
- *Resume and Cover Letter Guide —Liberal Arts and Sciences*

> *"Be impeccable with your word. Don't take anything personally. Don't make assumptions. Always do your best." – Don Miguel Ruiz, from The Four Agreements: A Practical Guide to Personal Freedom*

PRESENTATION SKILLS

CERTIFICATE: Bronze (Required) | **INSTRUCTORS:** Dr. Joseph Bulsys, Professor of Communication, and Dr. Andrew Herman, Associate Professor & Chair of Communication Department

"This workshop helped me to become a better public speaker, because of the techniques and tricks that the instructor taught."

Mike, junior, 2011

WORKSHOP DESCRIPTION

This workshop is designed to help students learn how to develop effective speeches and presentations, work on strategies to overcome fear of speaking in public, and utilize resources to make effective presentations. Using mini-lectures to set up hands-on activities, participants explore the working components of an effective public presentation or speech. Concepts covered within the workshop include preparing effective presentations and speeches, developing and organizing a thesis and main points, overcoming anxiety through preparation, and learning a strategic approach for organizing presentations.

LEARNING OUTCOMES

Upon completion of the workshops, participants will:
- Demonstrate knowledge and understanding of the components of an effective presentation or speech.
- Be aware of available resources they can use to help create effective presentations.
- Be able to compare organizational structures in speechmaking.
- Be able to describe strategies they can use to overcome a fear of public speaking.

WORKSHOP ACTIVITIES

- The instructors discuss why presentation skills are important for our personal and professional lives.
- The instructors discuss the components of a presentation and basic principles of design. Topics include:
  - Determining the specific purpose of the presentation
  - Considering what an audience would remember most out of a presentation
  - Balancing speech timing:10% introduction, 85% body, 5% conclusion
  - Understanding the importance and function of an effective introduction and conclusion
- After a brief lecture about topic development, participants use mind-mapping to brainstorm their own core idea and appropriate sub-categories. The discussion is supported by personal examples from the instructor.
- Another lecture segment prepares and encourages the participants to organize their core idea and sub-categories into an effective speech structure.
- A final segment addresses issues of speech timing and creating an appropriate introduction and conclusion. Participants craft an introduction and conclusion related to their core idea and anticipated audience.

RESOURCES USED

Bulsys, J. (2010). *Handout on Presentation Skills.*

PRESENTATION SKILLS II

CERTIFICATE: Silver | **INSTRUCTOR:** Dr. Andrew Herman, Associate Professor and Chair of Communication Department

"In the future, I am planning to use this program in my Residence Assistant position to give more captivating speeches, and express the points I need to make in a more elaborate way, to really captivate people's interest and to make what I'm saying entirely clear."

James, junior, 2011

WORKSHOP DESCRIPTION

This interactive workshop builds on the foundational skill of organizing presentations as discussed in Presentation Skills. Topics include reducing anxiety, developing self-awareness, and using the voice and body. Workshop activities and student practice will reinforce skills.

LEARNING OUTCOMES

Upon completion of this workshop, participants will:
- Demonstrate an understanding of basic issues of vocalics, eye contact, and nonverbal behavior.
- Recognize and better handle the "anxiety inducers" of public speaking.

WORKSHOP ACTIVITIES

- The instructor gives an overview of how the workshop will run and then distributes pages from a children's book to the participants.
- The instructor lists the "anxiety inducers" of public speaking and talks about several ways to deal with them.
- The instructor splits the audience into groups of three to four participants each. These groups go into separate rooms to work on the same interactive activities. Upper-level students assist by leading the activities in each room.
- The first activity focuses on vocal production and manipulation. Participants quickly practice and read a children's story in the packet. Afterward, the instructor discusses manipulating the voice, such as pitch, rate of speech, and pauses, in different areas of the story. After a small amount of practice, each participant reads his/her story again, trying to change his/her voice as needed to improve the impression of the story.
- The instructor of the group reviews eye contact while speaking. Each person of the group is encouraged to tell a short story during which s/he makes eye contact with each other person in the group for two to three seconds before moving on. Each listener holds up a hand until the speaker maintains proper eye contact. Participants learn that short periods of eye contact are possible and beneficial.
- To develop an awareness of nonverbal communication, all groups come back together in one room and split into new groups of three to four people. First, people in the groups talk for a few minutes about what they have learned so far in the workshop. The instructor stops the conversations and asks questions about what the audience members were doing non-verbally, and emphasizes being conscious of non-verbal behaviors and observing oneself. Before concluding the workshop the instructor has each group talk again for two minutes, but this time being observant of their non-verbal signals.

RESOURCES USED

Excerpts from any "read-to" children's book.

Herman, A. (2010). *Handout on Teacher's Guide for Presentation Skills II.*

PROBLEM SOLVING

CERTIFICATE: Bronze or Diamond or Sapphire | **INSTRUCTOR:** Barbara Wale, Class of '75, President/CEO, Arc of Monroe County

> *"When solving a problem, it is important that the solution does not act like a Band-Aid®, but that it eliminates the cause of the problem."*
>
> *Sam, freshman, 2012*

WORKSHOP DESCRIPTION

Have you ever played the "whack-a-mole" game? In this session, participants will learn a methodology to solve problems so that they do not feel as if they are constantly hitting the same concerns, only in different areas. The workshop will discuss the process of problem solving in detail and participants will have some fun at the same time.

LEARNING OUTCOMES

Upon completion of this workshop, participants will:
- Be able to select and use appropriate problem-solving techniques.
- Be able to use the problem-solving process to address problems and opportunities facing their organizations and/or quality improvement teams.
- Be able to identify quality improvement projects that the participants and their teams can initiate.

WORKSHOP ACTIVITIES

- After the instructor introduces a problem-solving methodology, the participants are split into groups.
- Each group works together in a brainstorming session to brainstorm problems in the SUNY Geneseo community and write them on a piece of posterboard-size paper. The instructor explains the ground rules for brainstorming, which include: "Don't over-think; every idea counts; and every member contributes—get others involved!" The instructor offers an example of a well-defined problem: Mary is late to work 50% of the time. This does not allow her to participate in the initial briefing meeting. Coming to work promptly 100% of the time will increase teamwork and allow Mary to remain on the job. The group chooses only one problem to focus on and writes out the problem statement, desired state, and impact statement regarding that issue.
- Participants work together to identify the root causes of the problem through use of a fishbone chart, which is also called *ishikawa*.
- Participants brainstorm solutions to the root causes of the situation using specific criteria from the handout.
- Each group plans a solution, then implements and evaluates it. The instructor leads a large-group discussion about the activity.

RESOURCES USED

Wale, B. (2012). *Handout on Problem-Solving Process.*

> *"Have you got a problem? Do what you can where you are with what you've got." —Theodore Roosevelt*

PROFESSIONALISM IN THE WORKPLACE: DRESS AND IMAGE

CERTIFICATE: Emerald | **INSTRUCTOR:** Kerrie Bondi, Career Counselor

"I hope to make a very good impression at interviews by dressing appropriately and continuing my appearance throughout any internships or jobs that I acquire."

Katrina, freshman, 2012

WORKSHOP DESCRIPTION

What kind of impression do you make on people? What kind of impression do you want to make? This workshop will introduce you to the typical do's and don'ts for dress and image in the workplace. In addition, you will gain an understanding of what casual dress and professional dress mean and will walk away with ideas on how to make a lasting impression with your appearance.

LEARNING OUTCOMES

Upon completion of the workshop, participants will:

- Have discussed the roles, varieties, and acceptance of self-expression in the workplace.
- Demonstrate an understanding of how to learn workplace culture and adapt accordingly.
- Be able to self-assess and constructively critique their outward appearance and self-expression in various work settings.

WORKSHOP ACTIVITIES

- After copies of the PowerPoint presentation are passed out, the instructor discusses first impressions. Participants are asked to shake hands and introduce themselves to someone else in the room. The instructor asks participants to critique each other's first impressions.
- The instructor leads a discussion about the "Four As" of workplace dress (appropriate, affordable, attractive, and assured), starting with appropriate interview attire. Examples of traditional business attire do's and don'ts for men and women are shown on the PowerPoint. The difference between business casual and traditional business attire is covered. The discussion about appropriate dress is wrapped up with advice on what not to do and the suggestion to pay attention to the culture at your organization.
- For the remainder of the workshop, the instructor presents the PowerPoint slides and talks about image in reference to "how you sound," "what you say," and "how you act," and how these factors influence employers' perception of participants.
- The workshop concludes with the suggestion to dress, speak, and act on the side of caution, both in and outside the workplace, especially when starting a new career.

RESOURCES USED

Bondi, K. (2011). *Professionalism in the Workplace PowerPoint.*

"The world sums you up by the clothes that you wear, and treats you accordingly." –Al Koran

RECOGNITION OF CHILD ABUSE: WHAT HAPPENS NEXT?

CERTIFICATE: Sapphire | **INSTRUCTOR:** Kay Fly, Coordinator of Volunteerism & Service Learning; Livingston County Department of Social Services staff & Child Protective Services staff member

> *"Child abuse is a serious and sad situation and it's a tough topic to talk and think about, but I'm glad that I took this workshop so I can be prepared in case I ever need to report something."*
>
> *Gabrielle, senior, 2012*

WORKSHOP DESCRIPTION

Volunteers sometimes observe and need to deal with their suspicions of child abuse. This workshop will review the signs of child abuse and help participants sort through who is responsible for reporting the alleged abuse, and what happens after the reporting. This session is a must for students who volunteer to work with children. Working with children is a common and rewarding volunteer opportunity, but also one that comes with the added responsibility of being part of protecting their well being. This workshop brings in a guest instructor who is a child-protective case worker from the local County Social Services Department to discuss the rules, regulations, and realities of not only recognizing signs of abuse, but also the role of mandated reporters. Participants are given numerous real-life examples and the opportunity to ask questions, work through decision-making styles, and process feelings and experiences relating to issues surrounding child abuse and how reporting abuse impacts relationships. Further, each participant is given an orientation regarding what social services are available and how these services operate on a day-to-day basis.

LEARNING OUTCOMES

Upon completion of the workshop, participants will:
- Demonstrate an understanding of social services.
- Be able to explain the importance of volunteers within the system of mandated reporters.
- Know the signs of physical and sexual abuse.

WORKSHOP ACTIVITIES

- Participants are asked what they know about child abuse and Supplemental Programs and Services. The presenters share the responses, and the instructor explains that it could be as simple as an uncle or older sibling who abuses a child. The instructor briefly discusses the mandated reporter list.
- The instructor talks about when an individual is mandated to report an incident, and discusses what is considered abuse and maltreatment. The presenter explains that abuse is the more serious and involves all of the sex crimes. Abuse means physical injury, while maltreatment is neglect. Most of the time maltreatment involves substance abuse cases. Maltreatment also involves a lack of food and shelter.
- The participants learn how to recognize child abuse and maltreatment, and are asked what signs they think are associated with physical abuse and sexual abuse. Participants share their responses
- Appropriate people to contact to make a report is discussed along with what happens when the New York State Central Register is called. The protection and liability that the person who makes the call has is explained and who provides training for mandated reporters.

RESOURCES USED

Livingston County Department of Social Services Child Protective Unit. (2009). *Handout on Mandated Reporters in New York.*

Livingston County Department of Social Services Child Protective Unit. (2009). *Handout on Responding to Disclosures of Child Sexual Abuse.*

Livingston County Department of Social Services Child Protective Unit. (2009). *Handout on Normal/Suspicious Bruising Areas.*

REFLECTING ON YOUR COLLEGE EXPERIENCE AND MARKETING YOUR SKILLS

CERTIFICATE: Emerald (Required) | **INSTRUCTOR:** Elizabeth Seager, Associate Director of Career Development

"As the presenter went through the list of questions we should think of when analyzing our skills, I realized those were the same questions I was asking myself last summer when preparing my resume for pharmacy school applications."

Kirsten, senior, 2011

WORKSHOP DESCRIPTION

This session will focus on evaluating your college career and preparing you for life after Geneseo. Learn how to identify soft skills and transferable skills you've built as a student and employee and how to communicate those to a future employer or graduate program. This process will help you build stronger resumes and cover letters, in addition to improving your interviewing skills.

LEARNING OUTCOMES

Upon completion of this workshop, participants will:

- Gain an understanding of the importance of marketing skills to prospective employers.
- Gain an understanding of and identify self-management, functional, and work content skills.
- Be able to understand how to communicate and apply those skills to an employment situation through the resume, cover letter, and interview.

WORKSHOP ACTIVITIES

- This workshop is lecture-based and includes defining the three types of skills; a review of the top skills employers seek in new hires; questions to help students identify their skills from employment, academic, and extra-curricular experiences; and examples of how to communicate those skills on a resume and in an interview.
- After the lecture on skills and identifying experiences, students complete a group exercise. Students are instructed to (1) List five experiences where they have done something well and enjoyed completing it; (2) In groups of two–three, discuss at least two of those experiences with each other and brainstorm to identify the skills and personal qualities utilized and developed during that experience; (3) In the group, brainstorm and identify how these skills are linked to their career goals.
- The instructor conducts a brief wrap-up of the exercise, asking students for feedback in relation to the top 10 skills employers are seeking and what skills students would like to develop further.

RESOURCES USED

Bondi, K., & Seager, E. (2010). *Reflecting on Your College Experience and Marketing Your Skills PowerPoint.*

Downing, S. Identifying Skills Exercise. Retrieved from www.oncourseworkshop.com/Student%20Success%20Strategies. htm.

Seager, E. (2010). *Questions to Help You Analyze an Educational and/or Work Experience.* Office of Career Development, SUNY Geneseo.

"Success is the sum of small efforts, repeated day in and day out." –Robert Collier

RELATIONAL THEORY OF LEADERSHIP

CERTIFICATE: Gold | **INSTRUCTOR:** Wendi Kinney, Assistant Dean of Students for Fraternal Life & Off Campus Services

"I really like the relational model of leadership because it emphasizes the process and the purpose in a way that makes team members feel needed and useful. In addition, because the process is the overarching key, group members are able to think outside the box and make discoveries en route to the ultimate goal."

Jesse, junior, 2011

WORKSHOP DESCRIPTION

Positive relationships are critical to effective and thriving organizations. The GOLD program defines leadership as a relational process of people together attempting to accomplish, change, or make a difference to benefit the common good. In this session, participants will learn the major components of the Relational Leadership Model. This workshop serves as an introduction to one of several contemporary theories of leadership. As part of the Gold-level certificate, students are expected to explore a number of leadership theories and determine which theories they identify with. This workshop is split between a lecture seminar by the instructor and a series of interactive activities that are designed to foster reflection and interpretation of the relational theory of leadership in the framework of the participants' own leadership journey.

LEARNING OUTCOMES

Upon completion of this workshop, participants will:
- Be able to define relational leadership and have a good understanding of the key components.
- Have a deeper understanding of relational theory applications.
- Have begun the active process of forming a personal leadership model.

WORKSHOP ACTIVITIES

- Participants are each given a sticker to be used during a later activity. The instructor provides an introduction to relational leadership using the PowerPoint presentation and explains the key ideas of the theory.
- Participants will form their groups based on their sticker (one circle, triangle, oval, and square per group). Each student is given an instruction sheet based on their particular shape. The purpose is to demonstrate the concept of inclusion with specific types of group members (new member vs. experienced member, "negative Nancy" versus the peppy member).
- Participants are given five to eight minutes to conduct a scenario with their group to plan an event by using the information they have about each member of the group. After this is completed, each group is given a list of reflection questions to examine regarding the activity.
- After a few minutes, the instructor brings the groups back together and leads a discussion about how this activity relates to participants' experiences within student organizations. Emphasis is placed on a role of a leader to make others feel included in a group setting.

RESOURCES USED

Kinney, W. (2010). *Handout on Leadership Components.* Adapted from Komives, S., Lucas, N., & McMahon, T. R. (1998). *Exploring leadership: For college students who want to make a difference.* San Francisco, CA: Jossey-Bass.

Kinney, W. (2010). *Handout on Relational Leadership Activity.* Adapted from Komives, S., Lucas, N., & McMahon, T. R. (2007). *Instructor's guide for exploring leadership.* San Francisco, CA: Jossey-Bass.

Kinney, W. (2010). *Handout on Relational Leadership Questions.*

Kinney, W. (2010). *Handout on Relational Symbols.* Adapted from Komives, S., Lucas, N., & McMahon, T. R. (2007). *Instructor's guide for exploring leadership.* San Francisco, CA: Jossey-Bass.

Kinney, W. (2010). *Relational Theory of Leadership PowerPoint.*

Komives, S., Lucas, N., & McMahon, T. R. (2007). *Instructor's guide for exploring leadership.* San Francisco, CA: Jossey-Bass.

REMEMBER THE TITANS

CERTIFICATE: Opal | **INSTRUCTOR:** Isaiah Tolbert, Residence Life Resident Director, and Matthew Jordan, Residence Life Resident Director

"I realize that how I lead people is going to affect how they respond in times of adversity and how efficient they are going to be at doing their job, so it is up to me to instill the positive attitude necessary for us to be successful."

Toby, junior, 2011

WORKSHOP DESCRIPTION

Strong leadership can come in many different styles and from a wide variety of people. Particularly in times of crisis, leadership is essential to help quell a potentially dreadful situation. This interactive workshop will involve discussion of leadership as it pertains to the award-winning film, *Remember the Titans*, and some of the lessons it provides for individuals today and in the future. After taking this workshop, participants will always remember the Titans!

LEARNING OUTCOMES

Upon completion of this workshop, participants will:
- Understand the discrimination that occurred during the civil rights movement (and that which still occurs today).
- Be able to recognize and address different leadership styles.
- Be informed about the current state of prejudice in the world.
- Consider incorporating the values learned in *Remember the Titans* into their own lives.

WORKSHOP ACTIVITIES

- Using a PowerPoint presentation, the instructor outlines the goals of the workshop.
- The instructor discusses the historical context during which *Remember the Titans* is set, and the major events of the civil rights movement. The workshop mainly focuses on the differing views of the two coaches: One wishes to nurture the players to instill self-confidence; the other seeks to replicate the hardships of society on the players.
- The instructor plays clips from the movie and provides quotes from different characters. Participants are asked to discuss the quotes.
- At the end of the workshop, participants brainstorm ways to incorporate the ideas discussed during the workshop into their personal lives. The instructors share some of their own wisdom and helpful ideas.

RESOURCES USED

Jordan, M., & Tolbert, I. (2009). *Leadership in* Remember the Titans *PowerPoint*.

"It is in times of crisis that good leaders emerge." –Rudolph Giuliani

RESEARCHING LAW

CERTIFICATE: Ruby | **INSTRUCTOR:** Tom Ottaviano, Reference & Instruction Librarian, Milne Library

"When I interned at a Rochester law firm over winter break, I did not feel confident in my ability to help research law cases; however, after taking this workshop, I am able to take on those responsibilities."

Luke, junior, 2010

WORKSHOP DESCRIPTION

Law and legislation can potentially have a profound impact on much of what we study, yet finding information about them is often both confusing and difficult. Learn where to find discussion about federal and state codes, information about court cases, and reviews of legislation and how to use the powerful yet intimidating resources that hold this information. With a focus on the creation and interpretation of law, this workshop addresses the basic steps of passing a law and the various databases used for researching bills and judicial documents. Each student has a laptop, and the instructor's computer is projected onto a screen. This is an interactive workshop that facilitates hands-on learning.

LEARNING OUTCOMES

Upon completion of this workshop, participants will:
- Have an understanding of the process of turning a bill into a law.
- Know the specific types of information available for each step of the lawmaking process.
- Be able to use efficient databases to research legal information.

WORKSHOP ACTIVITIES

- The instructor describes the steps from turning a bill into a law: Proposed to Congress, goes to subcommittee, back to committee, back to Congress, House and Senate special committee to agree on legislation, President's desk. (Note: This is a simplification of the process, but this makes it easier to understand what documents are produced in the process and why.)
- The instructor explains the types of information available for each step, and how to find the desired information.
- Students select a bill that interests them or the instructor gives them one and they follow it from its introduction into Congress through to becoming an actual law.
- The instructor discusses the databases that these resources can be found in: THOMAS (Thomas.loc.gov), and FDSys (http://www.gpo.gov/fdsys/).

RESOURCES USED

Ottaviano, T. (2011). *Handout on Researching Law Worksheet.*
Ottaviano, T. (2011). *Handout on the Legislative Process: Tracking Legislation.*

"At his best, man is the noblest of all animals; separated from law and justice he is the worst." —Aristotle

RIGHTS AND RESPONSIBILITIES OF VOLUNTEERS

CERTIFICATE: Sapphire (Required) | **INSTRUCTOR:** Kay Fly, Coordinator, Volunteerism & Service Learning

"As a volunteer, it is your responsibility to give a 100 percent effort to the task at hand because you are there to help, and you must do it graciously with a smile."

Sam, freshman, 2012

WORKSHOP DESCRIPTION

As a volunteer, people have rights and responsibilities. This session will provide participants with both a set of expectations for them as a volunteer and expectations from the people that direct their volunteer work. Participants will learn the basic do's and don'ts of volunteer work.

LEARNING OUTCOMES

Upon completion of the workshop, participants will:
- Be able to explain the rights and responsibilities of volunteers.
- Utilize this understanding through individual volunteering opportunities.
- Be able to critically analyze volunteering opportunities and experiences.

WORKSHOP ACTIVITIES

- The instruction asks participants to describe their own experiences with volunteering and what volunteer experiences they have encountered.
- The participants split into small groups and get potential volunteer organization case problems. The instructor asks them to discuss and present how the example problem could be best handled with respect for both the volunteer and the agency.
- The participants remain in small groups for the next exercise and are given a difficult topic (e.g., teenage pregnancy, adult illiteracy, homelessness) to discuss. They are asked to think of possible solutions, who would object to that solution, why the solution may not have been tried yet, and who is responsible for this issue (individual, community, or federal government). The answers are then discussed with all of the participants.

RESOURCES USED

Fly, K. (2010). *Handout on Volunteer Rights.*
Fly, K. (2010). *Handout on Volunteer Responsibilities.*
Fly, K. (2010). *Handout on Personal Experiences of Homelessness.*

"Volunteers are paid in six figures…S-M-I-L-E-S." –Gayla LeMaire

ROLE OF STUDENT ORGANIZATIONS IN PROMOTING THE VALUES OF DIVERSITY & COMMUNITY

CERTIFICATE: Silver or Opal | **INSTRUCTOR:** Dr. Robert Bonfiglio, Vice President for Student and Campus Life

"The members of my fraternity serve as role models to our community and, as a student organization, it is our job to create a positive image for our society."

Basil, junior, 2010

WORKSHOP DESCRIPTION

The report *Campus Life: In Search of Community,* by the late former SUNY Chancellor Ernest Boyer, defined the fundamental elements of a highly functioning academic community. This workshop will examine the ways in which student organizations can demonstrate the values of diversity and community and contribute to Boyer's vision of a purposeful, just, open, disciplined, caring, and celebrative community. This discussion-based workshop is designed to encourage students to think about how their organizations can effectively promote values and impact the community.

LEARNING OUTCOMES

Upon completion of this workshop, participants will:

- Have an awareness of the values and characteristics of effective campus organization and campus communities.
- Have an increased understanding of how student organizations can impact member diversity and participation in its sponsored programs and activities.
- Have an increased understanding of how individual student organizations can contribute to the effective functioning of a campus community.

WORKSHOP ACTIVITIES

- The instructor explains Boyer's vision of a purposeful, just, open, disciplined, caring, and celebrative community. Participants are asked to reflect upon and discuss each attribute.
- The instructor distributes *Community Attributes Part I* and leads a discussion about how these values are reflected in the internal functioning of the organizations in which the participants are members.
- *Community Attributes Part II* is distributed, and the instructor leads a discussion about how others from outside the participants' organizations may perceive that these values are reflected in the functioning of the organizations.
- Participants are encouraged to critically analyze how their organizations need to change in order to better represent the characteristics of a highly functioning campus organization.
- Participants will consider a series of questions related to the role of the organizations in promoting the values of diversity and community.

RESOURCES USED

Bonfiglio, R. (2011). *Handout on Community Attributes Part I.* Adapted from Boyer, E. (1990). *Campus Life: In Search of Community.* San Francisco: Jossey-Bass.

Bonfiglio, R. (2011). *Handout on Community Attributes Part II.* Adapted from Boyer, E. (1990). *Campus Life: In Search of Community.* San Francisco: Jossey-Bass.

RUNNING EFFECTIVE MEETINGS

CERTIFICATE: Silver (Required) | **INSTRUCTOR:** Barbara Stewart, Lecturer, Mathematics Department

"I knew that a leader must prepare for the meeting in advance in order to run an effective meeting, but I have never thought about preparing for the next meeting as soon as that meeting is over."

Renee, sophomore, 2012

WORKSHOP DESCRIPTION

Effective and efficient meetings will keep your organization on track and encourage your members to keep coming back. This program will provide tips on setting the agenda, meeting procedures, interacting with participants, and following up.

LEARNING OUTCOMES

Upon completion of the workshop, participants will:
- Understand how to create a meaningful and purposeful meeting agenda.
- Be able to critically analyze good and bad elements of meetings.
- Know how to stimulate effective discussions in organizational meetings.

WORKSHOP ACTIVITIES

- The instructor notes that an effective meeting is one that meets its goals and that the purpose of a meeting will determine the agenda, the participants, and the logistics.
- In small group discussions, participants make lists of characteristics of good meetings. The participants generate a combined list on the board while discussing how these items help to make meetings run more smoothly and lead to accomplishing the objectives.
- The instructor distributes a worksheet that asks each participant to evaluate a recent meeting that s/he attended.
- To formalize these ideas, the group discusses the steps to an effective meeting in chronological order—what should be done before, at the beginning of, during, at the end of, and after the meeting. A handout is distributed and participants are encouraged to add to the list provided.
- Agenda writing is highlighted while addressing what to do before the meeting, and the instructor shares an agenda from a student organization meeting.
- While talking about what occurs during a meeting, a discussion is held regarding how participants want to be treated. Dealing with long-winded or unruly members is also addressed.
- The instructor leads participants in a brief review of the workshop. Emphasis is placed on writing a goal-oriented agenda, interacting with participants, and making sure that everyone is aware of the next steps.

RESOURCES USED

Stewart, B. (2011). *Handout on Evaluate a Meeting.*
Stewart, B. (2011). *Handout on Running Effective Meetings.*

"An effective meeting is 80 percent planning, 20 percent execution. Too often people spend most of their time in the meeting and the least amount of time getting ready for it. Plan better meetings. They don't just happen." Tim A. Lewis, Manager of Knowledge & Culture, Eddie Bauer

SAFE ZONE TRAINING

CERTIFICATE: Silver or Opal | **INSTRUCTOR:** Dr. Alexandra M. Carlo, Staff Psychologist, Health & Counseling

"In the future, I hope to use this content in order to make others and myself more aware of LGBT students and the daily obstacles they face, and also to make them feel more comfortable."

Maria, senior, 2011

WORKSHOP DESCRIPTION

This program is designed to develop a deeper awareness of and comfort level with sexual diversity, along with ways individuals can be supportive of gay, lesbian, bisexual, and transgender (GLBT) individuals. Personal ideas and assumptions related to GLBT topics will be addressed in an interactive format with ideas and reactions being openly discussed, along with ways to address sexual oppression. Through critical analysis of personal thoughts and feelings and group discussion, participants will examine their attitudes toward GLBT individuals. They will learn what terms are politically appropriate and comfortable to use, and how to provide a safe environment for GLBT individuals.

LEARNING OUTCOMES

Upon completion of this workshop, participants will:

- Be able to define heterosexism and homophobia.
- Be able to describe steps toward self-identification and self-acceptance.
- Understand the challenges faced during the "coming out" process.
- Know how to make a safe environment for someone who is GLBT.

WORKSHOP ACTIVITIES

- The instructor asks participants to provide responses to specific terminology. The instructor says a word and participants write down the first thing that comes to mind when they hear that word.
- The instructor asks participants to think about the time in their life when they first noticed that there was a difference in people and how significant that difference was. A group discussion follows.
- The instructor asks participants to write down things that identify who they are. They pick one of them and describe how they display that particular quality. Participants are asked to imagine that the government has just outlawed that quality and asks participants to think about how they would feel. The instructor also asks participants what they would do and how they would respond.

RESOURCES USED

Carlo, A. (2012). *Handout on Safe Zone.*
Carlo, A. (2012). *Safe Zone PowerPoint.*

"I hid for years. I was afraid. Hiding my life took more energy than I had imagined. I needed to stop. I was weary. I didn't know you had prepared this safe place." –Anonymous

SERVANT LEADERSHIP

CERTIFICATE: Gold or Diamond or Sapphire | **INSTRUCTOR:** Tamara H. Kenney, Assistant Dean of Students for Student Conduct and Community Standards

"This workshop made me want to integrate servant leadership into all areas of my leadership. I like the idea of it, of being a leader by prioritizing the needs of the people I work with and serve."

Iwona, junior, 2011

WORKSHOP DESCRIPTION

Robert K. Greenleaf defined servant leadership as the natural feeling by an individual to serve first and everything else will fall into place. This leadership model values the education, inspiration, and development of others. In a relaxed, fun, and participatory atmosphere, participants are given a brief introduction to the concept of servant leadership, are offered examples of servant leaders, and encouraged to explore other leaders and leadership opportunities for the elements of servant leadership. One of the principal benefits of this workshop is that it provides a different context and new language for participants to learn in discussing and analyzing leadership.

LEARNING OUTCOMES

Upon completion of the workshop, participants will:
- Know the components of servant leadership.
- Be able to apply these components to existing systems they are aware of.
- Have assessed personal leadership experiences and opportunities regarding how the elements of servant leadership could positively impact them.

WORKSHOP ACTIVITIES

- The instructor provides a brief introduction to servant leadership and shows a 7-minute video of *Dateline's* special on servant leadership.
- The instructor uses the PowerPoint and handout to help explain these ideas. The concept of servant leadership can be transformative to new participants because it provides yet another vehicle toward leadership and overall involvement in society by showing that sometimes, being part of the system is leadership.
- The instructor discusses the seven pillars of a servant leader, while inviting questions and examples from participants.
- Participants are asked to think of a club or organization to which they belong. On one side of a piece of paper they are asked to write down what they get from that organization. On the other side, they are asked to write what they give to that organization. Responses are shared and discussed in the context of servant leadership.
- Participants are asked to work together to come up with another working definition of servant leadership based on what they have shared and learned in the workshop.

RESOURCES USED

Greenleaf, R. K. (1996). *On becoming a servant leader.* San Francisco: Jossey-Bass.

Greenleaf, R. K. (1977). *Servant leadership: A journey into the nature of legitimate power & greatness.* Mahwah, NJ: Paulist Press.

Kenney, T. (2012). *Servant Leadership PowerPoint.*

Silverstein, S. (1964). *The giving tree.* New York: Harper Collins.

Sipe, J. W., & Frick, D. M. (2009). *Seven pillars of servant leadership: Practicing the wisdom of leading by serving.* Mahwah, NJ: Paulist Press.

SEVEN HABITS OF HIGHLY EFFECTIVE PEOPLE

CERTIFICATE: Silver | **INSTRUCTOR:** Dr. Elizabeth Hall, Associate Professor of Education & LIVES Program Project Director

"In order to have effective relationships with others, it is necessary to distinguish between your wants and needs, and work to ensure that the needs of both you and others are being met."

Sarah, junior, 2010

WORKSHOP DESCRIPTION

Stephen Covey developed a plan for building true success and personal leadership. This workshop will help participants to understand, through examples and a self-test, their strengths and weaknesses within each of the seven habits of highly effective people. This process should help clarify participants' vision and values and align their lives with these timeless Covey principles. In this lecture-based and interactive workshop, participants learn how to use the Seven Habits as a guideline to improving their own productivity. The activities provide participants with an opportunity to realize how the depth of information available can drastically change the opinions they hold. This inspires participants to seek out as much information as possible before making decisions and passing judgment.

LEARNING OUTCOMES

Upon completion of this workshop, participants will:

- Have learned the seven habits of highly effective people.
- Have awareness of their own strengths and weaknesses in order to create a plan to improve upon their weaknesses.
- Be able to strengthen their time-management skills.
- Have an understanding of the importance of considering other points of view before passing judgment.

WORKSHOP ACTIVITIES

- The instructor explains the history and the ideas of the Seven Habits model using a PowerPoint presentation.
- The instructor leads a visualization exercise that helps participants understand that one must understand others before expressing one's view. The instructor does this by telling everyone to close their eyes and listen to a scenario. Each scenario uses a paradigm shift, in which one half of a story is told, people explain what they think, and then the other half is told, which may change people's perceptions.
- The instructor asks participants to provide input to hear how opinions may have changed.
- The instructor also hands out a Time Management Matrix, in which participants can classify activities into one of four variables, ranging from Important & Urgent to Not Important & Not Urgent.
- The instructor asks each attendee to write down what they think their best friend, parent, and employer would give them as their top three characteristics. By doing this activity, the instructor tries to get people to stand back and look at themselves through another's eyes.

RESOURCES USED

Hall, E. (2012). *Seven Habits of Highly Effective People PowerPoint.*

Hall, E. (2012). *Handout on Seven Habits Profile.* Adapted from S. Covey, (2004). *The seven habits of highly effective people.* New York: Free Press.

SEXUAL HARASSMENT

CERTIFICATE: Opal | **INSTRUCTOR:** Gloria Lopez, Director of Affirmative Action, and Leonard Sancilio, Dean of Students

"It was very important for me to learn the policy of sexual harassment and to understand that actions or advances are not welcome and tolerated here, and it makes me feel safer as a college student."

Kristin, senior, 2011

WORKSHOP DESCRIPTION

Sometimes people who are being sexually harassed feel that if they ignore the problem it will go away. The truth is that the situation could continue or get worse. Learn what sexual harassment is and what steps you can take to have it addressed and make sure it stops. This workshop is intended to furnish participants with the tools needed to recognize sexual harassment as well as the means to report incidents.

LEARNING OUTCOMES

Upon completion of this workshop participants will:
- Understand the definition and terminology associated with sexual harassment.
- Identify situations and behaviors that could be perceived as sexual harassment.
- Understand their obligation and responsibility to create and maintain a harassment-free environment.
- Understand SUNY Geneseo's specific policy and procedures regarding sexual harassment.

WORKSHOP ACTIVITIES

- The instructor outlines why the issue of sexual harassment is so important and indicates which laws sexual harassment violates.
- Differences between all unlawful discrimination and sex discrimination are discussed.
- Participants learn how to recognize and report workplace harassment.
- The possible effects of sexual harassment are brainstormed by students and then discussed.
- Ways in which students can intervene at Geneseo are also discussed and participants are shown a list of resources available to them on campus.

RESOURCES USED

Lopez, G. (2010). *Sexual Harassment PowerPoint.*
Lopez, G. (2010). *Handout of the Sexual Harassment PowerPoint.*

"Sexual harassment is uncivil behavior. It expresses disrespect. It abuses authority. It exploits and undermines relationships based on trust. It interferes with learning and productive work. In short, it is a breach of community." Hunter R. Rawlings III, former president of the University of Iowa and Cornell University

SHACKLETON: LEADING ON THE EDGE

CERTIFICATE: Silver | **INSTRUCTOR:** Carey Backman, Associate Director College Union and Activities

> *"A leader should hold everyone accountable for their actions and not fall apart when people make mistakes. Instead, the leader should take that opportunity to learn from the situation and re-adjust plans to be successful next time."*
>
> Adam, freshman, 2008

WORKSHOP DESCRIPTION

Using the story of Shackleton and his ship the *Endurance*, this workshop focuses on 10 strategies for helping you lead at "the edge"—the extreme of what your organization is capable of accomplishing. Strategies like tenacious creativity and vision can help you to maximize your group's potential and push your organization to be the best it can be. We'll identify the 10 strategies, discuss how you can implement them within your own organization, and talk about how you can continue to develop your leadership abilities through a personal leadership plan.

LEARNING OUTCOMES

Upon completion of this workshop, participants will:

- Use the example of Shackleton to examine their own leadership techniques.
- Identify areas of leadership that need cultivating through the Critical Leadership Skills survey.

WORKSHOP ACTIVITIES

- The instructor asks students to reflect on a situation in which they were stretched to the limits of performance or endurance, and what qualities they used to persevere.
- The instructor shares the Ernest Shackleton and the *Endurance* story and goes over 10 strategies of leadership used.
- The instructor reviews the qualities and actions that contribute to living, learning, and thriving at the edge.
- Workshop participants take the Critical Leadership Skills survey and share results.
- The instructor suggests a personal development plan for students based on their results.

RESOURCES USED

Backman, C. (2012). *Leading at the Edge PowerPoint*.

Critical Leadership Skills Survey. (n.d.). Retrieved March 26, 2012, from http://vialogue.files.wordpress.com/2012/01/ critical leadership-skills-survey.pdf.

> *"Don't let anyone rob you of your imagination, your creativity, or your curiosity. It's your place in the world; it's your life. Go on and do all you can with it, and make it the life you want to live." –Mae Jemison, first African American female astronaut*

SITUATIONAL LEADERSHIP

CERTIFICATE: Gold | **INSTRUCTOR:** Kevin Hahn, Assistant Director of Residence Life

"This workshop changed my perspective and I now believe that it is important to adjust leadership styles and tactics based on the group you are working with, which was something I often struggled with. I look forward to implementing and developing these leadership styles with other groups and various situations. "

Krista, junior, 2011

WORKSHOP DESCRIPTION

As leaders, participants need to make adjustments in their leadership style based on the needs of the group or organization. This adjustment can be made in response to the group's demonstrated capacity level and its confidence and willingness with regard to performing tasks at the time they must be performed. This session will show ways to work with groups in different situations/levels.

LEARNING OUTCOMES

Upon completion of this workshop, participants will:
- Have gained an understanding of the premise of situational leadership.
- Know the characteristics and appropriate use of four different leadership strategies.
- Recognize the various developmental stages of individuals and groups.
- Be able to effectively use various leadership strategies to navigate a variety of situations.

WORKSHOP ACTIVITIES

- The workshop is a lecture-based overview of situational leadership theory. The instructor presents a summary and evaluation of the four leadership strategies—Directing, Coaching, Supporting, and Delegating. The instructor compares and contrasts the different strategies after participants are familiar with them and encourages participants to offer examples of each from students' lives.
- The instructor splits the workshop participants into two-person groups for "Drawing With Directions." One partner is given a semi-complex geometric drawing that the other partner is not allowed to see. The partner has to describe the drawing in order to get the other partner to draw the same drawing. Afterward, the group gets back together to discuss how this activity demonstrates people's different ways of thinking, understanding, and describing tasks. (Note: With a smaller group, all participants can draw while the instructor gives directions.)
- The instructor delivers a development levels lecture. Because this theory is based on the idea that different people are at different developmental levels, a theory of four different levels is discussed. These include Low Competence/High Commitment (needs Direction); Some Competence/Variable Commitment (needs Coaching); High Competence/Variable Commitment (needs Support); and lastly High Competence/High Commitment (needs delegating).
- The workshop splits up into two teams. The set-up, object, and rules of "A Twisted Game of Leapfrog" are described. After the challenge, groups discuss who took the role of the leader and what strategies were used.
- The instructor leads a discussion about playing the leader. A sample situation is provided by the instructor and participants must decide what leadership strategy is appropriate and why. This is a large group discussion.
- The last activity is a discussion of applying the four different leadership strategies.

RESOURCES USED

Blanchard, K., Zigarmi, P., and Zigarmi, D. (1985). *Leadership and the one minute manager: Increasing effectiveness through situational leadership.* New York: Morrow.

Hahn, K., and Klein, A. (2011). *Situational Leadership From Theory to Practice PowerPoint.*

Hahn, K. (2009). *A Twisted Game of Leapfrog: Situational Leadership.*

Hahn, K. (2011). *Drawing With Directions.*

SMART GOALS

CERTIFICATE: Bronze | **INSTRUCTOR:** Tamara Kenney, Assistant Dean for Student Conduct and Community Standards

"Creating a specific goal, such as completing a certain workout program, will be more attainable than a broad goal, such as running every day. By laying out my plans day by day I will be able to stay interested and complete my goal."
Matthew, freshman, 2012

WORKSHOP DESCRIPTION

Goals should be Specific, Measurable, Action-oriented, Relevant and Time-bound. Participants will learn how to create SMART goals and use them effectively to establish priorities that meet the needs of a group or organization. This workshop presents a strategy for creating and reviewing goals that is known as SMART. The application of the SMART goals strategy ensures that goals can be used by a person working on a short- or long-term task. In addition, a person can guarantee that their task is fulfilled to the desired level of quality while not wasting resources or time. Participants practice creating SMART goals and receive feedback from the instructor.

LEARNING OUTCOMES

Upon completion of this workshop, participants will:
- Have the ability to easily create effective and powerful goals.
- Know how to create step-by-step plans.
- Be able to critically evaluate their own plans.
- Understand how to revise goals and plans when needed.

WORKSHOP ACTIVITIES

- The workshop begins with an open discussion on what goals are, why goals are used, and how goals can help people.
- The instructor delivers the PowerPoint presentation and facilitates a group discussion about SMART goals.
- Participants are divided into two groups. Each team works together to create a SMART goal and writes it down on a large piece of posterboard. The instructor asks participants to start with a general statement and then list S, M, A, R, and T down the page, with a short description of how each component will be met.
- The two groups then rejoin in order to share their goals. The instructor leads an evaluation and discussion and adds constructive criticism and helpful suggestions.

RESOURCES USED

Doran, G. T. (1981). There's a S.M.A.R.T. way to write management's goals and objectives. *Management Review,* 70:11, 35–36.

Kenney, T. (2012). *S. M. A. R. T. Goals PowerPoint.*

Meyer, P. J. (2003). What would you do if you knew you couldn't fail? Creating S.M.A.R.T. Goals. Adapted from *Attitude is everything: If you want to succeed above and beyond.* Meyer Resource Group, Inc.

"I've worked too hard and too long to let anything stand in the way of my goals. I will not let my teammates down, and I will not let myself down." –Mia Hamm

SOCIAL CHANGE MODEL OF LEADERSHIP

CERTIFICATE: Gold or Diamond or Sapphire | **INSTRUCTOR:** Wendi Kinney, Assistant Dean of Students for Fraternal Life & Off Campus Services

"If a leader isn't sure of what his or her goals, beliefs, and motivations are, it is difficult to motivate a group effectively."
Brittany, junior, 2011

WORKSHOP DESCRIPTION

Do you aspire to be a change agent to make a difference in the world? The Social Change Model of Leadership will help you understand the basics of social change and the roles that leaders and followers play in the process of making changes for the common good. The workshop introduces the Social Change Model of Leadership, which encompasses 7 Cs: Consciousness of Self, Commitment, Congruence, Collaboration, Common Purpose, Controversy With Civility, and Citizenship. Participants discuss which of the Cs to focus on in certain situations, and how to implement the Social Change Model of Leadership.

LEARNING OUTCOMES

Upon completion of this workshop, participants will:

- Have a concrete understanding of the social change model and feel comfortable explaining it.
- Be able to compare the social change model to other theories of leadership.
- Know how to correctly and effectively implement this theory.

WORKSHOP ACTIVITIES

- The instructor divides participants into five small groups. Each group discusses an assigned aspect of social change: culture, conflict, ideas, demographics and social movements. The groups talk for several minutes, then each group shares examples of their topic with the rest of the workshop.
- Using the PowerPoint presentation and the handout, the instructor provides an overview of the social change model. The instructor focuses on the 7 Cs of the model.
- In small groups, participants evaluate case studies. The instructor gives each group one note card with one case study written on it. Each group is charged with determining how to use the model to tackle the issue, and agreeing on which of the 7 Cs needs to be given the most attention.
- Tips for the implementation of the model are discussed (see handout).
- A short video provides information about famous leaders using the social change model.

RESOURCES USED

Astin, A., & Astin, H. *Leadership reconsidered: engaging higher education in social change.* Battle Creek, MI: W. K. Kellogg Foundation.

Brungardt, C. (1999). *Social change leadership inventory.* (Expanded 2nd ed.) Longmont, CO: Rocky Mountain Institute for Leadership Advancement.

Higher Education Research Institute. (1996). *A social change model of leadership development.* Version III. Los Angeles: University of California.

Kinney, W. (2011*). Social Change Model of Leadership PowerPoint.*

Kinney, W. (2011). *Handout on the Social Change Model of Leadership.*

Knobloch, L. (Ed.). (1996). *Leadership for the new millennium: citizens of change program.* DePere, WI: St. Norbert College.

SOCIAL NETWORKING FOR PROFESSIONALS

CERTIFICATE: Ruby (Required) | **INSTRUCTORS:** Tracy Paradis, Reference & Instruction Librarian, and Justina Elmore, Business & Data Librarian

> *"Keeping up on the latest tools for social networking in the professional setting is also proof that I can adapt to change and am able to communicate with people who are potentially beneficial to a common cause."*
>
> *Abigail, freshman, 2012*

WORKSHOP DESCRIPTION

Become familiar with some of the social media technologies the savvy professional will need, including social networks, social bookmarking, and other relevant Web 2.0 applications. The focus of this workshop is to encourage students to establish good habits that lead to a professional online representation of themselves. Participants are encouraged to take advantage of presenting themselves in a positive manner in order to reap the benefits later in life.

LEARNING OUTCOMES

Upon completion of this workshop, participants will:

- Demonstrate knowledge of social networking sites.
- Be able to present themselves professionally by means of an online profile.

WORKSHOP ACTIVITIES

- The instructor explains Web 2.0 and how it allows users to interact, share, communicate, and even change the online content of some web pages.
- Participants are introduced to many different online resources:
    - Mashable.com, a social media guide
    - Go2web20.com, very updated page about available tools
    - Facebook
    - Twitter
    - Socialooomph.com, which allows individuals to schedule tweets
    - LinkedIn, a professional social networking site that has 2.9 million users in the United States
- Participants are instructed to use the same default profile picture for all social networking sites to establish an identity. Some say that "business" posed pictures may make a bad first impression and that a relaxed pose is better.

RESOURCES USED

Paradis, T., & Elmore, J. *Social Networking for Professionals*. Milne Library, SUNY Geneseo. 11 November 2009. Web. 3 February 2012. <http://www.geneseo.edu/~paradis/GOLD.SocialNetworking.html>

> *"Networking is not about hunting. It is about farming. It's about cultivating relationships. Don't engage in 'premature solicitation'. You'll be a better networker if you remember that." –Dr. Ivan Misner, bestselling author & founder of BNI*

STARPOWER®

CERTIFICATE: Opal | **INSTRUCTOR:** Kevin Hahn, Assistant Director of Residence Life

"In the future, as a leader, I must be very aware of the people in a group who might have less of a say and to never exploit them for my own monetary gain."

Bridget, senior, 2011

WORKSHOP DESCRIPTION

This provocative leadership game allows participants to play with power. It is a simulation of the distribution of power in society. Students with majors in education, political science, business, sociology, psychology, and communication may find this game of particular interest, but all students are welcome to attend.

LEARNING OUTCOMES

Upon completion of the workshop, participants will:
- Demonstrate an understanding of power in society and how that impacts individuals and groups.
- Generate ideas on changing power dynamics within society for the betterment of others.
- Be able to relate what happened during the simulation to how members of the Geneseo campus community are affected by differences in power.
- Be able to explain how understanding power makes individuals better leaders.

WORKSHOP ACTIVITIES

- After a brief introduction, the instructor explains that Starpower® is a simulation of the distribution of power in society. Participants should expect to have fun and contribute to discussions.
- The instructor explains that the game involves trading and bargaining. The goal is to have the highest score. Each player receives five chips and they can trade for different chips. Participants are given an explanation as to how the game is scored.
- Participants trade their chips as part of the first round and the scores are recorded. After the trading round, the participants break up into three groups: squares, those with the highest scores; triangles, those with the lowest scores; and circles, those in the middle.
- After participants are divided into groups based on their scores from the first trading round, a bonus round occurs. Each team is given three bonus chips and told that each chip counts for three points that can be added to any member on their team's score. The participants take a few minutes to decide who gets the bonus points from the bonus round.
- Another trading session occurs, and the scores are recorded. If needed, some members may shift from one group to a different one based on their results from the second trading round. Another bonus session occurs.
- The participants find out that the squares are given the opportunity to make the rules that will be carried out for the rest of the game. The triangles and circles have the chance to petition rules they would like to see happen, but the squares do not have to accept the rules.
- Another trading session occurs and the scores are recorded.
- The remainder of the workshop is spent discussing the main ideas of the workshop and what the participants learned and got out of the workshop.

RESOURCES USED

This workshop requires the purchase of materials from Simulation Training Systems. To purchase these materials, please visit www.stsintl.com/business/star_power.html.

Feld, S. L. (1997). Simulation Games in Theory Development, Sociological Forum. *Simulation Training Systems: Simulations for Businesses, Schools, and Charities*. Retrieved May 14, 2012, from http://www.simulationtrainingsystems.com

STARTING A NEW ORGANIZATION

CERTIFICATE: Bronze | **INSTRUCTOR:** Lauren Dougherty, Assistant Director, College Union & Activities

"I believe it is important to have the ability as students to start new groups, and it is a good thing to be familiar with the process. This GOLD workshop taught me that process."

Olivia, freshman, 2010

WORKSHOP DESCRIPTION

This workshop intends to inform students about the process of official recognition of organizations by the college. From the beginning of an organization as an idea and to finally earning school recognition, the workshop provides a step-by-step explanation of the process. This workshop is tailored to a small group of students interested in starting an organization.

LEARNING OUTCOMES

Upon completion of this workshop, participants will:

- Know how to increase their involvement in the college community.
- Have an understanding of how to start an organization on campus.
- Have developed some leadership skills, such as assertiveness.

WORKSHOP ACTIVITIES

- The instructor introduces herself and her position as Coordinator of Student Organizations & Campus Activities at the College Union.
- The instructor uses a PowerPoint slideshow that covers the steps to achieve recognition:
  - General facts about existing campus organizations
  - History of the New Organization Recognition Committee and the criteria NORC uses in whether to grant recognition or not
  - The actual application
  - Finding/the importance of an advisor
  - The necessary two GOLD workshops that must be taken
  - Working with the constitution template
  - Having the interest meeting
  - Getting the approval from impacted departments
  - Allowing the paperwork to move forward
- After the PowerPoint, the instructor shows students how to navigate and find things like the application and constitution template on the College Union website.
- The workshop concludes with a discussion as the instructor asks participants to share why they decided to attend the workshop, what potential organizations they were thinking about, and whether the recognition process had begun for their idea.

RESOURCES USED

Taraska, L. (2010). *Starting a New Organization PowerPoint.*

STARTING YOUR RESEARCH PROJECT USING MULTISEARCH & OTHER TIME-SAVING STRATEGIES

CERTIFICATE: Ruby | **INSTRUCTORS:** Michelle Costello, Education & Instructional Design Librarian, and Justina Elmore, Business & Data Librarian

"During the workshop I found myself thinking back on all of the times this past semester I was struggling to find effective supporting information and thought of how simple it would have been if I had already taken this workshop."
Alexandra, freshman, 2010

WORKSHOP DESCRIPTION

This workshop intends to help participants begin research for class assignments and to introduce participants to some of the more important resources and services. A new tool, MultiSearch, and a few databases, including Credo and CQ Researcher, will be discussed.

LEARNING OUTCOMES

Upon completion of this workshop, participants will:

- Know how to efficiently navigate the library's website.
- Understand how to identify and access the appropriate databases to find books and articles relevant to their research project.
- Know how to quickly access the full text of an item.

WORKSHOP ACTIVITIES

- The instructors begin the workshop by showing a brief clip from *The Da Vinci Code*. They explain the relevance of the clip to the workshop by saying that Robert Langdon was trying to solve a puzzle by going through different parts in his mind of places and things he previously encountered.
- The instructors distribute the handout "Starting Your Research Project—Ruby Workshop" and explain some basic tips listed on the handout. The instructors ask the participants to fill in Section 1 of the handout. After several minutes, the answers are discussed as a group.
- After explaining section 2 of the handout, the instructors show the participants the Books and Articles Quick Search section on the library website.
- The instructors draw a web chart on the board. "Research topic" in the middle, with four bubbles off of that which contain article bibliography, key concepts, topic overview, and Credo and other reference material for more terms. The main concept of the chart is to demonstrate that research is not always a linear process; it can be cyclical.
- The instructors show participants resources by subject page on the library website and explain some of the resources available, emphasizing the importance of picking different subjects by different disciplines.
- Participants then complete section 3 of the handout and the instructors explain the difference between the databases and Google Scholar.
- Sections 3 and 4 of the handout are discussed before the instructors talk about the Journals tab on the library website.
- To conclude the workshop, the instructors show participants how to request a student research consultation with a member of the library faculty.

RESOURCES USED

Calley, J., Grazer, B., & Howard, R. (2006). *The Da Vinci Code* [Motion picture]. United States: Imagine Entertainment and Columbia Pictures.

Costello, M., & Elmore, J. (2010). *Handout on Using Multisearch and Other Time-Saving Strategies.*

STRATEGIC PLANNING

CERTIFICATE: Silver | **INSTRUCTOR:** Carey Backman, Associate Director, College Union & Activities

"Maintaining motivation is one of the most crucial aspects of strategic planning because many people can lose focus or are resistive to change in general."

Ashley, junior, 2011

WORKSHOP DESCRIPTION

With so much organizational turnover each year, it's hard to have consistency unless you have a strategic plan in place. This workshop expands on students' already existing goal-setting knowledge by introducing them to strategic planning and challenging them to let their strategic plan become their legacy. Students will be guided through the process of developing a mission statement and vision and will learn how to use these as tools for long-term planning. They will also better understand the impact long-term planning has on the viability and success of an organization.

LEARNING OUTCOMES

Upon completion of the workshop, participants will:

- Be able to write a mission statement.
- Create a long-term vision using COWS (Challenges, Opportunities, Weaknesses, and Strengths).
- Hold a strategic planning meeting.
- Develop an action plan using SMART goals.

WORKSHOP ACTIVITIES

- The instructor starts the workshop by giving out a handout for participants to use to take additional notes.
- The instructor delivers a PowerPoint presentation addressing the planning process and the ideas behind strategic planning.
- Workshop attendees are asked to form small groups and to practice each of the steps outlined in the planning process.
- The instructor asks participants to provide feedback and examples regarding clubs or organizations in which they are involved with in and around campus.

RESOURCES USED

Bacal, R. (2009). Work911.com—Workplace, Business, Career Help. Retrieved September 1, 2009, http://work911.com/articles/change7.htm.

Backman, C. (2011). *Handout on Strategic Planning: Additional Notes/Information.*

Backman, C. (2011). *Electronic Presentation: Strategic Planning: How to Keep Your Organization Moving Forward.*

Doran, G. T. (1981). There's a S.M.A.R.T. way to write management's goals and objectives. *Management Review,* 70:11, 35-36.

George, C. *The Road Map to Success: Strategic Planning for Student Organizations.* Campus Events Professional, September 2005, 1-8.

Kralles, A. *Leading Organizational Change lecture.* SUNY Brockport. Spring 2007.

Meyer, P. J. (2003). What would you do if you knew you couldn't fail? Creating S.M.A.R.T. Goals. *Attitude Is Everything: If You Want to Succeed Above and Beyond.* Meyer Resource Group, Inc.

Ritchie, B. Retrieved September 1, 2009. http://www.consultpivotal.com/lewin's.htm.

STRESS AND YOUR HEALTH

CERTIFICATE: Bronze | **INSTRUCTOR:** Dr. Steven Radi, Medical Director, Health & Counseling

"Throughout college, I have experienced stress from leaving home, tons of schoolwork, a new environment, and taking biology classes. After taking this workshop, my stress levels have decreased."

Stephanie, junior, 2011

WORKSHOP DESCRIPTION

This seminar will explore the mind/body links as they apply to specific physical illnesses and anxiety states. Learn more about the relationship between anxiety/stress and physical symptoms of illness and clinical disease syndromes. Recognition of specific syndromes and intervention strategies will be discussed. This lecture-style workshop addresses an issue that is extremely relevant to the daily lives of college students. Many students struggle with anxiety and stress, and this workshop brings these issues out into the open. Students will be able to identify problems and learn where to turn for help. Plenty of time is allotted for students to ask questions, seek advice, and share personal experiences.

LEARNING OUTCOMES

Upon completion of this workshop, participants will:
- Understand how to take care of their bodies and minds to avoid illness.
- Have an awareness of the resources they can turn to for help.
- Know how anxiety affects physical health.

WORKSHOP ACTIVITIES

- The instructor begins the workshop by asking if anyone has any health-related questions.
- After answering questions, the instructor delivers a lecture in which he explains the link between anxiety and health, medical conditions which can mimic or cause anxiety, and types of medication that can help.
- The instructor explains the handout.
- The instructor leaves time at the end of the workshop for questions or personal experiences to be shared.

RESOURCES USED

Radi, S. (2009). *Handout on Anxiety Attacks and Disorders: Symptoms, Types, and Treatment.*

"I believe that stress is a factor in any bad health." –Christopher Shays, former Congressman

STRESS MANAGEMENT

CERTIFICATE: Bronze | **INSTRUCTOR:** Dana Minton, Coordinator of Health Promotion, Health & Counseling

"This workshop taught me how important it is to deal with stress in a healthy way and gave me the skills with which to do it."

Natasha, junior, 2011

WORKSHOP DESCRIPTION

Explore the basic techniques of stress management and alternative therapies for coping with stress. Guided imagery, breathing exercises, and progressive relaxation are all included, so comfortable clothing is recommended. This informal interactive workshop is held in a room with carpeting that is conducive to performing stress-relieving floor exercises.

LEARNING OUTCOMES

Upon completion of this workshop, participants will:
- Be more aware of the negative effects of excessive stress in their lives.
- Recognize some common factors that contribute to high stress levels in college students.
- Be able to use new methods of stress management (guided imagery, deep breathing, or progressive muscle relaxation) to control their own stress levels.

WORKSHOP ACTIVITIES

- The workshop begins with an active discussion of the following questions: What is stress, anyway? What stresses you out? How do you know you are stressed? What do you do to relieve stress?
- Most college students are stressed and can learn from each other how to handle and manage their individual stress loads. The instructor states that there is not one definition for stress and explains how each individual has optimal levels of stress that can be handled well. Stress management, then, is unique to the individual.
- The instructor provides a handout, *How Can You Manage Stress Better?* and explains each point, giving examples for several of them.
- The instructor asks participants to put their personal belongings away and find an open area or couch on which to sit or lie down. Diaphragmatic breathing is demonstrated by the instructor and practiced by participants, who are now relaxing comfortably on the floor or couches.
- The relaxation exercise from *Thirty Scripts for Relaxation Imagery & Inner Healing, Vol. 1,* is read by the instructor.
- The instructor reminds participants that by practicing these exercises, they will be able to recall the benefits in any time of stress and use them whenever needed.

RESOURCES USED

Lusk, J. T. (1992). *Thirty scripts for relaxation imagery & inner healing, Vol. 1.* Duluth, MN: Whole Person Associates.
Health Promotion. (2012). *Handouts.*
Minton, D. (2011). Geneseo Health and Counseling Center. *Handout on How Can You Manage Stress Better?*

"It's not stress that kills us, it is our reaction to it." —Hans Selye

STUDENT LEADERSHIP PRACTICES INVENTORY (SLPI™)

CERTIFICATE: Silver (Required) | **INSTRUCTOR:** Dr. Tom Matthews, Associate Dean of Leadership and Service

"This workshop reminded me that leadership can be learned and changed over time when necessary. I now know that it is dynamic, and involves constant involvement and input. This workshop gave me input about my own skills and has given me room to grow."

Iwona, junior, 2011

WORKSHOP DESCRIPTION

In order to participate in this workshop, you must be registered one month in advance. Students need to be involved in one or more organizations or groups in order to effectively utilize the Student Leadership Practices Inventory (SLPI™) instruments. You will receive a code to go online and complete the Leadership Practices Inventory and to invite specific individuals (observers) to provide feedback on your leadership practices. This inventory is provided FREE to students who complete the process! There will be a $15 fee billed to individuals who do not complete the process after the code has been assigned. A printed inventory report will be provided to each individual at the workshop.

LEARNING OUTCOMES

Upon completion of this workshop, participants will:

- Be aware of how observers view their leadership practices.
- Be able to critically self-assess their own areas of strength and weakness in their personal leadership practices.
- Develop and implement a dynamic plan to improve two of the components of their leadership practices that are identified as the weakest.

WORKSHOP ACTIVITIES

- Prior to attending the workshop, participants receive an email containing instructions on how to access the SLPI™ online survey tools. In order to attend the workshop, each participant must have a minimum of five observers complete the online observer survey and provide feedback on their leadership practices.
- As participants arrive at the workshop, they are asked to read a section from a workbook on the SLPI™ that describes each of the five leadership practices: model the way, inspire a shared vision, challenge the process, enable others to act, and encourage the heart. Participants are given approximately seven to eight minutes to read the four pages. Even though the online student license provides each student one year's full access to the materials on the five exemplary practices, very few students seem to take the time to read the materials prior to the workshop.
- The instructor briefly explains the background on the research conducted by Kouzes and Posner and published in *The Leadership Challenge*. The instructor also explains that students completing the GOLD Program should be able to demonstrate progress in improving the five leadership practices from the SLPI™. The database provides an opportunity to compare individual practices with thousands of successful leaders, including student leaders, who were asked to describe a peak leadership moment and to indicate what they did to make it a successful experience
- The instructor asks participants to focus on a great leadership moment or experience that they are most proud of and willing to share with others. Participants are assigned to triads and instructed to share their leadership moments with each other. After everyone has had a chance to share, the instructor asks a few participants to share their stories with everyone at the workshop.
- Before moving to the SLPI™ inventory results, the instructor shares a series of motivational quotes connected to each of the five leadership practices.

- The instructor distributes the printed SLPI™ reports to each participant and asks them to focus on the last page of the report, which contains a summary sheet of their SLPI™ profile. Each participant is given SLPI™ worksheets and a set of SLPI™ suggestions for each of the five exemplary practices and instructed to select two of the practices that his/her profile data suggests might need the most attention. Participants are asked to complete an action plan to work on the two practices within the next few weeks. The instructor moves around the room and reviews student profiles with each participant as they are working on their action plans.
- Each participant is asked to share one action step from each of the two practices with everyone in the workshop.
- The instructor hands out a slip of paper providing specific instructions for writing journal reflections for the SLPI™ workshop. Participants are asked to write about their proudest leadership moment and describe what role they played. The story could be the one they shared in the workshop or another positive leadership experience. The second part of the journal should be a report on their action plan describing what they did to improve their practices and whether or not it worked.
- The instructor instructs the participants to delay writing the journal for a few weeks in order to include the report on their action plan.

RESOURCES USED

This workshop requires the purchase of the SLPI™ online license for each student registered for the workshop. Emails are sent to each participant approximately 30 days in advance asking them to drop the workshop within a few days if they are not able to complete the process. The licenses are then purchased and instructions are sent directly to each student from SLPI™. Progress is monitored and reminders are sent to students and their observers.

Kouzes, J. M., & Posner, B. Z. (2010). *The leadership challenge*. San Francisco, CA: Jossey-Bass. This material is reproduced with the permission of John Wiley & Sons, Inc.

Leadership Practices Inventory. https://www.lpionline.com

"To achieve greatness, start where you are, use what you have, do what you can." –Arthur Ashe, tennis champion & philanthropist

STUDENT ORGANIZATION EXPO

CERTIFICATE: Bronze | **INSTRUCTOR:** GOLD Leader Mentor Staff

"Attending the Student Organization Expo was a very rewarding experience because I learned more about the GOLD Program from GOLD Mentors, which ultimately got me interested in participating in the program and other organizations on campus."

Kaho, junior, 2011

WORKSHOP DESCRIPTION

Each semester the Student Organization Expo, sponsored by the College Union & Activities Department, provides an opportunity for new and returning students to talk to leaders of student organizations and volunteer for membership. New students in the GOLD Program may earn Bronze Certificate credit by registering for this program, obtaining an instructional handout at the GOLD Student Organization Expo Fair Table, and visiting at least 10 organizations' tables. The purpose of this workshop is to encourage students to become involved in organizations where they can practice the leadership skills they are learning in GOLD workshops.

LEARNING OUTCOMES

Upon completion of this workshop, participants will:
- Have an awareness of the wide variety of student organizations on campus and the goals of each.
- Realize which organizations they would like to become involved with and take the necessary steps to do so.

WORKSHOP ACTIVITIES

- Participants walk around and speak with representatives from all of the student organizations on campus.
- Participants are instructed to write a journal reflection on their experience at the Student Expo. They are asked to name the organizations they visited and reflect on which of them they either plan to join or have already joined.

RESOURCES USED

Center for Community. (2008). *Instruction Sheet for Student Organization Expo.*

"I don't know what your destiny will be, but one thing I know: the only ones among you who will be really happy are those who have sought and found how to serve."
—Albert Schweitzer

SUSTAINABILITY: DEBATING THE ISSUES

CERTIFICATE: Jade | **INSTRUCTOR:** Dr. Chris Annala, Professor of Business, and Dr. Harry Howe, Professor of Business, Coordinator of Accounting

"We need to preserve this planet for the next generation and thus sustainability is very important. However, we must also be aware of the costs associated with changing to sustainable ways."

Vishal, senior, 2012

WORKSHOP DESCRIPTION

This workshop will help participants better understand the issues surrounding sustainability and sustainability practices. The focus of the seminar will be on the balance between environmental concerns and business. There is a clear need to balance the future welfare of the environment with the needs of the present. Businesses often believe that the use of excessive regulations restrains a firm's ability to provide the economic growth needed to raise the standard of living for people in the present. Proponents of sustainability argue that improvements in environmental quality will not only increase standards of living for the current generation, but also for future generations.

LEARNING OUTCOMES

Upon completion of this workshop, participants will:

- Be able to articulate the arguments in favor of sustainability initiatives.
- Be able to articulate the arguments against sustainability initiatives.
- Understand the basic concepts of cost-benefit analysis and the importance of considering scarcity when allocating scarce resources.
- Understand that technological advances have allowed for ever-increasing standards of living, despite resource constraints.
- Recognize the importance of free markets and capitalism to direct resources to their highest valued uses.
- Understand the term "externality" and recognize that the existence of externalities inhibits the efficient use of resources without some form of intervention.

WORKSHOP ACTIVITIES

- Participants listen to a debate of the issues.
- Participants are given an opportunity to ask questions of the presenters.
- Participants are asked to provide comments related to both sides of the argument.
- If time allows, the class is divided and students from each side of the debate are asked to argue in favor of the other side, and against their own side.

RESOURCES USED

No additional resources.

"I left Earth three times and found no other place to go. Please take care of Spaceship Earth." —Wally Schirra, Jr., astronaut in Mercury, Gemini, & Apollo programs

TAKING THE NEXT STEPS

CERTIFICATE: Opal (Required) | **INSTRUCTOR:** Fatima Rodriguez-Johnson, Coordinator, Multicultural Programs & Services

"This workshop helped me prepare for the different people I will face in the future and gave me the tools of how to solve problems or differences, and how to be accepting of other people and their culture."

Karina, junior, 2011

WORKSHOP DESCRIPTION

This workshop is the conclusion of the Opal Certificate Program. Participants will share their experiences by reflecting on the workshops they participated in and explain growth that they experienced. Participants will also create a Personal Action Plan for the future. The purpose of this workshop is to review what participants of the Opal Certificate have learned thus far and how they can improve in the future.

LEARNING OUTCOMES

Upon completion of the workshop, participants will:

- Have a solid understanding of the topics discussed throughout the Opal Certificate workshops, including the formation of personal identities and how it relates to their relationships with others.
- Learn about the existence of racial and cultural acceptance in society.
- Develop a Personal Action Plan for the future that will help guide them to achieving their goals related to taking the next steps.

WORKSHOP ACTIVITIES

- The instructor asks participants to introduce themselves and share their name, year, and major.
- The instructor explains that this workshop is an opportunity to reflect on the Opal series. What have you learned? What are you still struggling with?
- Participants are encouraged to join in an open discussion of the questions on the handout. They are asked to talk about their experiences (both past and present) and how they have applied what they have learned.
- The instructor guides participants as they formulate a realistic action plan that they can apply in the next 30 days.
- The participants are asked to put their name and campus box number on the top of the sheet and the instructor collects the students' worksheets. These worksheets will be mailed to the participants approximately one month after the workshop so they can be reminded of their goals and can measure their success.

RESOURCES USED

Johnson, F. (2009). *Handout on Action Planning Worksheet.*

"Tolerance implies no lack of commitment to one's own beliefs. Rather it condemns the oppression or persecution of others."
—John F. Kennedy

TEACHING/COACHING LEADERSHIP

CERTIFICATE: Silver | **INSTRUCTOR:** James Lyons, Head Men's Lacrosse Coach, SUNY Geneseo

"Being part of a team means that you must understand that you are attempting to achieve a common goal together, and you must work together and be able to have efficient communication."

Kimberly, freshman, 2012

WORKSHOP DESCRIPTION

This session will discuss changing one's leadership style from delegating and decision making to coaching and enabling your "team." Emphasis will be on interpersonal skills such as communication, listening, and involving every member as part of the process.

LEARNING OUTCOMES

Upon completion of this workshop, participants will:

- Have developed a sense of the importance of communication, listening, and involving every member as part of the process of being a coach and teacher.

WORKSHOP ACTIVITIES

- The instructor presents examples of how he manages a team, focuses on what characteristics he looks for in a team, and explains the process of selecting captains.
- The instructor discusses how to develop good team values. He shares some additional advice stemming from first-hand experiences as a coach.

RESOURCES USED

Lyons, J. (2011). *Handout on Teaching/Coaching Leadership.*

"Michael, if you can't pass, you can't play."
—Coach Dean Smith to Michael Jordan in his freshman year.
"Talent wins games, but teamwork and intelligence wins championships."
—Michael Jordan, later in his career.

TEAMBUILDING

CERTIFICATE: Silver (Required) | **INSTRUCTOR:** Two to three GOLD Leader Mentors

"By realizing that our group needs to work together in order to be successful, I will strive to make everyone feel welcome and comfortable with one another."

Christopher, freshman, 2009

WORKSHOP DESCRIPTION

Teambuilding is critical to the success of any group that must work together. This session will cover the appropriate sequencing of activities and some basic tools for developing and enhancing teamwork. This workshop is an active learning session.

LEARNING OUTCOMES

Upon completion of the workshop, participants will:

- Have gained exposure to a variety of teambuilding activities that can be adapted for use in their own organizations.
- Know the five basic stages of group development: forming (getting acquainted), storming (struggling forward), norming (becoming personal), performing (working together), and transference.
- Understand the characteristics of effective teams.

WORKSHOP ACTIVITIES

- After the instructors welcome the participants and introduce themselves, they pass out a handout on teambuilding. The mentors deliver a short lecture on what makes an effective team, the difference between team building and team development, and the basic stages of group development.
- Participants are then split into groups of four or five and were given a length of rope (~15–20 feet). Each participant is instructed to unravel the rope and talk about themselves to their group for the whole length of time that it takes them to wrap the rope back up. Each participant has the opportunity to wrap the rope up in their respective group.
- Participants partner up and receive a piece of rope (~2 feet) that has loose loops at the end that can be wrapped around each wrist. After looping the two pieces of rope together, participants put the loops around their wrists and are instructed to work together to disconnect the ropes.
- Participants are split into two large groups. The groups form circles and are instructed to keep a ball up in the air despite challenges such as using one's non-dominant hand to hit it, having to clap before touching the ball, or not being allowed to catch the ball.
- Participants are split into small groups and each group gets a bag of PVC piping (various joints and lengths in each). The participants are challenged to build the highest free-standing tower among the groups. At first, the groups are given two minutes to talk and strategize, but are not allowed to touch the pipes. Participants are then allowed to talk and build for approximately four to five minutes. Finally, participants are allowed to continue building but are instructed not to talk for approximately two to three minutes.
- The instructors discuss the remainder of the handout on teambuilding with the participants.

Possible additional activities:

- The Bean Bag Name-Learning Challenge: A small group is arranged in a circle and everyone goes around introducing themselves. One person gets a bean bag and throws it to someone else, but before s/he or throws it, s/he has to say the receiver's name. The person who catches it says someone else's name and throws it to that person. More bean bags are added after a couple of minutes.
- The Tennis Ball Tarp: The group picks up a small tarp with five tennis-ball sized holes in it. A tennis ball is thrown onto the tarp, and the group has to work together to have the ball circle all five holes, but never fall through. Another challenge is to throw the tennis ball on and ask the group to get the ball on the other side without the ball ever touching the ground.

- Four Person Train: In a group of four, participants line up in a "train" and walk around with their eyes closed. When the instructor says "rotate," the train reverses direction. When s/he says "switch," the person leading the train goes to the back. When the instructor says "change," the two individuals in the middle of the train switch places. It gets tricky when the instructor starts combining the action words into a single command.

RESOURCES USED

Cain, J. H., & Joliff, B. (1998). *Teamwork & teamplay: A guide to cooperative, challenge, and adventure activities that build confidence, cooperation, teamwork, creativity, trust, decision making, conflict resolution, resource management, communication, effective feedback and problem solving skills.* Dubuque, IA: Kendall Hunt.

Cain, J. H., Cummings, M., & Stanchfield, J. (2005). *A teachable moment: A facilitator's guide to activities for processing, debriefing, reviewing and reflection.* Dubuque, IA: Kendall Hunt.

Cavert, C. (1999). *Affordable portables: A working book of initiative activities and problem solving elements.* Oklahoma City, OK: Wood 'N' Barnes.

Matthews, T. (2011). *Handout on Team Building and Basic Stages of Group/Team Development.* Adapted from Tuckman, B. W. (1965). Developmental sequence in small groups. *Psychological Bulletin, 63*, 384–399.

Rohnke, K. (2010). *Silver bullets: A revised guide to initiative problems, adventure games, stunts, and trust activities.* Beverly, MA: Kendall Hunt.

Scannell, M., & Cain, J. H. (2012). *The big book of low cost training games: Quick, effective activities that explore communication, goals setting, character development, team building and more—and won't break the bank!* New York: McGraw-Hill.

"The way a team plays as a whole determines its success. You may have the greatest bunch of individual stars in the world, but if they don't play together, the club won't be worth a dime." –Babe Ruth

THE INDIRECT LEADER: HOW TO BOSS PEOPLE AROUND WITHOUT BEING BOSSY

CERTIFICATE: Silver | **INSTRUCTOR:** Dr. Kenneth Kallio, Associate Professor of Psychology

"The key is not to order people to complete their assigned tasks, but to convince them to want to succeed at the job out of their own volition."

Jesse, junior, 2011

WORKSHOP DESCRIPTION

Overtly directing people to attain a work or organizational objective (bossing) can backfire as a leadership tactic. Indirect leadership relies on shared vision and intrinsic motivation to achieving objectives. This workshop will compare direct and indirect leadership styles.

LEARNING OUTCOMES

Upon completion of this workshop, participants will:
- Be able to identify behaviors that may be perceived as bossy.
- Appreciate that the leadership style that one adopts can be attributed to either or both personal traits and situational factors.
- Understand that the use of high levels of assertion may not be an effective leadership style in all cases.
- Be able to identify the qualities of individuals/situations that form the foundation for effective use of an indirect leadership style.
- Recognize when direct (assertive) leadership may be necessary.

WORKSHOP ACTIVITIES

- The workshop opens with participants contributing examples of their own experiences with bossy bosses.
- The instructor leads participants through a consideration of key ideas from psychology and research literature on direct and indirect language, assertiveness in leadership, and related concerns. The PowerPoint presentation is liberally sprinkled with comic strips from *Dilbert* to illustrate ideas.
- The workshop concludes with a question-and-answer session from the participants.

RESOURCES USED

Ames, D. R., & Flynn, F. J. (2007). What breaks a leader: The curvilinear relation between assertiveness and leadership. *Journal of Personality and Social Psychology, 92,* 307–324.

Fast, N. J., & Chen, S. (2009). When the boss feels inadequate: Power, incompetence, and aggression. *Psychological Science, 20,* 1406–1413.

Kallio, K. (2010). *The Indirect Leader PowerPoint.*

"You do not lead by hitting people over the head—that's assault, not leadership." –Dwight D. Eisenhower

THE JOB SEARCH

CERTIFICATE: Emerald | **INSTRUCTOR:** Kerrie Bondi, Career Counselor

"By knowing more information about the online job resources and effective job search strategies, I will be able to put this knowledge to use and set a goal of sending out my resume and cover letter to five different companies a week."

Michael, junior, 2011

WORKSHOP DESCRIPTION

This workshop is designed for juniors and seniors beginning their professional job search. A typical job search for a college senior takes three to six months to land that first professional position in a field related to their major. Attend this workshop to learn about job search tools, plans, and strategies to get you started. We will discuss the importance of having a clear assessment of your interests, skills, values, and goals and the typical steps you will take in developing your job search plan. You will also learn about the resources available in the Career Development office and beyond.

LEARNING OUTCOMES

Upon completion of this workshop, participants will:

- Have analyzed interests, skills, personality, and values as a foundation for a job search.
- Have created personal Plans A, B, and C for initiating a job search.
- Be able to utilize both on- and off-campus resources appropriately for job searches.

WORKSHOP ACTIVITIES

- The instructor delivers a PowerPoint on "Getting a Job Is a Job" and focuses on the following points:
  - The National Association of Colleges and Employers' top 10 skills that employers are looking for in today's job market, and the importance of identifying the skills you have and how to provide evidence of these skills.
  - The value of being able to confidently market yourself and your skills.
  - The importance of knowing what you want to do before you start the job search because most employers are not willing to figure it out for you.
  - The importance of having a Plan A (ideal job/career), a Plan B (a related job/career), and a Plan C (a back-up job/career).
  - Cover letters, resumes, interviewing skills, and networking talents.
  - Statistics and facts about the current job market.
  - The resources that are available at Geneseo's Career Development office, and the websites that are available to participants looking for jobs.
  - The instructor highlights certain websites listed on the PowerPoint presentation and then hands out a hard copy of these websites and others.
- The instructor has each participant write down a short description of his/her plans of action (Plans A, B, and C) for their own job searches.

RESOURCES USED

Bondi, K. (2011). *Getting a Job Is a Job PowerPoint.*
SUNY Geneseo Office of Career Development. (2011). *Handout on Effective Job Search Strategies.*
SUNY Geneseo Office of Career Development. (2011). *Handout on Effective Job Search Strategies for Educators.*
SUNY Geneseo Office of Career Development. (2011). *Handout of Online Job Search Resources.*
SUNY Geneseo Office of Career Development. (2011). *Handout on Networking.*
SUNY Geneseo Office of Career Development. (2011). *Handout, Goal Setting Worksheet.*

THE PRIVILEGE WALK

CERTIFICATE: Opal | **INSTRUCTOR:** Ray Fedora, Residence Hall Director, Residence Life

"This workshop taught me how to recognize where the concept of white privilege appears in my life."

Erin, sophomore, 2011

WORKSHOP DESCRIPTION

This workshop will discuss the notion of privilege and how it manifests itself in the world around us. Participants will be challenged to see privilege as something that exists beyond money, but is inherent in interactions, systems, and society. We will explore the privileges that we each have and don't have, as well as discuss what this means for our daily lives.

LEARNING OUTCOMES

Upon completion of this workshop, participants will:

- Understand privilege as a collection of unearned advantages bestowed upon some.
- Explore the privileges they have as well as the privileges they lack.
- Discuss the impact this has on their lives and hear how privileges, or their lack, impacts other students.

WORKSHOP ACTIVITIES

- All participants introduce themselves.
- Ground rules are established, which include honesty, respect, openness, and confidentiality.
- The Startling Line/Privilege Walk Activity is conducted.
- There is a discussion to debrief the activity. This includes the definition of privilege, assuaging the guilt, validating the discomfort in the room, and encouraging each individual to speak.
- The workshop concludes with a short discussion on the next steps that participants can take.

RESOURCES USED

Johnson, A. (2011). *Privilege, power, and difference.* Mountainview, CA: Mayfield Publishing Company.

McIntosh, P. (1989). *White privilege: Unpacking the invisible knapsack.* [S.l. : s.n.]

"Working at the Food Bank with my kids is an eye-opener. The face of hunger isn't the bum on the street drinking Sterno; it's the working poor. They don't look any different, they don't behave any differently, they're not really any less educated. They are incredibly less privileged, and that's it." —Mario Batali, chef

THE SMART NEGOTIATOR!®

CERTIFICATE: Silver | **INSTRUCTOR:** Deb Rapone, President, bc&j solutions, LLC

"The saying that 'your reputation will precede you' is very important in the negotiating world and first impressions can go a long way."

Patrick, freshman, 2012

WORKSHOP DESCRIPTION

We all negotiate every day with our friends, parents, spouses, classmates, professors, bosses, and members of our organizations. Learn how to and why you should continuously improve your skills from a Geneseo alumna who offers corporate training in negotiations skills to Fortune 500 companies.

LEARNING OUTCOMES

Upon completion of this workshop, participants will:

- Know strategies for successfully negotiating with other people.
- Have practiced negotiation skills.

WORKSHOP ACTIVITIES

- The instructor provides some background information about negotiation and shares some helpful strategies with the participants by using a PowerPoint presentation.
- Participants split up into pairs and complete either the *Seymour Sales'* or *Ida Dealmaker's* situation brief.
- The instructor leads a discussion about successful and unsuccessful strategies that participants demonstrated during the activity.

RESOURCES USED

Rapone, D. (2012). *Handout of Seymour Sales' Situational Brief.* bc&j solutions, LLC.

Rapone, D. (2012). *Handout of Ida Dealmaker's Situational Brief.* bc&j solutions, LLC.

Rapone, D. (2012) *The Smart Negotiator!® PowerPoint.*

"During a negotiation, it would be wise not to take anything personally. If you leave personalities out of it, you will be able to see opportunities more objectively." –Brian Koslow, founder and president/CEO of Breakthrough Coaching, Inc.

THE TOOLKIT FOR ETHICAL DILEMMAS

CERTIFICATE: Silver or Emerald | **INSTRUCTOR:** Mark S. Kane, MBA, CPA—Class of '80, President of The Kane Firm CPA PC; Co-founder—Column of Hope (public health charity)

"By strengthening my networks that give highest preference to an ethically run business, as well as being pragmatic by rationally considering all the facts before making a decision, I will uphold a business culture that includes ethics in all facets of its decisions."

Ryan, sophomore, 2009

WORKSHOP DESCRIPTION

Ethical behavior may seem difficult, but pays off in every career. Our guest presenter will work through real-world examples of ethical dilemmas. The presenter draws upon experiences in various endeavors: including founding a CPA firm, advising bio tech and IT start-up enterprises, and managing sales and operations of a national manufacturer, as well as serving as lead negotiator in several mergers and acquisitions (M&A) transactions.

LEARNING OUTCOMES

Upon completion of this workshop, participants will:

- Be better prepared to deal with ethically complex situations.
- Have a perspective on the importance of ethics in the workplace by listening to an experienced speaker who has worked in different fields.
- Use the Ethical Dilemma Toolkit to increase the chances of achieving a positive outcome in difficult situations.

WORKSHOP ACTIVITIES

- The guest speaker begins the workshop by sharing anecdotes which demonstrate the positive long-term results of maintaining a high ethical standard.
- The use of the "tool kit," which is a set of procedures to follow when dealing with ethically complex situations, is explained. Participants are encouraged to ask questions.
- For the remainder of the workshop, small groups discuss how the "tool kit" could be used in various hypothetical situations and share their conclusions with the full group.

RESOURCES USED

Kane, M. S. (2012). *Handout on The Ethical Dilemma Toolkit.*

"Non-violence leads to the highest ethics, which is the goal of all evolution. Until we stop harming all other living beings, we are still savages." –Thomas A. Edison

TIME MANAGEMENT

CERTIFICATE: Bronze or Sapphire | **INSTRUCTOR:** GOLD Leader Mentor Staff

"This workshop started with a quote by H. Jackson Brown that really hit me. It was, 'You have exactly the same amount of hours per day that were given to Helen Keller, Pasteur, Michelangelo, Mother Teresa, Leonardo da Vinci, Thomas Jefferson, and Albert Einstein.' When I start to stress about how much I have to do, this quote will help me to remember that I really do have enough time for it all."

Sarah, sophomore, 2010

WORKSHOP DESCRIPTION

As an involved and active student, it can be challenging to fulfill the responsibilities of both the "student" and the "leader" parts of your life! This session, facilitated by an active student leader, will provide tips and strategies on reconfiguring your time to effectively balance your academic, social, and leadership lives.

LEARNING OUTCOMES

Upon completion of this workshop, participants will:

- Have an awareness of the three common time wasters—interruptions, procrastination, and waiting.
- Understand the importance of prioritizing.
- Have discussed the differences between urgent/important activities and non-urgent/unimportant activities.
- Have received tips and advice on the most effective ways to manage and save one's time, thereby avoiding, reducing, and relieving stress.
- Be able to plan a weekly schedule.

WORKSHOP ACTIVITIES

- The instructors ask each student to introduce himself/herself and to name one thing that he/she does that wastes time.
- The GOLD Mentors go through the Time Management packet with the participants.
- As a wrap-up, each instructor gives an example of one thing s/he does to save time or maximize his/her time.

RESOURCES USED

Bly, R. W. (2010). *Make every second count: Time management tips and techniques for more success with less stress*. Pompton Plains, NJ: Career Press.

Leland, L., & Bailey, K. (2008). *Time management in an instan*t. Pompton Plains, NJ: Career Press. http://www. exse;.mtu.edu/UN1000/Activities/Time%20Management%20Activities.pdf.

Muscarella, K., & Singer, H. (2012). *Handout on Time Management for Student Leaders.*

"All that we have to decide is what to do with the time that is given to us." –Gandalf, in J.R.R. Tolkien's The Lord of the Rings: The Fellowship of the Ring

TRUE COLORS®: WHAT COLOR ARE YOU?

CERTIFICATE: Silver or Emerald | **INSTRUCTOR:** Kimberly Harvey, Director of New Student Programs, and Luke Haumesser, Jones Hall Residence Hall Director, Residence Life

"No one category is inherently more desirable in a leader, but members of an effective team understand the varying needs that each kind of person has, and act accordingly."

Jared, sophomore, 2012

WORKSHOP DESCRIPTION

In building relationships with members of your organization or team, you help others to connect and recognize how personality plays a role in the overall effectiveness of your team. This workshop will examine various personality assessment tools, look at ways in which personality affects relationships and work styles, and provide suggestions for using these tools to create a stellar team that works collaboratively based on individual assets. This highly participatory workshop offers one perspective on personality type and its impact on teambuilding and teamwork. Participants are encouraged to share experiences with one another and to see this model not as an explanation for all behaviors and interactions, but as another component for looking at interpersonal dynamics.

LEARNING OUTCOMES

Upon completion of the workshop, participants will:
- Be able to identify characteristics of a highly effective team.
- Understand the benefits to a group leader of understanding personality type.
- Have assessed their own personality type and what it means.
- Have demonstrated how to create effective teams through an understanding of personality type.

WORKSHOP ACTIVITIES

- Each participant takes the True Colors® Personality Assessment and comes up with two individualized colors (primary and secondary color).
- The instructor leads the group through an exploration of what each of the four colors means and how those traits can work as positives and negatives within the constructs of teams.
- Participants are divided into four groups based on their color and prompted to plan a party.
- Groups are redivided into groups containing a few of each color and use their insights to work with different personality types to form effective teams.

RESOURCES USED

Lowry, D. (1979, 2001). *True Colors® Successful Leadership Handbook and Word Sort.*
Lowry, D. (1979, 2001). *Keys to personal success.* Riverside, CA: True Colors® Publishing. www.truecolors.org
Harvey, K. (2010). *True Colors®: What Color Are You? Power Point.*

"Learning about our Personality Type helps us to understand why certain areas in life come easily to us and others are more of a struggle. Learning about other people's Personality Type helps us to understand the most effective way to communicate with them and how they function best."
David W. Keirsey, psychologist and personality type researcher

UNDERSTANDING YOUR LEARNING STYLE

CERTIFICATE: Silver | **INSTRUCTOR:** Dr. Elizabeth Hall, Assistant Professor of Education & LIVES Program Project Director

> *"Speaking to students I know who have the same learning style as me will also help me in the future in planning my schedule and how I intend to do homework, study, etc."*
>
> *Jacqueline, junior, 2011*

WORKSHOP DESCRIPTION

A good leader knows his/her learning style. Each person has a distinct learning style in which s/he learns best. You may be surprised by your preferred learning style. Are you a visual learner—someone who learns through seeing? Are you an auditory learner —someone who learns through listening? Are you a tactile/kinesthetic learner—someone who learns through moving, doing, and touching? We will explore the various styles and you can determine your preferred learning style or the way you learn best. Through a series of quizzes and activities, participants will learn if they tend to use more of the left part of their brain or the right part of their brain. Participants will discuss their tendencies in certain situations and will learn how to become more "middle brained." Participants will also learn if they tend to learn better visually, auditory, kinesthetically, or multi-modally (a combination of learning styles).

LEARNING OUTCOMES

Upon completion of the workshop, participants will:

- Have an understanding of how to approach studying and interacting with others by considering their learning styles.
- Know how to increase awareness of and incorporate the "opposite" side of the brain in order to become more "middle brained."

WORKSHOP ACTIVITIES

- The instructor writes left-brain characteristics (sequential, time oriented, detail oriented, likes order, specializes in logic, enjoys analytical thinking, etc.) on the left side of the whiteboard and right-brain characteristics (alerts us to novelty, tells us when someone is lying or telling a joke, specializes in understanding the whole picture, enjoys art, music, and spiritual things, etc.) on the right side of the whiteboard.
- The instructor asks participants to move to the side of the room that they tend to identify with. Participants introduce themselves and share their college majors. The instructor explains the positive and the negative attributes of being left brained, right brained, or (ideally) a bit of both.
- After completing the "Cognitive Style Quiz: Brain Dominance" activity, participants are instructed to move to the side of the room that is synonymous with their results.
- The participants complete the "Which Side Are You On?—Brain and Behavior" and VARK questionnaires.

RESOURCES USED

Hall, E. (2011). *Handout on the VARK Questionnaire*. Adapted from http://www.vark-learn.com/english/page asp?p=questionnaire.

Hall, E. (2011). *Handout on Study Strategies Packet*.

Hall, E. (2011). *Handout on Which Side Are You On? Questionnaire*.

Hall, E. (2011). *Handout on Interpreting the Questionnaire*.

USING IMOVIE TO CREATE WINNING VIDEOS

CERTIFICATE: Ruby | **INSTRUCTOR:** Joe Dolce, Coordinator of Instructional Support, Computing & Information Technology

"This interactive workshop taught me about many tricks and tools involved in iMovie, which will allow me to create better movies that leave a more lasting impression on the viewers."

Melissa, junior, 2012

WORKSHOP DESCRIPTION

Learn how to use iMovie '11 to spice up your video for YouTube, PowerPoint, DVDs, and more! This class will teach you the basics of video ingestion, how to trim your footage, and add transitions and effects, as well as how to share your video with the world.

LEARNING OUTCOMES

Upon completion of the workshop, participants will:

- Understand the basic tools of iMovie '11 and be able to make basic movies.
- Be able share with others the tools involved in iMovie '11 when working on a group project.

WORKSHOP ACTIVITIES

- Participants use iMac computers with iMovie '11 installed and a folder with videos, pictures, and audio clips of the instructors dog. These were demo files that allowed the students to create a movie during the workshop.
- The instructor explains the basics of iMovie, such as adding and editing clips, adding and editing audio, adding title pages, and adding and formatting pictures into the clip.
- Participants are able to try out these features and make a video while the instructor teaches participants how to use it.
- Features such as exporting and converting videos to various file types to make them compatible with many computers, using templates, and other more advanced features are explained.
- Time is left at the end to continue working on the videos and ask specific questions.

RESOURCES USED

iMac computers are provided for all students for this workshop.

"But having a really good understanding of history, literature, psychology, sciences—is very, very important to actually being able to make movies." –George Lucas

USING PERSONALITY TYPE FOR CAREER EXPLORATION: THE MYERS-BRIGGS TYPE INDICATOR

CERTIFICATE: Emerald | **INSTRUCTOR:** Elizabeth Seager, Associate Director of Career Development

"I was surprised at how well the assessment pinpointed certain challenges that I have faced in the past in the workplace and greatly appreciated the advice provided for how to overcome them."

Sarah, senior, 2012

WORKSHOP DESCRIPTION

The Myers-Briggs Type Indicator® (MBTI) is a premier tool to help you understand yourself and how your personality relates to career choice. Exploring your type will tell you from where you draw your energy and how you process information, make decisions, and approach time. The MBTI Career Report will then assist you with career exploration, development, and management. In addition, it will identify strengths and weaknesses of your type for the career search process. This assessment is appropriate for all students regardless of where you are in the career exploration process. Completion of the MBTI Form M questionnaire is required prior to the workshop. You will receive instructions on how to access Form M one week prior to the workshop. Class size is limited to 20.

LEARNING OUTCOMES

Upon completion of the workshop, participants will:

- Be able to verify their MBTI four-letter type and understand each type.
- Understand how type affects career choices and influences one's approach to career exploration and development.
- Know how to utilize the job families and occupations for further career exploration.

WORKSHOP ACTIVITIES

- Students are required to complete the MBTI Step 1 Form M prior to attending the workshop. The Office of Career Development pre-purchases the Myers Briggs Type Indicator® Career Report and distributes it to participants at the beginning of the workshop. The instructor conducts a review of each type to help participants verify their own type.
- The instructor discusses the Introversion/Extraversion scale: Participants are asked to move to the left or right side of the room, each representing a large party with many people they don't know or a party of four to five people of people they do know. The instructor and participants discuss why they selected their party and how it relates to the I/E characteristics.
- The instructor discusses the Sensing/Intuition scale: Participants are shown an abstract painting from the MBTI teaching materials. Each type is asked to describe the painting. A discussion compares descriptions to the S/N characteristics.
- The instructor discusses the Thinking/Feeling scale: Thinking and Feeling types are asked to separate into groups. They are assigned to discuss a scenario in which they are coaching a team that has a rule that if a member is late to practice three times, s/he cannot play the next game. A team member breaks the rule, but begs to be permitted to play. The groups are brought together to discuss how they would handle the situation. The T/F characteristics are discussed in relation to the exercise.
- The instructor discusses the Judging/Perceiving scale: Each type is divided into their respective groups. They are told they have the entire day off and to discuss how they would approach their day. The groups are brought back together to discuss what they would do with their day off. The characteristics of J/P are discussed.
- A lecture is held instructing participants on how to interpret the career planning, career exploration, career development, and Job, Families, and Occupations portions of the assessment.

RESOURCES USED

http://www.myersbriggs.org/my-mbti-personality-type/take-the-mbti-instrument/

USING THE PATH-GOAL APPROACH TO LEADING

CERTIFICATE: Gold | **INSTRUCTOR:** Dr. Avan Jassawalla, Professor, School of Business, SUNY Geneseo

"Since taking this workshop, I will try to adapt my style according to other members' internal and external behaviors rather than just try to make the most out of the group's personalities."

Bareeqah, freshman, 2011

WORKSHOP DESCRIPTION

Different leadership approaches are suitable to different situations. This session covers some of the major concepts of the path-goal approach and help students determine strategies for what might work best in a variety of leadership situations.

LEARNING OUTCOMES

Upon completion of this workshop, participants will:

- Have an awareness that there is not one single "right way" to lead.
- Know about four different leadership styles and the situations where they are most effective.
- Have practiced using the path-goal approach to arrive at the most effective leadership model.

WORKSHOP ACTIVITIES

- The instructor explains that the old approach to leadership was identifying and using "one best way" to lead, while the more current approach is to consider a variety of ways and choose those most effective for any given situation.
- The workshop reviews the path-goal approach to leadership and explains the four leadership styles therein: Directive, Supportive, Participative, and Achievement-Oriented. The instructor explains how to match style to situation by analyzing characteristics of the task/environment and characteristics of followers.
- The workshop participants are split into small groups and provided mini-cases through which they practice applying the path-goal approach and determining the most effective leadership style(s) in each situation.

RESOURCES USED

House, R. J. (1971). A path-goal theory of leader effectiveness. *Administrative Science Quarterly*, 16(3), 321–328.

House, R. J. (1996). Path-goal theory of leadership: Lessons, legacy, and a reformulated theory. *Leadership Quarterly*, 7(3), 323–352.

Jassawalla, A. (2009). *Handout on Path-Goal Model of Leadership.* Adapted from *House's Path-Goal Theory.*

Jassawalla, A. (2009). *Handout on Case Studies.*

McShane, S. L., & von Glinow, M. A. (2013). *Organizational behavior* (6th ed.). Boston, MA: McGraw-Hill.

"The final test of a leader is that he leaves behind him in other men the conviction and the will to carry on…the genius of a good leader is to leave behind him a situation which common sense, without the grace of genius, can deal with successfully."
—*Walter Lippmann*

VOLUNTEER FAIR

CERTIFICATE: Sapphire (Required) | **INSTRUCTOR:** Kay Fly, Coordinator, Volunteerism & Service Learning

"I plan to not only become more active in volunteer organizations myself, but I also plan to involve my residence hall, advertise organizations, and encourage my residents to get involved early in their college career."

Meghan, junior, 2011

WORKSHOP DESCRIPTION

Representatives from college and community organizations will be present to recruit volunteers and explain their programs and services. Students involved in the GOLD Program and the Sapphire Certificate should attend and visit with as many organizations as possible in order to discover the range of possibilities for volunteer involvement. Sapphire students will need to sign in at the GOLD table and submit a reflection. As opposed to a traditional workshop format, this fair, offered once each semester, features over 30 organizations and agencies from on campus and in the community that offer volunteer opportunities. Students wishing to obtain credit for the Volunteer Fair must visit a minimum of 10 representatives and then reflect on the Volunteer Fair in a journal.

LEARNING OUTCOMES

Upon completion of the workshop, participants will:
- Have compiled an individualized list of available volunteer opportunities.
- Have compared differing volunteer opportunities.
- Be able to summarize a variety of opportunities and their motivations for volunteering.

WORKSHOP ACTIVITIES

- Participants register for the "workshop," obtain an instruction handout at the GOLD Volunteer Fair table, and visit at least 10 organization/agency tables.
- Participants are encouraged to commit themselves to one or two volunteer opportunities by signing the registration sheets at the tables.
- Participants earn credit for this required "workshop" by writing a journal reflection on their experience at the Volunteer Fair. They are instructed to name the organizations they visited and reflect on which opportunities they either plan to join or have already joined.

RESOURCES USED

Center for Community. (2008). *Instruction Sheet for Volunteer Fair.*

"One is not born into the world to do everything but to do something."
–Henry David Thoreau

VOLUNTEER INVOLVEMENT REFLECTION

CERTIFICATE: Sapphire (Required) | **INSTRUCTOR:** Kay Fly, Coordinator, Volunteerism & Service Learning

"In the future, I plan to ask better questions before committing to a volunteer opportunity so that my time and efforts are used in the most effective manner."

Elizabeth, junior, 2011

WORKSHOP DESCRIPTION

All students pursuing the Sapphire Volunteerism & Leadership Certificate are required to complete a minimum of 10 hours in a volunteer activity. The activity should be an approved volunteer opportunity from the College's Volunteer Center. This workshop gives participants who have completed volunteering activities an opportunity to share experiences with fellow volunteers and those interested in getting involved in volunteering. During this moderated discussion, participants will give brief public presentations on the volunteer work that was done and share impressions on the experience with everyone. Questions are encouraged as participants come together to collaborate and share knowledge. Additionally, participants will be asked to brainstorm and share journal reflection questions and ideas as a means to prompt further discussion and exploration.

LEARNING OUTCOMES

Upon completion of the workshop, participants will:
- Demonstrate formal and informal presentation skills.
- Have compared volunteer experiences with individuals from other organizations.
- Have prepared individual volunteer reflection questions.

WORKSHOP ACTIVITIES

- The first activity in this workshop is very informal. All of the participants talk about their volunteer experiences and share what they learned, tell a story connected to their experience, and discuss how they plan to use what they learned in the future.
- In the second activity, participants either make up an experience or use a real experience that they have had to write a letter to a person or organization that they helped. In the letter, the participants include details such as how they felt, express how much they hoped they helped, and anything else they feel they may want to include.

RESOURCES USED

No additional resources.

"It is our choices, Harry, that show us what we truly are, far more than our abilities."
–Albus Dumbledore in J.K. Rowling's Harry Potter

VOLUNTEERISM, ENGAGEMENT, & SERVICE

CERTIFICATE: Sapphire (Required) | **INSTRUCTOR:** Kay Fly, Coordinator of Student Volunteer & Service Learning

"I realized that I need to find a service opportunity that is the right fit for me so I can help the most people."

Gabrielle, senior, 2012

WORKSHOP DESCRIPTION

Volunteerism is an active form of exercising leadership for the common good. This session is an introduction to volunteerism, community engagement, and service learning. You will learn a conceptual framework for volunteer service and explore a myriad of opportunities through which you can volunteer in the Geneseo and Greater Livingston and Monroe County area, or in the Livingston County CARES programs and projects in Harrison County, Mississippi. Learn how to get the most out of your volunteer experience by choosing a volunteer and service opportunity that will benefit you as well as the recipients.

LEARNING OUTCOMES

Upon completion of this workshop, participants will:
- Be able to recognize their personal underlying values driving them to volunteer.
- Have become more aware of the various volunteering opportunities offered through the college and the local community.

WORKSHOP ACTIVITIES

- The instructor has workshop participants introduce themselves and share one example of how they have volunteered in the past. This sharing of personal experiences facilitates meaningful conversations focusing on volunteerism.
- Following this introduction, the instructor shares her personal experiences with volunteerism, starting with the beginning of her engagement in the community.
- The instructor asks the participants what career field they are interested in pursuing and how it is related to volunteerism.
- After discussing volunteerism, the instructor asks what the participants do to relax from work and volunteering, and poses the question, "Why do you want to volunteer?"
- The instructor indicates that she is very willing to meet individually with students to help them discover volunteer opportunities that they might pursue.
- The instructor provides an overview of opportunities locally available and then asks each participant to share a word of wisdom from the handouts.
- The instructor has the participants write what they believe is the difference between charity and service.

RESOURCES USED

Ellis, S. J. Finding the right volunteer opportunity for you. *Service Leader.* Retrieved February, 9, 2012, from http://www. serviceleader.org/volunteer/finding.

Fly, K. (2012). *Handout on Volunteer Center: Learning, Service, and Community.* Center for Community, SUNY Geneseo.

Fly, K. (2012). *Handout on Why Volunteer?* Center for Community, SUNY Geneseo.

Fly, K. (2012). *Handout on How Do I Start?* Adapted from United Way of the Greater Seacoast Volunteer Action Center (2012). Retrieved February 8, 2012, from http://www.uwgs.org/.

Fly, K. (2012). *Handout on What Kind of Opportunities Are Available?* Center for Community, SUNY Geneseo.

Fly, K. (2012). *Handout on Volunteer Quotes.* Center for Community, SUNY Geneseo.

Fly, K. (2012). *Handout on What Is the Difference Between Charity and Service?* Center for Community, SUNY Geneseo.

WHAT IS CIVIC AND COMMUNITY ENGAGEMENT?

CERTIFICATE: Diamond (Required) | **INSTRUCTOR:** Dr. David Parfitt, Director of Teaching & Learning Center

"I plan to find more creative ways to give back and make a difference, whether it be in my own community or somewhere else in the country or even the world."

Lindsey, junior 2012

WORKSHOP DESCRIPTION

Engaging in one's community includes personal action to join a group that is interesting to you, work on a cause or social justice issue that you are passionate about, help with community projects, participate in local political party activities, or simply serve on the planning or clean-up committee for a community event. Practicing civic and community leadership develops from engaging with others in the leadership process.

LEARNING OUTCOMES

Upon completion of this workshop, participants will:

- Have explored students' personal view on civic engagement activities.
- Have discovered the range of various types of civic and community engagement activities that one can participate in.
- Have an understanding of possible projects they could take on for the completion of the Diamond Certificate.

WORKSHOP ACTIVITIES

- The instructor begins the workshop by asking the participants the opening question, "What is civic and community engagement?"
- After a few responses, the instructor presents a PowerPoint which describes various definitions of civic and community engagement.
- The instructor passes out a handout with 20 examples of civic and community engagement.
- Participants are then asked to list the examples from 1 to 20 in terms of how civically engaged each example is. 1 corresponds to the highest form of civic engagement and 20 corresponds to the lowest.
- Based on the worksheet, participants create a human histogram for various examples in order to see where those examples ranked for the workshop population.
- The instructor stresses the benefits of connecting academic course work and service to both students and recipients.
- After discussing the results, the instructor returns to the PowerPoint and shows a YouTube video about Cal State's civic and community engagement.
- As a group, participants discuss the video and relate it to their campus's involvement.
- The instructor explains the GOLD Diamond Certificate, including: (1) The remaining three required workshops; (2) The required civic/community engagement project; (3) The GREAT day involvement as a result of participating in the certificate.

RESOURCES USED

Ehrlich, T. (Ed.) (2000). *Civic responsibility and higher education.* Westport, CT: Oryx Press.
Parfitt, D. (2011). *Handout on Various Forms of Civic and Community Engagement.*
Parfitt, D. (2011). *What Is Civic and Community Engagement? PowerPoint.*

WHO KNOWS YOU: SPEED NETWORKING ON THE CLOCK

CERTIFICATE: Bronze or Emerald | **INSTRUCTOR:** Kim Harvey, Director, New Student Programs

> *"I am planning on using what I learned from this workshop in the future to pitch offers to people while under the tight confines of a time limit. I know I will be successful because I took this GOLD Workshop."*
>
> *Jason, junior, 2011*

WORKSHOP DESCRIPTION

So you think you can network? Come learn basic networking techniques and put them to practice during this workshop. Participants will beat the clock by engaging in speed networking to put those skills to practice. This high energy and interactive workshop is invaluable for anyone who wants to learn how to network and make a good impression. Participants learn the proper ways to greet others, the keys of small-talk, and how to be confident in this often frightening situation. The program includes an interactive discussion of the do's and do not's of social networking where students learn valuable skills and techniques.

LEARNING OUTCOMES

Upon completion of this workshop, participants will:
- Understand what networking is.
- Understand basic networking etiquette.
- Know the ways to make a good first impression and have a strong handshake.
- Know how to self market and develop a personal sales pitch.
- Understand the basics of small talk and become more comfortable with default topics.
- Know the Seven Rules and Three Steps to Small Talk.
- Be able to understand and overcome stumbling blocks in networking.

WORKSHOP ACTIVITIES

- The instructor leads an interactive discussion and presents a PowerPoint about networking skills.
- The instructors and participants discuss first impressions, handshakes, and tips to remember names, body language, and small talk. The instructors interact with the participants by acting out situations and scenarios.
- Participants are asked to make sure they are seated across from another participant for the speed networking activity. The workshop participants have three minutes to talk in pairs (the time can be increased or decreased depending on the number of participants), utilizing the small talk and introduction skills they learned at the beginning of the workshop to become more comfortable in networking situations. After three minutes, one side of the table moves down one seat and the process continues.
- The instructors lead a discussion about the activity. They focus on what was difficult, what was easy, and helpful hints picked up throughout the activity.

RESOURCES USED

Harvey, K. (2012). *Who Knows You: Speed Networking on the Clock PowerPoint.*

Kintish Ltd. (2007, February 14). *How not to network* [Video file]. Retrieved from http://www.youtube.com. watch?v=XuM0KtW73WU.

Ramsey, L. (2005). Six stumbling blocks to networking at events and how to overcome them. *The Talking Stick*, 22(7).

WHO MOVED MY CHEESE?®

CERTIFICATE: Silver | **INSTRUCTOR:** Wendi Kinney, Coordinator of Greek Affairs and Off-Campus Living

"This workshop clearly demonstrates that one must be able to adjust to change to be successful, and I will certainly heed this advice in the future."

Cory, junior, 2011

WORKSHOP DESCRIPTION

We all get comfortable with routine and many of us like to repeat things and do things the way we did them last year. However, change happens, and we have to be flexible and ready to adapt to new situations. This workshop is based on the best-selling book *Who Moved My Cheese?*® by Spencer Johnson, author and consultant to major corporations. Learn what corporate executives are taught about dealing with change in work and in life.

LEARNING OUTCOMES

Upon completion of this workshop, participants will:
- Have an understanding of the four ways people react to change.
- Be able to identify how leaders react to change.
- Know the best way to handle change in a leadership position.

WORKSHOP ACTIVITIES

- The presenter starts the workshop by showing a 15-minute video. It is a light-hearted cartoon, which is informative and uses humorous examples.
- The participants are then divided into four small groups. Each group is given one of the four characters in the movie. There are four characters to match each of the four ways one can react to change. Each group evaluates its designated character on the basis of what intimidates it, what it likes, how it dealt with change, etc.
- The instructor stresses that the four types of reaction are not on a hierarchy—no one is better than another. There are benefits in each one. Furthermore, there is benefit in having different employees be different types. It is not advantageous for an entire organization to be homogeneous in this regard.
- As a large group, participants brainstorm and contemplate strategies for dealing with different types of people in an organization.
- The final section of the workshop is for personal reflection and self-evaluation: What type of reaction do I typically have?
- The instructor leads a discussion on what participants' "cheese" is and where they are looking for it.

RESOURCES USED

This workshop requires the purchase of materials from Who Moved My Cheese?® To purchase these materials, please visit www.whomovedmycheese.com.

Johnson, S. (2002). *Who moved my cheese? An amazing way to deal with change in your work and in your life.* New York: Putnam.

Johnson, L. D., Pileggi, S., Germer, W., Burnett, B., Smith, B., & Johnson, S. (2003). *Who moved my cheese? The movie* (Motion Picture). United States: LDJ Film Productions.

"In times of profound change, the learners inherit the earth, while the learned find themselves beautifully equipped to deal with a world that no longer exists." –Eric Hoffer

WORK-READY PROTOCOL: HOW TO DELIVER SOFT SKILLS

CERTIFICATE: Emerald | **INSTRUCTOR:** Elizabeth Seager, Associate Director of Career Development

> *"Soft skills are those things that we seem to overlook from day to day, such as common sense, determination, courage, commitment, passion, and sincerity."*
>
> *Raymond, junior, 2008*

WORKSHOP DESCRIPTION

You've learned how to market your skills to get the job offer. Now, how do you deliver those skills to your employer to ensure early career success? Employers are surveyed each year regarding the skills they seek in new employees. Of those top 10 skills, at least half are considered soft skills. This session will address how to apply your soft skills in the workplace. The concept of "soft power" and applying it to developing into an effective leader will also be discussed.

LEARNING OUTCOMES

Upon completion of the workshop, participants will:

- Know soft skills that will lead to success.
- Understand the difference between hard power and soft power.
- Have reflected on their soft skills and be able to identify their strengths and weaknesses.

WORKSHOP ACTIVITIES

- The instructor begins the workshop with a brief introduction and explains the goals of the workshop and the importance of time management.
- The instructor presents the PowerPoint slide on soft skills and explains the importance of these skills. Participants are asked which of the skills they see in themselves. After the participants give their responses to the question, the instructor emphasizes the importance of problem solving, integrity, and honesty.
- The instructor asks the participants which soft skills they need to work on and after a few minutes they share their answers in small groups.
- The instructor introduces the top 10 skills employers are seeking and points out 90% of them are soft skills.
- The instructor continues to lecture using the PowerPoint presentation as a guide. Participants are encouraged to join in on the discussion prompted by each new topic.

RESOURCES USED

Seager, E. (2008). *How to Deliver Soft Skills PowerPoint.*

> *"The most important single ingredient in the formula of success is knowing how to get along with people."* —Theodore Roosevelt

WORKING WITH THE BRADY BUNCH: HOW BIRTH ORDER AFFECTS YOU AND YOUR ORGANIZATION

CERTIFICATE: Silver | **INSTRUCTOR:** Tamara Kenney, Assistant Dean of Students for Judicial Affairs

"The information I learned from this workshop will better enable me to work with my different staff members in terms of their strengths and weaknesses and thus focus on tasks that match skills based on birth order."

Kerisha, junior, 2011

WORKSHOP DESCRIPTION

Come and learn how to manage your "Brady Bunch" by understanding the impact that birth order has on you and on the members of your organization. Birth order can help you understand all the players and can be a tool in motivating and organizing your group to meet your goals. There are a number of interesting and fun theories available about working with team dynamics. One such theory is how your birth order impacts your personality and thus impacts how individuals of differing birth orders interact in teams. In this interactive, informative, and fun workshop, participants use the timeless example of the "Brady Bunch" to get to know the differences, strengths, weaknesses, and interactions of differing birth orders.

LEARNING OUTCOMES

Upon completion of the workshop, participants will:

- Be able to compare the differing impacts of birth order.
- Know how to utilize this knowledge to form more effective teams and manage them more effectively.
- Be able to critique anecdotal and scientific data.

WORKSHOP ACTIVITIES

- The group is split up by their birth order (oldest, middle child, youngest, only child), and asked as a group to write qualities about themselves that they like, don't like, and what they think others do and don't like about them. The instructor provides statistics and information regarding studies on birth order. The group shares stories relating to these findings, such as whether they agree or disagree with them. The instructor explains how different types of people can complement each other and how differences can make groups and organizations function well.
- The instructor breaks participants into four random groups and assigns each group a different question to answer. For example, what are the challenges of working with an only child in a group? Or with a middle child? Each group answers their question and shares their answer with the rest of the workshop.

RESOURCES USED

Leman, K. (1985). *The new birth order book: Why you are the way you are.* Grand Rapids, MI: Fleming H. Revell (a division of Baker Book House Company).

Kenney, T. (2012). *Working With the Brady Bunch: How Birth Order Can Affect You and Your Organization PowerPoint.*

Sulloway, F. J. (1997). *Born to rebel: Birth order, family dynamics, and creative lives.* New York: Vintage Books (a division of Random House, Inc.).

"In families children tend to take on stock roles, as if there were hats hung up in some secret place, visible only to the children. Each succeeding child selects a hat and takes on that role: the good child, the black sheep, the clown, and so forth." —Ellen Galinsky, president and co-founder of Families and Work Institute (FWI)

WRITE FOR SUCCESS

CERTIFICATE: Bronze or Emerald | **INSTRUCTOR:** Dr. Celia Easton, Dean of Residential Living and Professor of English

> *"There are many things in my life that become mountains from molehills due to my inability to write an email to someone. After taking this workshop, I feel more confident in my ability to express my concerns and effectively communicate using informal writing."*
>
> *Kaelyn, junior, 2011*

WORKSHOP DESCRIPTION

This workshop on effective professional writing focuses on the importance of strong written communication skills outside the classroom and the formal expectations of business and professional communication both within and outside the workplace. Participants will have the opportunity to critique and revise business memos and letters and think about the keys to writing for success: directness, succinctness, clarity, and correctness.

LEARNING OUTCOMES

Upon completion of this workshop, participants will:

- Demonstrate an understanding of the appropriate conventions of professional written communication.
- Have practiced selected forms of written communication.
- Be able to edit written drafts to create accurate documents that serve as records and/or contracts and that foster contact and good will.

WORKSHOP ACTIVITIES

- The instructor references an article about the inappropriateness of wearing flip-flops to the White House as an analogy for knowing appropriate conventions when writing. Writers need to keep their audience in mind, follow appropriate formal conventions, and pay attention to even the smallest detail in order to write effectively. Successful writing is not about "good English" or "proper grammar"; it's about knowing the conventions for the writing context. The workshop practices composing "good news" and "bad news" letters, following appropriate conventions.
- The instructor shares a handout that compares wordy and pretentious words or phrases to words of equivalent or more direct meanings to cut back on wordiness and bureaucratic over-writing. The focus of the discussion is the use of Plain English (a movement that gained momentum during the Carter Administration), including re-writing passive voice sentences in the active voice, using active verbs rather than "to be," addressing an audience as "you" when giving directions, and honestly identifying agency.
- The participants break into small groups to edit and rewrite short and realistic writing samples, paying attention to the detail and form of correct, effective, and appropriate writing.

RESOURCES USED

Baker, S. (1985). *The practical stylist*. New York, NY: Harper & Row.

Daniels, N. (1992). *Guide to style & mechanics*. Fort Worth, TX: Harcourt Brace Jovanovich.

Flesch, R. (1979) *How to write Plain English: A book for lawyers and consumers*. New York: Harper & Row.

Lunsford, A. A., & Horowitz, F. E. (1999). *The everyday writer*. Boston, MA: Bedford/St. Martin's.

Oliu, W. E., Brusaw, C. T., & Alred, G. J. (1988). *Writing that works*. New York: St. Martin's Press.

Schacht, P., & Easton, C. *SUNY Geneseo Online Writing Guide* (http://writingguide.geneseo.edu).

WRITING GRAD SCHOOL APPLICATION ESSAYS

CERTIFICATE: Emerald | **INSTRUCTOR:** Dr. Celia A. Easton, Dean of Residential Living and Professor of English

"I think a lot of undergraduate students assume graduate school application reviewers expect much the same thing undergraduate school application reviewers expect, and this workshop showed that this is not the case."

Kevin, sophomore, 2012

WORKSHOP DESCRIPTION

This workshop helps writers identify the role, audience, and purpose of their graduate school application essays, encouraging clear and direct writing and avoiding writing pitfalls such as clichés and lack of concreteness.

LEARNING OUTCOMES

Upon completion of this workshop, participants will:

- Understand the need for multiple drafts of a grad school or scholarship application essay.
- Practice general skills that help an essay make a good impression on a selection committee.

WORKSHOP ACTIVITIES

- The instructor uses a PowerPoint presentation and a handout to discuss essay writing strengths and pitfalls.
- Participants work together in one large group to revise a poorly conceived graduate school application letter.

RESOURCES USED

Gasman, M. (2010, November 15). Dos and Don'ts in Graduate-School Essays. *The Chronicle of Higher Education.*
Sword, H. (2012, April 6). Yes, Even Professors Can Write Stylishly. *The Wall Street Journal.*

"You can make anything by writing." –C.S. Lewis

BIBLIOGRAPHY: PART 1

Baker, K. C., & Mazza, N. (2004). The healing power of writing: Applying the expressive/creative component of poetry therapy. *Journal of Poetry Therapy*, 17(3), 141–154.

Burns, J. M. G. (1982). *Leadership*. New York: Harper & Row.

Cain, J. (2012). *Teamwork and teamplay*. Retrieved from http://www.teamworkandteamplay.com

Dugan, J. P., Komives, S. R., & Owen, J. E. (2009). *Multi-Institutional Study of Leadership Programs*. Center for Student Studies and the National Clearinghouse of Leadership Programs.

Fisher, R., Ury, W., & Patton, B. (1991). *Getting to yes*. New York: Penguin Books.

Goethals, G. R., & Sorenson, G. L. J. (2007). *The quest for a general theory of leadership*. Cheltenham: Edward Elgar Pub.

Hiemstra, R. (2001). Uses and benefits of journal writing. *New Directions for Adult and Continuing Education*, 90, 19–26.

Huber, N. S. (1998). *Leading from within: Developing personal direction*. Malabar, FL: Krieger Publishing Company.

Komives, S. R., Lucas, N., & McMahon, T. R. (2007). *Exploring leadership: For college students who want to make a difference*. San Francisco, CA: Jossey-Bass.

Komives, S. R., Dugan, J. P., Owen, J. E., Slack, C., Wagner, W., et al. (2011). *The handbook for student leadership development*. San Francisco, CA: Jossey-Bass.

Northouse, P. G. (2004). *Leadership: Theory and practice*. Thousand Oaks, CA: Sage.

Rost, J. C. (1991). *Leadership for the 21st century*. New York: Praeger.

State University of New York at Geneseo GOLD Program. (2012). *Mission statement*. Retrieved from http://gold.geneseo.edu/index.php?pg=missionstatement

State University of New York at Geneseo. (2012). *Mission statement*. Retrieved from http://www.geneseo.edu/about/mission-values-goals

W. K. Kellogg Foundation. (2000). *Leadership reconsidered: Engaging higher education in social change*. Astin, A. W., & Astin, H. S. (Eds.) Battle Creek, MI: Kellogg Foundation.

INDEX OF TERMS